Justine Kolata is a writer and philosopher educated at Yale University (B.A.) and the University of Cambridge (Ph.D.). Her scholarly research focuses on the Enlightenment and Romantic Era philosophy of the Beautiful Soul and the salon culture in which it was enacted.

Justine is founder of *The Beautiful Soul*, a cultural organisation which revives the Beautiful Soul and salon culture, applying this philosophy's timeless wisdom on self-improvement to further human flourishing today. Justine and her husband, a concert pianist, host philosophical salons and music *soirées* in London and throughout Europe.

In Pursuit of
the Beautiful Soul

The Philosophy of the Beautiful Soul,
Salon Culture, and the Art of Creating a Beautiful Life

Justine Kathryn Kolata

Double A Group Publishing
First published in Great Britain in this edition
by Double A Group Publishing, 2023

A CIP catalogue record for this book is available from the
British Library.

ISBN 978-1-7391482-0-1

Typeset in 11/13pt Times New Roman by Geoff Fisher
geoff.fisher@yahoo.co.uk

Papers used by CPI Books are from well-managed, sustainable sources.

*Printed and bound by CPI Group (UK) Ltd,
Croydon, CR0 4YY*

Double A Group Publishing
is part of The Double A Group,
The Hive London
Camrose Avenue
HA8 6AG

ACKNOWLEDGEMENTS

This book is dedicated to my loving family, my mother, Anna, my father, Alan, my husband, Louis, my daughter, Anastasia, and Putti, the beautiful souls who have inspired my life's work.

I would like to thank my Ph.D. supervisor, Dr. Martin Ruehl, for his exceptional mentorship in guiding my research on the Beautiful Soul at the University of Cambridge and Dr. Jessica Frazier for her invaluable insights as a reader. I would also like to express my deep gratitude to Anthony Kleanthous, Philomena Muinzer, Natasha Kaye, and Christian Kleanthous for their dedication to the publication of this book.

Now, this harmonious cultivation of my nature, which has been denied me by birth, is exactly what I most long for...with this, there is combined my love for poetry and all that is related to it; and the necessity I feel to cultivate my mental faculties and tastes, that so, in this enjoyment henceforth indispensable, I may esteem as good the good alone, as beautiful the beautiful alone.

— Wilhelm Meister's Apprenticeship and Travels,
Johann Wolfgang von Goethe

TABLE OF CONTENTS

Part 1. The Beautiful Soul and Salon Culture

Part 2. Cultivating a Beautiful Soul

Part 1

The Beautiful Soul and Salon Culture

CHAPTER 1

Introduction

O<small>NE</small> spring afternoon in London, a group of strangers seeking the address on a mysterious invitation walked down an elegant street lined with white-columned, Thomas Cubitt houses. Magnolia blossoms fell to the ground beneath them under billowing, illuminated clouds. Upon approaching 95 St. George's Drive, they heard a concert pianist in a flat above playing Chopin's nocturnes while people on the balcony, sharing a bottle of wine, watched life pass below. "It's flat three!" cried out one jovial man to those who approached in curious anticipation.

They rang the buzzer and clambered up the stairs. The *salonnière* greeted them with elation, inviting them inside. The flat had high ceilings delineated by crown moulding, soaring windows and a marble fireplace with a mirror that reflected the colourful *mise en scene*. A Bechstein piano on a Persian carpet was the centrepiece of the room. To its right was a long table with a profusion of peonies and fragrant hyacinths in a large Chinese ginger jar. Pungent cheeses, succulent oysters, grapes spilling from porcelain platters, half opened pomegranates, and cream cakes were displayed. A large candelabra illuminated the table with an amber glow, giving the impression that the scene was part of a Dutch still life.

The newcomers entered a room already filled with artists, tradespeople, intellectuals, politicians, and musicians engaged

1

in animated conversations. In one corner, an Indian accountant, an Ethiopian bodyguard, and an American professor of Hindu studies discussed the philosophy of love. On the other side of the room a Brazilian social anthropologist, a Japanese novelist, and a French poet debated how meaning is translated through different material mediums.

The *salonnière* introduced the guests to one another, moving from one group to the next to ensure that conversations had not lulled before she was drawn once again to the door where a new flood of people emerged. Some observed the busts of Goethe and Schiller that were placed on either side of the mantelpiece as if to frame the nature of the discussions that were to take place. Others browsed the bookcase, pulling out Plato's *Complete Works* and Shikibu's *The Tale of Genji,* perusing texts quietly before the salon. An occasional sharp outcry could be heard above the murmur from animated disputes that had already emerged on questions such as "do we have free will?" or "are humans naturally monogamous?"

Amidst these spirited discussions, the pianist was joined by another musician. They played Schubert's *Fantasy in F Minor*, occasionally pausing to drink from the glasses kept filled by the gregarious guests. The German opera singer, who was conversing with a Mexican actor and a Sudanese film-maker on the balcony, wandered into the room and offered to sing a *lieder*. Delighted by this spontaneous musical collabo-ration, the *salonnière* attracted the attention of her guests. Slowly people drifted over to chairs that had been placed in front of the piano. The singer introduced his chosen piece and sang with melancholic beauty, while the virtuoso pianist sight-read the score.

Passers-by on the street below stood under the window, listening to the impromptu performance. The *salonnière*

2

walked onto the balcony and beckoned them to join. The most adventurous person accepted her offer and the poetic afternoon was amplified by the bystander who had fortuitously stumbled upon the vibrant salon nestled away in the chaotic metropolis.

The *salonnière* introduced the topic for the afternoon's conversation on "The Philosophy of Wonder." She welcomed the speaker, an eminent intellectual who had completed a book of wonders that would soon be published. He gave a short talk, discussing everything from Francis Bacon's idea that wonder is "broken knowledge" to René Descartes' conviction that wonder is the first and most noble of the passions. He then interrogated the place of science in the experience of wonder and how, according to Richard Feynman, "science only adds to the mystery and the awe of a flower." He concluded by considering what it means to feel awe in times of disenchantment.

Without waiting for the dynamism of his discussion to subside, the *salonnière* catalysed a conversation among salon participants. She posed questions from a "conversation menu" which drew from the talk and offered a structure to the ensuing discussion. Many people contributed, offering their insights into personal experiences and philosophical reflections, while others pensively listened to what had been said. Everything from the fractals discovered in nature to cross-cultural under-standings of the experience of wonder and the way that children perceive the world was debated with great animation. The *salonnière* attempted to bring the distinct points into a cohesive whole while gently guiding the conversation. She probed ideas left unchallenged and encouraged the further exploration of the most interesting points. At times laughter erupted, disagreements were theatrically communicated, and accord was found. All the while drinks flowed, food was passed around, and spirits remained high.

When the discussion came to a close, an eccentric Indian artist, who had written an ode inspired by the conversation as it was occurring, stood on the coffee table and read his creation aloud, much to the delight of the guests. While jazz performances welcomed the dusk, less formal discussions emerged organically in response to what had been said. The salon continued into the early hours of the morning with conversation and dancing as love affairs blossomed and friendships burgeoned around the green chaise longue.

The guests who took part in this cosmopolitan space for intellectual exchange imagined that they had been transported to the salons of Paris during the Enlightenment. For a moment they were suspended from an awareness of time or space, enveloped in moments of self-discovery and intimate exchanges that lingered in an animated room of beauty. But, upon departing this enchanted space as the sun of a new day rose, a harsher reality confronted them once more, for this was not the Age of Enlightenment and the times were not those that could be characterised by reason or wisdom, kinship and good faith.

This was the twenty-first century, at a moment of profound tension when irrationality and wilful misunderstanding had been accelerated by information technologies and increasingly hostile forms of political debate; when enervating streams of superficial interactions in the virtual realm threatened meaningful connections in physical space. The anachronistic space on St. George's Drive was not part of a thriving network of salons, as had once been the case throughout Europe. It was an anomaly that appeared in stark contrast to the values and aesthetics of the modern age.

The salon in this story, and the characters who transformed it into the vibrant space that it became, was one of the first that

I organised in two thousand and fourteen when I began my cultural organisation, *The Beautiful Soul*, dedicated to the revival of the philosophy of the Beautiful Soul and salon culture. I was in the process of refining my ability to create and sustain a community. I explored new ways of structuring the small but beautiful universe of the salon. I experimented with eliciting positive qualities in salon participants through diplomacy, reason, and a shared valued system that undergirded the social interactions that took place.

I discovered that a salon is a microcosm of life: beauty and banality, elation and discord, questions and misgivings; all manner of human behaviour are condensed and intensified within this circumscribed space. The coexistence of disparate personalities and belief systems catalyse ideas, spark collaborations, and engender revelations that offer deep insights into the human condition. Character weaknesses and strengths are revealed, negotiated, and, in the best of outcomes, overcome or solidified within this discursive space. To be part of a salon is to attain a magnified understanding of oneself and of the social whole. This aesthetically and intellectually stimulating atmosphere encourages participants to envision the world as they wish it could be, collaboratively constructing a more perfect reality through the power of their minds and imaginative faculties.

My salons were not born in isolation. They represent a renaissance of ancient ideals. They compose part of a rich historical lineage inspired by a philosophical belief system and cultural tradition instigated by pioneering women centuries ago. In contemplating the myriad problems of contemporary society, I returned to ideas that were promulgated and practiced in the past, while refining and elaborating upon them to fit modern realities and contemporary social demands.

5

My endeavours were founded on the conviction that this is a most beautiful world and progress is possible if we elicit the inherent goodness in people by cultivating moral and intellectual faculties through positive community structures. To catalyse a new period of enlightenment, we will need to overcome the pervasive cynicism that has defined modern life in favour of a rational optimism that embraces the possibilities of existence. Such optimism is grounded in collaborative inquiry and the will to seek truth and beauty in the face of a culture steeped in derision and the bloodlust of unbridled competition.

For ours is a world of bright ideas and vital cultural creations, novel scientific discoveries, artistic inspirations, and sublime natural landscapes. Every day we are presented with the possibility to advance knowledge, feel wonder, find happiness, and experience love. Each person can appreciate the profound beauty of the universe and attain self-knowledge and meaning. Instances of human ingenuity across the globe, the emergent collective will to confront our most devastating social and environmental problems, the spontaneous demonstration of kindness and empathy in the face of catastrophes, all exemplify that we have just as much reason to believe in the promise that the future may hold than to fear what it may bring. A sanguine conviction in the ultimate goodness of people is neither naïve nor unfounded when we consider the historic progress that has been made and the boundless achievements that we can attain by virtue of the innate capacities with which every person has been endowed.

Yet collectively we have not lived up to the possibilities of our nature or fully realised the rich opportunities available to us. For, despite undeniable advances in medicine, technology and, for some, expanding economic opportunity, the moral

6

foundation of our actions appears increasingly divorced from deeper meaning within our society that idolises extreme individualism and materialism above all else. From rising economic inequality and environmental degradation to intensifying public hostilities and destructive political discourse, the modern world is fraught with seemingly intractable problems. As the ends that we prioritise become more superficial and self-seeking, a dangerous mixture of apathy, despair, and irrationality hinders human progress and a healthy public sphere.

Although the complicated issues that we face appear disparate, I argue that they ultimately derive from the same source: a lack of individual meaning and the loss of communal structures through which to cultivate this meaning. We are fortunate to live in an age in which we can reject the oppressive confines of dogmatic religion and social norms that have historically infringed upon personal liberties. But secularism and self-expression often come at the expense of belief in something greater than ourselves. Noble aspirations, worthy pursuits, and the most basic forms of human decency are too often undermined in the aggressive assertion of the self.

Surface-level interactions in the virtual sphere have replaced a deeper sense of community in physical space. Loneliness and anomie breed intolerance, ignorance, and lack of empathy. As social creatures, the trend towards individualism impelled by market realities and the dehumanising effects of information technologies have led to catastrophic consequences, fragmenting the bonds necessary to reach social accord. Until we reconsider our values and the means by which we choose to pursue them, the possibility of reaching *communitas* appears lost.

The underlying nature of the problems we face originates,

I suggest, from a crisis of values, a loss of worthy principles and beautiful ideals, rendering us divided, unhappy, and alone. This moral crisis is reflected in the evolution of our language. The change in the meaning of a single word exemplifies this trend towards superficiality.

Once the word "beauty" was synonymous with goodness and truth. Now it is often reduced to images of the body. The corporeal replacement of an immaterial beauty of soul is emblematic of the value system in which we find ourselves today: one that perpetuates an economy of desire focused on appearances, money, sex, and fame that negates higher ideals and our deeper responsibilities to ourselves and to each other.

We can observe the decline of society through the corruption of this word, its meaning devolving from an unquantifiable value inhering in nature and artistic expression, to the superficial possession of a selection of physical traits. That the concept of beauty has been so debased suggests that our global culture requires profound spiritual and moral awakening.

As an undergraduate at Yale University, I became passionate about exploring the importance of beauty for the human soul and how beautiful experiences in art and nature can fundamentally improve our character and our inclination towards moral law. My quest to address the problems that plague modern society through this lens entailed returning to ancient Greek philosophy, particularly Plato's aesthetics, in which beauty is inextricably bound to the noble and the good.

Intuitively I affirmed Plato's idea that life should be lived as a reflection of the forms of Beauty, Goodness, and Truth which exist in a realm unto themselves, independent of human fallibility. I became certain that this transcendental triad encompasses the universal ends worthiest of human pursuit and are the means by which to structure individual and collective action. I began to wonder what attempts had been made historically to apply Platonic ideals in a practical philosophy that could be used as a guiding principle for individuals and society itself.

Through extended historical inquiries, my quest led to a study of the intersection of aesthetics and morality within the German philosophical tradition. With the guidance of my professor, I discovered the lost, but once vibrant tradition of the Beautiful Soul, a philosophy of self-cultivation, and the salon culture of the Enlightenment, a space for conversation, which sought to enact its ideals.

Fascinated by the beautiful principles and utopic community that I discovered, I decided to interrogate this topic in depth by pursuing doctoral studies at the University of Cambridge on the intersection of the philosophy of the Beautiful Soul and salon culture in the Age of Goethe, a study that had never been undertaken. I did not, however, want this concept and the practical attempts to inculcate its ideals to remain in the ivory tower, for I believe that they have great potential to change the world. So, I simultaneously founded my cultural organisation, *The Beautiful Soul*, to revitalise salon culture and the practice of this philosophy. My inquiry into the theory and applications of this tradition has yielded insights that may offer solutions to some of the challenges that we face today.

The philosophy of the Beautiful Soul's fundamental tenet is that life should be lived as a work of art in the pursuit of beauty, goodness, and truth. When people develop a noble character through the cultivation of their moral, aesthetic, and intellectual faculties, they prosper and humanity flourishes. This humanistic philosophy offers an optimistic vision for reaching one's full potential, finding happiness and meaning in life, while positively shaping society as a compassionate, rational, and well-informed citizen.

The theorists of the Beautiful Soul dared individuals to preserve youthful ideals, to expand rational faculties, to feel deeply, to see beauty, and to experience great love. They challenged people to overcome the lethargy of intellectual immaturity, to question embedded prejudices, and to think critically for themselves. With a strong conviction in the human capacity for goodness, they believed that every individual could take part in forming a more beautiful and virtuous humanity through the art of self-cultivation.

The Beautiful Soul allows for different beliefs and ways of being, while also representing a set of universal ends. It embraces the creativity and dynamism of modernity with the moral rigour and intellectual acumen of great intellectual traditions of centuries past. This philosophy is conceived for all. It makes the universal, immaterial soul the basis for its social and political ideals. The Beautiful Soul reminds us that if we are committed to improving the world, we can no longer address symptoms alone. We must return to value systems that inform action. Nor can we simply blame others for the problems that exist. Changing society begins by observing the weaknesses within and sculpting them away, transforming ourselves into more beautiful minds and noble souls for the greater social good.

The Beautiful Soul remains extraordinarily progressive centuries after it was first conceived. It presciently furnished insights into the state of contemporary society. Anticipating the dangers of individuals blindly subscribing to ideologies, the perils associated with a loss of communal life, and the negative dimensions of industrialisation and cultural homogenisation, it offers solutions to the most challenging social issues we face.

In a global culture preoccupied with radical individualism, narcissistic presentations of self, extreme materialism, and incendiary political rhetoric, the ideal of the Beautiful Soul may appear elusive. Yet, to challenge the superficial values that have become commonplace, we may learn from intellectual history and elaborate upon knowledge-systems past, questioning what it means to be human and how to exist harmoniously in a social whole. Only by doing so will we reclaim the true sense of the word beauty and thus fulfil the promise it holds.

This book narrates the story of a luminous period in history when the ideals of Antiquity and the European Enlightenment were enacted in a space of enlightened exchange. The story unfolds in the late eighteenth and early nineteenth centuries within the circles of "noble souls" in Weimar and the illustrious salons of Jewish women in Berlin. Here, two of the most celebrated poets, philosophers, and playwrights in European history, Johann Wolfgang von Goethe (1749-1832) and Friedrich Schiller (1759-1805) were formulating a concept that was as politically revolutionary as it was idealistic: the philosophy of *Bildung* (self-cultivation) *and die schöne Seele* (the Beautiful Soul).

Inspired by the idealism and universality of this philosophy, Rahel Varnhagen (1771-1833) and Henriette Herz (1764-1847), the two most celebrated Jewish *salonnières* of post-revolutionary Berlin, fearlessly strove to bring this more beautiful humanity into being. They saw this philosophy as a force for emancipation and unity in a world fragmented by ethnic, religious, and class divisions. Overcoming formidable discrimination both as women and as Jews, they became the "leaders of souls" in the inclusive, egalitarian spaces that they created. Their role as *salonnières* was to help others self-cultivate in an ambitious attempt to draw out their humanity and to bring about a consonance of peoples through beautification of the world.

This book demonstrates that, in the Age of Goethe, the Berlin salons became a space in which beautiful souls were cultivated through the indefatigable, unsung idealism of the *salonnières*. I argue that the salons were projects of a radically political nature whose manifesto was the Beautiful Soul. I challenge the 'critical' depiction of the Enlightenment with this clearer vision of the utopian movements and aesthetic spirit that flourished at this crucial moment in the making of the modern world. By revitalising the ideals of Antiquity upon which this tradition was based and providing an intellectual lineage from Hellenism to German Romanticism to the present day, this book offers a pragmatic philosophy from which to inform individual action.

No single treatise by the proponents of the Beautiful Soul provides a comprehensive explanation of the theory. The most inclusive treatment is that of Schiller's *On the Aesthetic Education of Man* (1795) which offers insights that are pertinent to this tradition, but frames them in rather general terms. The concept was discussed within multiple contexts, such as reflections on the powers of the State, notions of personal liberty, and aesthetics as a pedagogical discipline. The expansive application of the Beautiful Soul suggests that it was a total philosophy, a grand theory that could be applied to everything from one's personal development to politics and the public sphere. But this philosophy was never articulated exclusively in manuscript form. Many of its propositions and practices were voiced and debated in the context of salon conversations. Since we lack a single, standardised text, I have constructed a comprehensive account of the features of a beautiful soul, assembled from the historical and literary fragments of multiple authors, that identifies the commonalities amongst them, and, I believe, most accurately captures the ethos of the philosophy.

In this endeavour, I focus primarily on the writings of Goethe and Schiller. Their conception of the Beautiful Soul, which, more than any other, proposed to transform life into a work of art was adopted by the Berlin *salonnières*, and most substantively connects this philosophy to the institution of the salon. The development of *die schöne Seele*, as well as public enthusiasm for it, was at its apex during the time of Goethe and Schiller. Arguably their work engenders its spirit in the purest sense. Apart from these two transcendent figures, I foreground the contributions of certain other thinkers who either influenced them or were heavily influenced by them. For instance, Immanuel Kant's reflections on aesthetics were instrumental in framing this concept, while Novalis' writing reflects the Beautiful Soul's turn towards Romanticism at a crucial moment when this philosophy flourished on the Continent.

In discussing the Beautiful Soul today, I focus particularly on social media and communication technologies because these twenty-first century tools have brought the most drastic changes to the way we live and relate to others. In fundamental respects, they stand in stark contrast to this philosophy and the institution of the salon. This contrast makes apparent the lessons that we can learn from past attempts to grapple with the meaning of the human condition.

Practicing this philosophy benefits from joining or establishing a salon-like community at a time when they are few and far between. Historically almost every society from Europe and Asia, to Africa, Latin America, and the Middle

13

East has had some form of a salon culture which contributed to a vibrant public sphere. This book shows how to revive a universal tradition. However, its reflections can be viewed more generally within friendships and family, in professional environments, and when exercising democratic rights. It serves as a guide for individuals and larger communities and its lessons can be applied to most situations in life.

In this book I discuss the features of the Beautiful Soul and the *salonnières'* implementation of them within their salons. These historical insights serve as examples of how to practice the Beautiful Soul in the modern age. I also explore the state of contemporary society and consider lessons learned during my experiments in reviving this concept and institution, as well as offer a framework for how to practice this philosophy today. This book is a practical philosophy for the present, one that examines an ancient theory and offers insights into its implementation in order to guide individuals to a life of constant self-improvement, deep empathy, commitment to human flourishing, and moral beauty in the modern age.

CHAPTER 2

The History of the Beautiful Soul

THE concept of *Bildung* first appeared in sixteenth century theology but was most fully developed in the eighteenth and early nineteenth centuries. *Die schöne Seele* emerged from the discourse on *Bildung* in the nineteenth century. Although there is no exact translation in English, *Bildung* is sometimes roughly translated as "formation" or "self-cultivation." It may be defined as a moral-aesthetic education, or more precisely, the rigorous cultivation of one's intellect and the formation of one's self. Education in this sense has a rich, multifaceted meaning; a process of intellectual, spiritual, and cultural *poiesis* that conjoins enrichment of one's own faculties with the objective of contributing to the commonweal. *Bildung* is an aesthetic ideal focused on developing human capacities and advancing knowledge and culture.[1]

Similarly, the concept of *die schöne Seele* entails a rigorous pursuit of personal cultivation to create a convergence of the individual aesthetic impulse with a collective, ethical ideal. The concept affirms "that a profound affinity exists between beauty and goodness; that there is a point at which aesthetic and ethical values commingle to form a new, indivisible unity."[2] A beautiful soul is a virtuous soul, one that possesses a sense of justice, pursues wisdom, and practices benevolence through an aesthetic proclivity for the good.

Bildung and *die schöne Seele* had their own history and

strands of thought that may be considered separately, but they are fundamentally convergent concepts. Self-cultivation is an active process, and the Beautiful Soul is its idealised form. But the pursuit of a beautiful soul is essentially synonymous with the pursuit of self-cultivation: both are directed towards attainment of the same enlightened state and the metaphysical ends of Beauty, Goodness and Truth. Together they may be defined as the aesthetic cultivation of one's intellectual, moral, and imaginative faculties for the purpose of self-realisation, cultural refinement, and collective human flourishing. Over the course of this book, I will use the terms *Bildung* and *die schöne Seele* interchangeably to emphasise their synonymous nature.

Many of the most prominent German intellectuals of the time, including Immanuel Kant (1724-1804), Christoph Martin Wieland (1733-1813), Johann Gottfried Herder (1744-1803), Johann Wolfgang von Goethe (1749-1832), Friedrich Schiller (1759-1805), Johann Gottlieb Fichte (1762-1814), Wilhelm von Humboldt (1767-1835), Friedrich Schlegel (1772-1829) and Novalis (1772-1801) were instrumental in advancing the concepts and practices of *Bildung* and *die schöne Seele*. They devoted much of their intellectual careers to the definition of these concepts through philosophical essays, letters, literary works, and the theatre. Although these concepts were elaborated in other European countries by philosophers like the third Earl of Shaftesbury (1671-1713) who greatly influenced their development, they remained a distinctly German tradition, one which engaged overlapping circles of intellectuals, artists, educators, politicians, and a critically debating public for over two centuries.

The development of *Bildung* and *die schöne Seele* in Germany can be traced to the contemporaneous revival of

Hellenism and an obsession with Greek ideals. Philhellenism penetrated all areas of philosophy from politics to ethics and epistemology. The core element of Greek philosophy that unified its different branches was its strong emphasis on aesthetics, which particularly attracted the Germans and led them to establish aesthetics as a separate discipline. Schiller and Goethe venerated the Beautiful; they respected the Greeks because they believed that their art and culture reflected this higher form.[3] German humanists turned to Hellenic ideals as a solution to the problems they identified in their increasingly materialistic society. The Ancients, they believed, had demonstrated that beauty could ennoble art, life, and politics. To have a historical model to lionise thus grounded their aspirations for a more beautiful and virtuous society in a possible world that could recover the poetic glory that they imagined Antiquity possessed.

The art historian Johann Joachim Winckelmann (1717-1768) was the scholar most responsible for initiating these developments. Archaeological excavations that took place at Herculaneum in 1738 and Pompeii in 1748 were the inspiration for his ground-breaking work, *Reflections on the Imitation of Greek Works in Painting and Sculpture* (1756) and later *History of the Art of Antiquity* (1764). Winckelmann believed that modern civilisation could only become great if it imitated the ancients. He famously argued that Greek art has a "noble simplicity and quiet grandeur" which makes it superior to the creations of other cultures and time periods. The beauty of Greek art comes from the greater freedom and harmony that it expresses. These claims catalysed a wealth of scholarship in this area.

Taking inspiration from Winckelmann, Schiller believed that Greek culture put modern society to shame by virtue of its simplicity and wisdom. He particularly admired its ability to unite fullness of form and fullness of substance, philosophising with creativity, gentleness with vitality, and to marry the excitements of youth with a matured faculty of reason.[4] The Greeks understood that the good life entails balancing the pleasures of the sensory world with intellectual endeavours. Schiller contrasted the harmoniousness with which they approached life with the inharmonious condition of modern man enslaved by economic realities that create artificial needs. The only way to restore this lost harmony is to refer to the Greeks for their wisdom and inspiration. His influential poem, "The Gods of Greece," is a tribute to the beautiful world that they created with the hope that their heightened states of aesthetic self-cultivation would once again inform society's course. Schiller claimed, "the Greeks are what we were; they are what we shall become again."[5]

Goethe, who also drew heavily on Winckelmann, echoed Schiller's sentiment when he argued that we must return to the ancient Greeks, contending that their model was the greatest.[6] He maintained that "of all peoples, the Greeks have dreamt the dream of life the best."[7] This, he believed, was because they were so highly cultivated that their daily realities were elevated by their poetic imagination.[8] Like Schiller, he considered the modern society in which he lived to be constrained and joyless in comparison. Goethe's nostalgia for antiquity informed most of his writings which often borrow from Greek themes. He endeavoured to reconstruct Ovid's *Metamorphoses*, a book he read as a young boy that greatly influenced his intellectual development. His play *Iphigenia in Tauris* (1779) is a rewriting of the tragedy by Euripides, and those literary works that are not as explicitly Greek, such as *Wilhelm Meister* (1795/1796), nevertheless have strong Greek undertones.

The unifying theme that informed his collective works was

his ambition to arrive at a concept of the perfected man. With their notions of *arete* (moral excellence) and *eudaimonia* (an enlightened state of happiness), the Greeks touched upon the issues that concerned him most. Related to this quest was his desire to discover the original plant from which all other plants derived.[9] This interest in human *Bildung* as mirrored in plant life, and his passion for nature more generally, was, again, the product of Greek inspiration from his interpretation of their natural philosophies.[10]

The Germans found particular inspiration in Plato's theory of the forms and Plotinus's notion of *kalokagathia*, roughly translated as a person who exhibits καλός (the beautiful) and ἀγαθός (the good or the virtuous).[11] The Platonic triad is systematically intertwined in this theory. Herder, for example, states that the ultimate purpose of a classical *Bildung* education is to imprint upon the youthful soul "the eternal, inviolable rule of the true, the good, and the beautiful."[12] He argues that:

> Truth, beauty, and love are the objects at which man aims in all his endeavours, even without being conscious of it, and often by the most devious paths; the perplexities of the labyrinth will be unfolded, the seductive forms of enchantment will vanish, and everyone will not only see the centre, far or near, to which his ways tends, but though, maternal Providence, under the form of the genius and friend he needs, wilt guide him to it themselves, with a gentle and forgiving hand.[13]

Herder understands the Platonic forms to be the teleological objective of humankind and argues that a *Bildung* education will bring humans closer to this objective. Schlegel concludes that the Greeks reached the highest level of *Bildung* of any people in history because of their interest in beauty for beauty's sake and because their self-determination was derived from the equilibrium which they had found in the Platonic forms.[14] The aim of *Bildung,* to strive towards a metaphysical state of Beauty, Goodness, and Truth, was first identified by Greek philosophers as the end worthiest of human pursuit.

From Winckelmann to Wieland, Schlegel, Schiller and Goethe, the Germans shared the belief that Greek art and philosophy are the foundation of *Bildung*. They were the first to acknowledge that the concept of *die schöne Seele* has its origins in Antiquity. They viewed their theory as an elaboration on ancient Greek ideas. Therefore, although it is true that the formal philosophy originated in the sixteenth century and reached its pinnacle in the late eighteenth and early nineteenth centuries, its genesis can be attributed to notions formulated in millennia long past.

The historical setting of this Hellenic burgeoning in the intellectual landscape of Germany that gave rise to the development of *die schöne Seele* was the *Aufklärung*, the German Enlightenment. In order to contextualise this concept, evaluations of the place of the *Aufklärung* within the European Enlightenment more generally merit consideration. Much of what we define as the Enlightenment today—especially that grounded in the critique of instrumental reason—comes specifically from interpretations of its emergence in France. Although the French may be seen as the initiators and driving force, the Enlightenment was a trans-European movement with a shared set of values in rationality, *fraternité,* individual freedom, and religious tolerance, as well as a rich variety of distinct ideas that appeared in different countries. Yet, the French Enlightenment has dwarfed others, such as the German

Aufklärung, which is often considered relatively insignificant by comparison. A central reason for this perception is that, as opposed to the French Enlightenment, the German Enlightenment was not defined by resistance to the state.[15] During the rule of Frederick the Great (1740-1786), there was a measure of intellectual freedom that allowed both intellectuals and servants of the state to engage with Enlightenment ideology without fear of repression. In certain cases, it was easier to advance these ideas with the support of a monarch sympathetic to the cause rather than to criticise the monarchy and risk freedom of expression.[16]

Later philosophers, such as Humboldt, Goethe, and Schiller, saw the negative effects of the radical political strands of the French Enlightenment that culminated in The Terror.[17] Their disillusionment with the revolutionary cause fuelled the perception that the *Aufklärung* was apolitical and therefore a less significant version than that of the French. But this is not an entirely accurate portrayal. The German *Aufklärung* was *inherently* political in nature, but its thinkers chose to develop their political philosophy along lines that they considered to be more sustainable, holistic and, in their eyes, imbued with the possibility of producing perpetual peace.[18]

An analysis of the *Aufklärung* through its tradition of the Beautiful Soul challenges this apolitical critique. It exemplifies the approach its theorists took, founded upon their conviction that every individual can master their destiny, not through violent social outbursts and political chaos, but through self-cultivation in the name of a greater social good. Kant, Schiller, and Humboldt did not believe that the Enlightenment's ideological ends could immediately be brought to fruition, but rather would only emerge through a continuous process of the education of its citizenry, thereby developing the capacity of the public to legitimately govern itself. Premature revolutionary action of the uninformed masses would only lead to despotism, more catastrophic for the public than monarchy. The theorists of the Beautiful Soul turned to aesthetic philosophy, not as a means of *avoiding* the political sphere, but for precisely the opposite reason. They wanted to engage directly with politics, incorporating everyone into a grand vision of human progress through an aesthetic impulse, elaborating upon notions of an Aesthetic State formed in Antiquity. A nuanced understanding of the experience of the beautiful upon the human soul was these theorists' political solution to the irrationality and chaos that they observed in France which overpowered and perverted the promising universal principles that the European Enlightenments had once shared.

In the tradition of Pico della Mirandola (1463-1494) and his *Oration on the Dignity of Man* (1496), the theorists of the Beautiful Soul believed that only by activating each person's potential could Europe reach its ends of equality, liberty and fraternity. The soul, while metaphysical and eternal, was reinvented within a humanistic framework such that the individual possessed the agency to shape it. Just as an individual might ask "what is the state of my physical health?" it was expected that they would pose the question "what is the present condition of my soul?" and work towards its improvement. What was once referred to as moral beauty became the Beautiful Soul, a revealing ontological evolution which placed greater emphasis on people's ability to better their condition and take the future of Europe into their own hands.[19]

The importance placed on subjectivity demonstrates that this was a time of transition in which Enlightenment thought was vividly coloured by Romanticism. Ideas from the *Sturm und Drang,* the German artistic and literary movement of the late 1760's to the early 1780's, which opposed the extreme rationality of the French and saw value in emotions, feelings, and the passions, influenced the theoretical development of the Beautiful Soul. Although its theorists' ideas were still firmly embedded within the Enlightenment tradition, they offered a more human, holistic approach to its ends, overcoming strict rationalism in favour of a balance between reason and feeling.

By reclaiming the soul and asserting the individual's innate freedom to govern their inner world, this philosophy liberated individuals from pre-existing social, religious, and political doctrine. It offered clear paradigms for lived experience that spoke directly to the individual and their circumstances in the world. If we assess the political dimensions of the *Aufklärung* from the perspective of the Beautiful Soul tradition, a substantive argument can be made that it was the strongest of the various strains of the Enlightenment. This tradition proposed a longer-term horizon for the triumph of reason, knowledge, and freedom from oppression based in the agency of individuals. As such, it was radically egalitarian and inclusionary. Deeper exploration of *Bildung* and *die schöne Seele* will expand our notions of what the Enlightenment meant historically and what it could mean today.

CHAPTER 3

The History of Salon Culture

MOST historians have identified the rise of salon culture in Old Regime Berlin with a specific moment of political transition in Germany, one associated with the reigns of Frederick the Great (1740-1786), Frederick William II (1786-1797) and Frederick William III (1797-1840). Prior to Frederick the Great's ascendance to the throne in 1740, the Holy Roman Empire lacked a courtly life that facilitated the development of salon culture.[20] There are several reasons why salon culture emerged later in Germany than in other European countries, such as Italy or France. One of the principal reasons was the political fragmentation of Germany into small princely states, territories, and cities. This fragmentation impeded the emergence of a cosmopolitan culture in which salons could flourish.[21] Another reason was the dominance of universities and the competition among German principalities to found them.[22] Male-controlled scholarly institutions had a stronghold on the intellectual climate of the time, inhibiting the possibility for a traditionally female-led intellectual institution to gain traction. Furthermore, the Prussian court's hostility towards Protestantism detached the monarchy from broader developments in Enlightenment ideology and fostered antagonism towards the influences of French society where salon culture was most prevalent.[23]

In Germany, the emergence of salons, and their heyday

from 1780 to 1807, is associated with several important social conditions and political developments that came immediately prior to and during this period. One such condition was the willingness of the government to utilise its resources for the advancement of ideas and the arts, rather than solely for military or economic purposes. This depended on a leader amenable to investing in culture. Frederick the Great, who established many spaces and institutions for the public to self-cultivate, was this leader. Prior to his rule, few places existed for social and intellectual exchange. But, by his death in 1786, countless public areas, including parks, theatres, and an opera house had been erected. The expansion of cultural institutions and their wider demographic reach was born from Frederick the Great's personal devotion to Enlightenment principles, his patronage of the arts, and his love of philosophy and music, all of which contributed to a revived intellectual and cultural landscape in Prussia. His proclivity towards enlightened absolutism, and his desire to be remembered as a "Philosopher King," advanced a political environment amenable to new intellectual developments, a communicative culture, and a better educated populace. His passion for French ideas and his efforts to bring French scholars to Germany peaked German interest in the intellectual life of France, including its salons.

Frederick the Great therefore contributed to a more enlightened and cultured Prussian society, which was a necessary precondition for salons to emerge. However, it was only with Frederick William II's assumption of power that the court actively took an interest in and encouraged different forms of sociability.[24] After the brief reign of Frederick William II from 1786 to his death in 1797, Frederick William III and his wife Louise of Mecklenburg (1776-1810), furthered this receptiveness to enlightened social exchange. The royal couple were avid supporters of the literary scene and salon culture in Germany. Queen Louise befriended several important *salonnières*, most especially the Duchess Dorothea von Courland (1793-1862), whose salon she attended on numerous occasions.[25] These changes in courtly and political life in Germany created a more amenable environment for intellectual exchange, but they were not necessarily the proximate cause for a vital salon culture.

Although not all salons in Germany were run by Jewish women, the majority and the most important ones were. Therefore, to understand their history, one must also attend to the history of the *Haskalah* and Jewish high society during this period. The *Haskalah*, from the Hebrew *sekhel,* "reason" or "intellect," which began in the 1770s and ended in the 1880s, was a Jewish intellectual movement inspired by the European Enlightenment. This movement promoted integration, religious tolerance, rationality, freedom of thought, and emphasised the importance of secular education. It sought simultaneously to preserve Jewish cultural identity and to integrate Jews into wider European culture and society. The *Haskalah* emerged during a moment of economic prosperity for the Prussian Jewish elite. They had the resources to invest in culture and possessed a more stable social position from which to consider the place of their people in society. Despite the hostile financial and legal conditions imposed on the Jewish mercantile class, and the extreme taxes they were forced to pay, a new kindred of affluent Jews came into being.[26] This golden age of Jewish economic prosperity allowed Jews to gain wider social and intellectual acceptance and influence.

The gradual maturation of salon culture in Prussia was

enabled by a number of important *Haskalah* intellectuals.[27] The most prominent of these was the philosopher and literary critic, Moses Mendelssohn (1729-1786) whose works ranged from subjects in metaphysics and epistemology to aesthetics and political theory. Mendelssohn's prolific writing and intellectual eminence made him the paragon of Jewish scholarship. He became a public personality celebrated by the Jewish community for his efforts to advance their civil rights. His encouragement of secular education catalysed an intense period of intellectualism and engagement with high culture.[28] Within the context of the *Haskalah,* under the guidance of Mendelssohn's intellectual leadership, affluent Jewish women became the visionaries of a vibrant culture of salons in Germany.

By the late eighteenth and early nineteenth centuries, salons were a relatively ubiquitous form of social gathering in the circles of high society in cosmopolitan areas. They appeared across the lands of the Holy Roman Empire in cities such as Weimar, Jena, Heidelberg, and Leipzig. I focus on the Berlin salons because we have more detailed historical information on the celebrated Berlin *salonnières*, Rahel Varnhagen and Henriette Herz. This is largely because their salons attracted publicly recognised intellectuals and, as a result, are more thoroughly documented. Moreover, the Berlin *salonnières* wrote autobiographies and extensive letters that aid us to better understand their motivations and ideological orientations. The Berlin salons were spaces where the literature on the Beautiful Soul was most fervently discussed; its primary theorists, including Humboldt, Goethe, and Schiller, frequented these salons and developed their ideas within them. Varnhagen and Herz had a particularly strong interest in *Bildung and die schöne Seele,* as well as a shared passion for the work of Goethe, which makes the powerful connection between institution and philosophy even more apparent. The Berlin *salonnières* were close friends and their salons formed an interconnected social network of Jewish intellectual elites in which their endeavours converged on the shared ideology of the Beautiful Soul.

Rahel Varnhagen is the central figure of this story, not only because she was the leading and arguably most influential of the German *salonnières*, but also because her direct concern with the philosophy of the Beautiful Soul, and her internal struggles to find a place and a purpose in the world, reveal the more ambitious socio-political ends towards which her salon was directed. Henriette Herz who established the first Berlin salon is another important figure in this story. Sara Levy (1761-1854), Sara Grotthuis (1763-1828), Dorothea Schlegel (1764-1839), and Amalie Beer (1767-1854), each of whom held their own smaller salons and were part of the intellectual circles of Varnhagen and Herz, provide a more comprehensive framework in which to explore the social intersection of institution and philosophy that emerged in Berlin.

Varnhagen and Herz emblemised the sisterhood that the *salonnières* established. These women maintained close personal relationships, strengthening their salons' foundations through demonstrations of camaraderie and mutual support. As childhood friends, relatives, or mentors, they began their salons after learning from others and they often attended their friends' salons for sustained periods over the course of their lives. They were not afraid to concede the successes and qualities of other *salonnières*: they viewed each other not as competitors, but as friends. Herz, for example, generously acknowledged that Varnhagen was "the highest blossom of the new spirit" and was profoundly impressed by her accomplishments.[29] The *salonnières* typically planned their activities on different days of the week in order not to interfere with each other's events, while also exchanging ideas and alternating topics. The spirit of reciprocity and the intersections that took place make an analysis of their shared aims and activities feasible.

At the core of salon culture was the exploration of ideas and the acquisition of new knowledge through the art of conversation in a participative community. The structure of the Berlin salons was modelled after those of the French in the Age of Enlightenment.[30] The topic of conversation changed each time and spanned the spectrum of disciplines from philosophy and the arts to the natural sciences. Usually during a salon, an invited speaker would read a text chosen by the *salonnière*, such as a philosophical treatise, a poem, or a scholarly article, and give a short lecture on the topic. Thereafter, salon participants would engage in conversation moderated by the *salonnière*. The presentation was meant to stimulate discussion and the emphasis was placed on the conversation that it inspired. This distinguished the salon from other cultural institutions of the time that instead separated the conveyor of knowledge from the listener. In a salon, everyone present both offered their ideas and heard those of others in a mutually rewarding meeting of minds. The *salonnière* artfully guided the conversation and gave it structure, but the atmosphere was natural and conducive to free-flowing dialogue. The salon was a space for polite sociability; a forum to meet other curious people who shared an affinity for culture and ideas, and an opportunity to encounter disparate perspectives and lived circumstances. Salons were the only institution of the time in which people of different classes, genders, and religions met as presumptive equals for mutual betterment—a defining feature that will be discussed in depth.

Salons were hosted in the intimate setting of the home, usually the drawing room. Although the setting was personal and informal, the *salonnière* took her role as host seriously, viewing it not as a pastime but as a career requiring apprenticeship.[31] *Salonnières* spent days preparing for their salons, reading the literature, speaking with experts, and writing in their journals so that they would be well versed on the topic in order to successfully conduct the conversations. Minutes of proceedings were generally not taken, so most of our knowledge of their contents and happenings derives from letters between the *salonnières* and participants. Unfortunately, these letters often assumed a familiarity with the structure and functioning of the salon so some useful historical information is missing.[32] Nevertheless, we have sufficient evidence to draw a vivid picture of what would have happened in the Berlin salons.

CHAPTER 4

The Beautiful Soul in the Salon

G ERMAN Jews of the late eighteenth and early nineteenth
centuries affirmed the basic principles of *Bildung* by
following the model of Mendelssohn and, through the practice
of this philosophy, endeavoured to integrate themselves into
broader German culture.[33] They professed the Beautiful Soul
both for the benefits it could bring for the assimilation of Jews,
as well as for the universal values that it held in promoting
tolerance, empathy, and understanding.[34] Its meritocratic
principles proffered a form of cultural assimilation that did not
require the negation of one's roots or personal identity.[35] This
philosophy did not depend on conditions set at birth, but rather
on choices made by the individual through the cultivation of
the mind. Although the Beautiful Soul was first formulated by
non-Jewish philosophers, the concept embraced essential
aspects of Jewish culture: a deep appreciation of art, music,
and novel ideas. It adhered to principles practiced through the
exercise of one's reason, integral to the Haskalah tradition. As
such, it could serve as a common point of reference for
Christian and Jewish communities.

The Beautiful Soul was also an attractive philosophy to a
Jewish elite for whom community was an important value
since it advocated moral development through friendship and
encounters with others. The possibility of finding common
ground through personal relationships, like the exemplary

friendship and intellectual collaborations between Moses Mendelssohn and Gotthold Ephraim Lessing (1729-1781), offered cooperation towards mutual goals and more immediate prospects for social assimilation. Given their commitment to secular education and the emphasis they already placed on cultivating intellectual faculties, if *Bildung* were to be adopted by the population, the Jewish people would naturally become integrated into German society and the tensions of religious difference would be diminished.

It was not simply the Beautiful Soul's meritocratic quality, alignment with basic Jewish values, and promises of assimilation that so greatly appealed to the Jewish gentry. This philosophy was also inherently attractive from an aesthetic and political perspective. Mendelssohn fervently believed in the power of beauty to improve the human soul and the capacity of aesthetic pleasure to advance moral faculties. He argued that "the delight in metaphysical perfection will outweigh all pain and attune man to a recognition of his moral duties," a sentiment at the core of this tradition.[36]

In his essay, "What Is Enlightenment?" (1784), Mendelssohn defines the terms "Aufklärung," "Kultur," and "*Bildung*," arguing that *Bildung* is the most essential of the three. Enlightenment, associated with knowledge and reason, and culture, affiliated with art and morality, are the two pillars of *Bildung*, but it is ultimately *Bildung itself* towards which humans should strive.[37] In this essay alone, we can see the centrality of the concept to the concerns of Jewish intellectuals and its position at the forefront of the Haskalah tradition.

The actors behind the institutional advancement of the Beautiful Soul became political and cultural leaders of the Jewish people. Prominent families such as the Mendelssohns were considered the human embodiment of *Bildung*: a model for a new, more enlightened German citizenship. The Jewish elite began to train their children according to its principles; they received a broad humanistic education that included literature, history, languages, music, and the liberal arts.[38] Many of the Jewish *salonnières* were educated within this pedagogical tradition.[39] Henriette Herz had a rigorous secular education that applied the values of *Bildung* with a special emphasis on music. Sara Grotthuis was educated by Moses Mendelssohn himself. Dorothea Schlegel was the daughter of Moses Mendelssohn, who also directed her *Bildung* education. Subsequently she married Friedrich Schlegel, one of the Beautiful Soul's most important theorists, whom she met at Herz's salon. When the *salonnières* became adults, the Beautiful Soul became the "guiding force" of their lives, shaping their identity, belief system, and aspirations.[40] Their letters reveal the centrality of this concept to their intellectual development as well as the psychological significance that they attributed to it.

Given the educational importance placed on the Beautiful Soul, the Jewish people's special reverence for its principles, and the *salonnières'* personal dedication to its teachings, we can clearly see how this philosophy became the foundational ethos and motivational force behind the establishment of their salons. Like the Jewish societies that promoted *Bildung* through their musical events, sustaining a community dedicated to mutual enlightenment was a pragmatic way to advance this philosophy. Salon participants viewed the pursuit of the refined and "cultivated personality" as the common element that brought coherence to the institution.[41]

The salon became the embodiment of the Beautiful Soul through the practice of its values as well as a space in which to debate its ideas in a diverse audience, marking an important practical development in the transition from concept to reality.

The *salonnières* used their salons for the theorists of the Beautiful Soul to congregate so that they could further these ideas in a receptive environment. One particularly evocative description depicts illustrious figures including Wieland, Schiller, Herder, and Goethe in a salon:

> And while we are still dreaming, thinking we see Wieland, meagre, the skull cap on his high forehead, striding toward us while haggard Schiller, one arm on the table, reads with his Swabian accent a philosophical theme, and Herder, portly but disapproving, makes discontented faces, and Goethe, with the sober dignity of a counsellor, listens attentively, leaning on the window-sill—we are bidden to enter a friendly looking room, whose pale green colouring is wonderfully restful to our eyes after the red, white and gold of the outer apartment.[42]

Another telling passage reveals the extent to which these theorists would have interacted with one another in this space, arguing, debating, and exchanging ideas:

> Mere nobility is almost barred at these dinners; one sees instead Wieland, Goethe, Herder, Schiller, Knebel, and anyone else who represents the arts. There are hot, wordy battles, for most of them have a grudge against some or all of the others; Herder against Schiller, Goethe against Wieland, Wieland against Herder. There are moments when Herder, through his arrogance, stirs the gall of the poet of Oberon, who will let his feelings have expression when he gets home.[43]

In Herz's salon alone, prominent philosophers such as Johann Gottlieb Fichte, Friedrich Schiller, Wilhelm von Humboldt, and Friedrich Schlegel were regular participants. They garnered greater fame and recognition in the salons.[44] The *salonnières* themselves should be included in this category of *Bildung* theorists because they reflected on and wrote extensively about this philosophy. Varnhagen produced a wealth of epistolary exchanges on *Bildung*, and Schlegel wrote her own *Bildungsroman, Florentin* (1801). And so, these *salonnières* accomplished a triple feat of enacting the Beautiful Soul by cultivating minds through conversations, by providing the necessary spaces for different people to discuss the theory, and by developing the theory themselves.

The male proponents of this philosophy often acknowledged the critical role that the *salonnières* played in inspiring their ideas and facilitating the interactions that allowed them to collaborate with others. Lessing, Herder, and Goethe, for example, praised Sara Grotthuis for the brilliance of her salon, as well as her personal qualities which reflected the beauty of her soul, such as her lively spirit and her talent for languages that allowed her to communicate with many different people.[45] The intense correspondence that these men maintained with the *salonnières* further influenced their work.

Many of the characters in the *Bildungsroman* were inspired by the *salonnières* and the participants in their salons.[46] As an artform itself, the *Bildungsroman* is similar in tone and style to salon conversations and may plausibly be interpreted as a mimetic tribute to the salon.[47] In a *Bildungsroman* the protagonists typically undergo a personality transformation through having their ideas tested by other people in new settings. From their formative experiences, they learn about themselves and the world, and, consequently, become more enlightened human beings. This was precisely the objective of salon conversation: to overcome ignorance and prejudice through interactions with others and to enrich one's intellectual perspectives.

Devotion to the Beautiful Soul in the salon can best be seen in the obsession the *salonnières* had with the cultural figure and the work of Goethe. Goethe was at once their God and their lover, their idol, and their friend. He provided them with a sense of purpose and belonging in the world. His formulation of *Bildung* rendered their own intuitions palpable and philosophically legitimate. Enthusiasm for Goethe was one of the most important aspects of the salons. The most famous *salonnières* had a personal relationship with him or, at least, had met him on several occasions and were deeply inspired by their encounters.[48] He frequently appeared at the salons and left a strong, and overwhelmingly positive impression.[49] Following their meeting in 1795, Goethe habitually visited the salon of Sara Grotthuis which he used as a space to promulgate his work.[50] They were in close correspondence from 1795 to 1824 and she often consulted him on the intellectual questions she found most important.

The author and essayist of the *Sturm und Drang* movement, Karl Philipp Moritz (1756-1793), who regularly attended the salon of Herz, installed a "cult of young Goethe" in this circle.[51] They practiced neo-humanism and the ideals of the "harmonious personality" which sought to achieve individual perfection of mind, soul, and body through salon society with its emphasis on music, literature, and art. Goethe's works continued to play a significant and recurring role in Herz's salon during its active decades.

But it was Varnhagen who was most in love with the spirit of

Goethe's work; so in love that after her first meeting with him in 1795, she feared what a personal relationship with him would mean, so powerfully did his presence affect her. In a letter to her friend David Veit (1771-1814) she wrote, "I cannot be blindly captivated by any person so that I don't go in for worship…because otherwise I would certainly have fallen in love with Goethe, and, you know, I only worship him."[52] Varnhagen understood that she had to obey "an impulse that comes from my innermost self, to keep a humble distance from Goethe" for fear that she would become so wholly devoted to him that she would lose all sense of self.[53] Her acute self-awareness demonstrates that the ideals of the Beautiful Soul, not simply the theorists themselves, captivated the minds of the *salonnières*.

Varnhagen remained intellectually devoted to Goethe for her entire life and defended him against the unfavourable commentary of the second school of Romantic writers. The power and charisma that she possessed as a *salonnière* was kindled by Goethe; she drew endless inspiration from his creative spirit and ability to show everything as essence.[54] She did more for the proliferation of his poetry in her salons than anyone else of her time.[55] She begged her generation to "listen to Goethe" and, indeed, they listened when she spoke.[56]

The intense relationship between Varnhagen and Goethe exemplifies the philosophical spirit in which her salon, and those of other Jewish *salonnières,* were born. These pioneering women were intellectually consumed by *die schöne Seele*. Their belief in its philosophy was genuine, impassioned, earnest. They gave themselves wholly to its ideals. The *salonnières'* creative act of maintaining their salons was sustained by the prospect of cultivating the beautiful souls that they had contemplated in the abstract but desired to produce in living form. The salons were their vision of a future in which individuals could take part in establishing a society founded upon the poetic ideals and noble values which they so passionately held.

By exploring the features of the Beautiful Soul which the *salonnières* systematically sought to embody and cultivate in others, we will see the extent to which they successfully created a more beautiful and virtuous world, elevating what it meant to be human. Their pioneering efforts will inform our examination of how to cultivate a beautiful soul in the modern age.

Part 2

Cultivating a Beautiful Soul

CHAPTER 5

On Inner Activity and Reaching One's Full Potential

T HE idea that every person possesses an innate cognitive potential is at the core of the philosophy of the Beautiful Soul. Subject to the force of personal volition, this potential can be cultivated to ennoble the soul, strengthen character, and ultimately improve the human condition. Potential is conceived in poetic terms as beautiful universes within the self; infinite realms of possibility that might positively inform one's life course and actions in the world.[57] Although theoretically limitless, most human potential lies dormant. The fundamental aim of this philosophy is to identify the most promising elements of one's latent state and to bring them into full realisation. By doing so, one enriches one's own life and plays a critical role in the formation of a just society.[58]

Schiller describes the wealth of ideas and possibilities held within a beautiful soul, remarking that "a soul of beauty bears in itself by anticipation all great ideas; they flow without constraint and without difficulty from its very nature-an infinite nature, at least in potency, at whatever point of its career you seize it."[59] Goethe similarly believed that the whole world exists within us. These thinkers argue that only once the individual is fortified with full knowledge of their internal nature can they grow nourished by the influences of the world around them. The first task of this philosophy, then, is to arrive at greater self-knowledge.

Among the innumerable potentialities in this infinite self are the ideal elements of one's own character and the qualities necessary to become an exemplary member of society. Schiller observes that every person carries within an ideal version of themself waiting to be awakened and to flourish in the world.[60] Humankind, he argues in his *Aesthetic Letters*, has the autonomy to discover and develop innate, positive characteristics that will improve their being.[61]

Intrinsic to this notion of potential is the belief that every individual has their own *telos*, a greater purpose or objective, one that they are meant to discover and to fulfil. Finding one's *telos* is the first aim of any cultivated individual, a highly personal task that no one else can assist in achieving. According to this philosophy, people ineluctably desire to discover their *telos* since this is what gives their life meaning.

Cultivating potential is considered natural and often analogised to organic processes in environmental systems. Much can be learned about *Bildung* from nature and vice versa. Indeed, the word *Bildung* may be translated as "formation" in reference to the shaping of natural forces.[62] Describing the process of self-cultivation through biological metaphors became a common practice around 1790 when Goethe's influential text, *The Metamorphosis of Plants*, tangibly illustrated otherwise opaque and immaterial processes. One of the most common organic metaphors is Humboldt's comparison of a person's development to a seed induced to blossom. If this "seed" (the soul) does not thrive, then it represents what Goethe analogises to the *Incompletae*, a species of plant that remains incomplete and imperfect.[63]

Schiller warns that people often develop only a part of their capacities, while the rest remain feeble like stunted plants.[64] But, unlike a plant whose *telos* is physiologically pre-determined, to be human means to dynamically evolve in an autonomous cognitive capacity in order to ascertain for oneself what constitutes those teleological ends. People harness the capacities of their nature and in doing so they may ultimately overcome limitations and achieve the full realisation of their potential.[65] Change that is analogous to organic transformations, yet exists through the capacity for self-determination, is the means by which one achieves one's *telos*.[66]

This philosophy places great faith in the power of human agency to achieve self-realisation. Its theorists reject deeply entrenched social hierarchies that envision most of humanity as passive agents in a predetermined social order. They adamantly deny the constraints of inherited personality traits on the capacity to change character, affirming an individual's capacity to transcend the deterministic trajectory of their life; thereby a person can construct themself in ways that align most closely with their personal aspirations.

Even during times of social or political turmoil, when an ideal of self-improvement is thwarted by imperfect environmental conditions, the interior activity of the individual can challenge an imperfect *status quo*; they can actively evolve based solely on their own volition. This philosophy shifts the conceptual locus of power from passive, impenetrable social structures to the active development of one's personhood.

Most people cultivate a fraction of the infinite possibilities of being that are inherently available to them. With time these possibilities narrow, and a static set of adopted characteristics and personality traits comes to define a person and their interactions with the world. Often these characteristics suppress the most promising potentialities from reaching fruition, while self-repression stymies personal growth. But there is no reason why this must be the case; other more beautiful and virtuous ways of being can be discovered, nurtured, and illuminated from within. The problem is not an incapacity to become intellectually cultivated or morally good. Rather, the problem resides in a lack of motivation and conviction. By harnessing one's will, these impediments may be successfully overcome.

A person who was raised by cruel and self-centred parents, for example, is not fated to become cruel and self-centred themself. Rather than replicating problems, they can break from this cycle and overcome their familial environment. Indeed, many of the characters of the *Bildungsroman* are depicted as escaping the conditions of their birth, ultimately triumphing over the constraints of their social contexts by exercising a self-determined identity.[67] Instead of yielding to the assumptions of the social worlds into which they were born, humans may defy them and reach more exalted states.

Evidently, it is easier to foster moral behaviour in a milieu that encourages it, rather than one in which the individual must fight against the odds. Therefore, the construction of environments that stimulate potential (such as the space of the salon) is fundamental to the wider attainment of the Beautiful Soul. Yet, if people do not first recognise the potential within themselves, the course of their development will be predicated on an overdependence on their original circumstances. Environments can greatly encourage potential, but only when the desire to improve comes from within can an individual achieve the autonomy necessary for self-cultivation.

Often people who have been fortunate in their social position will squander their advantages. A child who is wholly uninterested in learning will not miraculously excel academically by being enrolled in a resource-rich preparatory school. A person who is insensitive to beauty will not necessarily find

44

meaning in music if they attend a masterful symphony. Much of this process, then, relates to training one's mind to reject apathy rather than changing external environmental realities.

The universal agency that this philosophy espouses comes with the corresponding moral responsibility to cultivate inner faculties. If the individual neglects to develop their innate potential, they deny themself a more meaningful existence. They also shirk their duty to contribute to the betterment of humanity, which is considered a sign of moral frailty.

Action, therefore, begins inwardly with the cultivation of the self. In his *Monologues* (1800), the philosopher and theologian Friedrich Schleiermacher (1768-1834) captures how internal reflection leads to a felicitous external state:

> Oh, how much richer my life has become! What a happy self-consciousness of my inner worth, what a heightened feeling for my own life and existence, crowns my self-reflection now that I consider the rewards of so many beautiful days! Not in vain was my quiet activity, which externally seemed like idleness. It has nicely aided my inner development.[68]

In mentioning idleness, he alludes to the standard critique of this philosophy: that cultivating the soul surely cannot produce tangible results. Animalistic instinct and injudicious decision-making are quicker to action than any contemplative response. But just because cultivated activity takes longer to develop does not mean it is any less effectual. On the contrary, only meditated action can produce lasting results.

According to Schiller, there is nothing more agreeable to a beautiful soul than inner activity.[69] Likewise, for Goethe, all human worth is derived from doing: "How can a man come to know himself? Never by thinking, but by doing. Try to do your duty, and you will know at once what you are worth."[70] Humboldt similarly argues that the more activity one does, the more likely one is to do good. It is only man's active energy "that can turn the most promising seed into a full and precious blessing for himself."[71]

To self-cultivate is not a pursuit that one casually adopts; its ends can never be achieved in a desultory, cavalier fashion. Self-cultivation is the ultimate activity to which all one's thoughts and actions should be directed.[72] Beyond basic subsistence, what is the purpose of existence if not to improve morally and intellectually, and by doing so, to create beauty and goodness in the world? The concept may seem instinctual to any person with an inclination to use their higher faculties. Yet it appears striking and original in a world where often the most evident truths are the ones most occluded.

If one accepts the fundamental idea that it is our personal responsibility to improve ourselves, then not doing so shows a weakness of character, which, along with indolence, epitomises the human frailty these theorists so assiduously worked to overcome. As Friedrich Schlegel says "Whoever remains indifferent and lazy does not care for the dignity of art and humanity. What use are the achievements of *Bildung* without a secure foundation? What use is vitality without a sure direction, without proportion and balance?"[73] The Beautiful Soul demands indefatigable, lifelong dedication and practice. Personally constructed and continuous forms of self-improvement constitute the core reality of this concept.

In the literature, the figure of the Beautiful Soul is strong and active, with a mind constantly animated. Once the protagonist deemed the Beautiful Soul in Goethe's *Wilhelm Meister's Apprenticeship and Travels (1795)* discovers that her ends are those of a spiritual nature, she relentlessly gives herself up to their pursuit. It is not the ends she chooses but rather the passion with which she pursues them that distinguishes her and legitimises her personification as a beautiful soul. The fictional character's uncle acknowledges that this is what makes her so special.[74] He concludes that decision and perseverance are the noblest qualities and that man's primary vocation is activity.[75]

In the novel the activity that the uncle identifies as the purpose of humanity is represented by the characters of the Beautiful Soul and Wilhelm Meister, respectively. With her spiritual devotedness, which is meant to represent commitment to the non-physical dimensions of existence rather than to organised religion, the Beautiful Soul personifies the need to develop moral values. In contrast, Wilhelm Meister's adventures into the outer world and the evolution of his character by action, represents the value of experience. Each of these perspectives prove important to the formation of the self— but present their own challenges if not maintained in balance with the other. The Beautiful Soul, for example, is so adamant about her internal development that she forgoes important experiences in the world while Wilhelm Meister could at times benefit from greater self-reflection before acting. As Goethe demonstrates, the ideal soul of beauty must live up to their responsibility to balance their mental states with their worldly representations of these states.

Once their potential has been achieved, the individual is meant to integrate their actualised potential with that of their social milieu, like organisms in an ecosystem maintaining their functions to serve the larger whole. Human potential is represented by a conception that every individual strives towards the ideal version of themself by strengthening their inner qualities and synthesising them with the developed capacities of others. An enlightened society will be one in which the full breadth of human capacities is present, and a universal ideal of ultimate potential is symbolised by the individual who fulfils their own.

Part of what this means is to perceive the potential in oneself as well as in others and to help them attain their potential as well. As Goethe remarks:

> I have come to the frightening conclusion that I am the decisive element. It is my personal approach that creates the climate. It is my daily mood that makes the weather. I possess tremendous power to make life miserable or joyous. I can be a tool of torture or an instrument of inspiration, I can humiliate or humour, hurt or heal. In all situations, it is my response that decides whether a crisis is escalated or de-escalated, and a person is human-ised or de-humanised. If you treat an individual as he is, he will remain how he is. But if you treat him as if he were what he ought to be and could be, he will become what he ought to be and could be.[76]

Although the individual must discover their inner world, others can assist in drawing out their finer qualities—but only if they understand what they are capable of and believe in their abilities. Human possibility ultimately arises, then, from an optimistic spirit and an imagination vivid enough to see beyond the present. The philosophy of the Beautiful Soul understands human nature, not in terms of what it is, or what it seems to be, but in terms of what it *could* be according to moral ideals that are held to be universally true. This is the

48

difference between being and becoming—and the prospects associated with becoming are endless.

The Berlin *salonnières* adamantly affirmed this philosophy's ideas on potential. These ideas sustained their intellectual activities and were a main motivation for founding their salons. Rahel Varnhagen most strongly asserted the expansive development of the self and all its potentialities in a manner that corresponded closely to *Bildung*.[77] She believed that a truly cultivated person is one who uses their capacities to the fullest and amplifies the faculties inherent in them at birth.

Following Schiller, who argues that it is more admirable to assiduously develop oneself than to be a natural genius for whom these potentialities appear to emerge without effort, Varnhagen understood self-cultivation to be something that one does not inherit whole cloth. Rather it is a process of development that requires bringing dormant qualities into being through concerted effort. A highly educated person, she said:

> Is not one whom nature has treated lavishly: an educated person is one who uses the talents he has kindly, wisely and properly, and for the highest purpose…who can look firmly at where he is lacking and realise what he is lacking. In my mind this is a duty and not a gift; and constitutes for me solely an educated human being.[78]

In arguing that it is a duty to develop one's potential, she affirms the individual's agency to improve their condition, while also making explicit that with this agency comes a set of responsibilities to oneself and to others.

The correspondence between Varnhagen and her friend

David Veit are replete with hopeful references to human potential and *Bildung*. Veit's letters encourage her to self-educate and practice the principles of this philosophy in order to further Jewish social integration.[79] In his view, only by bringing her potentialities into being could she overcome the limitations of her social standing. Rather than wait for political tides to turn or social attitudes to change, she could contribute to shaping her personal destiny. She directly affirmed this sentiment by acknowledging her identification with *Bildung*.[80]

Varnhagen believed that the need to achieve one's ideal state should come naturally to all people. In a letter to her husband, the diplomat Karl August Varnhagen von Ense (1785-1858), she writes at length about the importance of his and her own self-cultivation as well as the all-encompassing nature of this pursuit:

> Yes, you are yourself what you judge best and most impartially and therefore you are also the person most capable of acquiring cultivation, perhaps I ought to say the most cultivated person…We are also cultivated; we must cultivate ourselves as water must rush, such cultivation is happiness…Yours is a noble act of your whole moral being; it is not only the morality imposed by your nature, but a morality that should be demanded of all rational creatures; from you and from your nature it emerges of its own accord.[81]

Varnhagen believed that, like a heart that must beat, the desire to reach one's full potential is a property intrinsic to any healthy organism. Varnhagen went as far as to say that if this desire is not present, then the person in question is dead.

Mirroring Goethe's metaphor of the plant that does not grow, she believed that a human whose faculties remain stagnant and who lacks the will to improve, cannot truly claim to be alive beyond the rudimentary functioning of their biological system. In referring to Fichte, she states, "Whoever believes in a fixed, permanent, and dead Being, believes in it only because he is dead in himself."[82] She asserts that "It depends upon ourselves to become human beings."[83]

From this perspective, to be human is not a pre-given or stationary state, but rather an earned condition that depends on the continual cultivation of latent qualities. Her ideas echo those of Fichte and Herder on the Enlightenment ideal of *Humanität*, a predestined state of human perfection that is not a given but one that individuals achieve, and, in doing so, fulfil a necessary historical process in the formation of humankind.[84]

According to Varnhagen and her fellow *salonnières*, all people are given the equal possibility of being both alive and fully human at birth. But most people fail to achieve what is available to them. Instead of developing as a human should, they remain dead inside and exist in an inhuman state, their faculties numbed to new knowledge, emotion, and experience. They mechanically fulfil functions, unmoved by the great beauty of their surroundings, uninterested in exploring the vast potentialities associated with their nature. Over time, the possibilities of being diminish.

The *salonnières* understood that a "dead being" can rarely escape its condition in isolation. Individuals cannot comprehend their own failings or live up to the promises associated with their nature when they are limited by restricted perceptions; neither can they understand the flaws in their engagement with a world where contingency and irrationality prohibit a linear path to personal development. Very few people have sufficient volition or a favourable set of circumstances to develop on their own. Cultivating human potential requires the active support of a community and a structure for self-improvement.

Salons were conceived as a distinct opportunity to save individuals from this invisible "soul-death" by providing them with an environment dedicated to the development of the latent potentials of selfhood. A small, enlightened community that acted according to the principles of the Beautiful Soul was uniquely suited to nurture these latent human qualities.

The *salonnières* attempted to overcome the lethargy of a world of unlived potential and regain the lost promise of a better future. In creating their salons to escape this state of "dead being," they re-envisioned their own fates and invited their salon guests to do the same by giving them new opportunities for self-actualisation. The *salonnières* were the catalysts of cultivation for their salons, perpetually considering the condition of their soul and working towards its improvement. They possessed the rare ability to bring incipient qualities into full maturation. They chose a specific *metier* from the infinite universe of potentiality: their salons and literary careers, which they ardently developed. But they also embraced the more expansive spectrum of possibilities available to them by playing musical instruments, learning new languages, reading widely, and, perhaps most important, engaging in conversations and social relations that expanded their intellectual horizons.

For those who recognised the "germ of potential" within and were determined to improve their condition, which was the antecedent requirement for anyone participating in a salon, the *salonnières* provided the regular occasion and structure for them to do so. They facilitated the development of the potential associated with character, morality, and intellect in curated conversations whose underlying motivation was to catalyse latent qualities and bring unborn ideas into being.[85] They contributed to the potential associated with artistic projects and intellectual pursuits by providing a space in which to develop the imagination and to present works for constructive critique and creative formation. Their aspiration was to make apparent the infinite possibilities of being, while helping each person reach their own version of an ideal self.

Salon participants understood that diligent self-cultivation requires continuous motion directed towards this end. Since the salons occurred regularly, usually every week with intervening visits to or correspondence with participants, salon culture encouraged personal development as an active process, an ongoing responsibility integrated into one's daily routine. Intimate interactions afforded all those who were present with the opportunity to strive towards a higher state of self-realisation through the continuous expression and development of their ideas.

Sustained interactions ensured that salon participants understood the core belief system and character of other participants so that they could first acknowledge one another's perceptions and then evolve from these assumptions. This proffered the possibility of developing more complex perspectives and nuanced ways of thinking that could not occur without ongoing socialisation. Questions could be revisited, and the various topics of different salons could be connected to shape a coherent intellectual trajectory.

Both the *salonnière* and her participants prepared for the conversations that would take place in the salon. Those who gained entrance once were expected to participate thereafter for the purpose of sustained self-development. Regular attendance ensured that a salon was not a singular event but rather a serious commitment that could achieve its stated goals. With admittance came the obligation to continuously engage within the space and actively contribute to it. Varnhagen expressed the importance of activity when she remarked "What makes the mind and soul of man older than inactivity?...Think always ceaselessly! This is the only duty, the only happiness."[86]

The *salonnières'* role as moral and intellectual educators extended beyond the salons themselves. They discussed the latest ideas, challenged perspectives, and maintained lengthy correspondences. This was a position that they took seriously because they understood that self-cultivation could not end at the conclusion of a salon, for this would diminish its significance in informing the trajectory of a person's life. Self-cultivation within the salon had to be an uninterrupted and life-long pursuit.

The *salonnières* engaged their participants in an individualised pathway towards improvement by continuing to discuss the subject matter of the salons and its members' own reflections throughout the week. The salon transformed the Beautiful Soul from an abstract theory into a tangible structure of human activity performed with diligence and devotion. Its ability to encourage sustained practice in the art of self-cultivation may be considered one of its greatest achievements.

The *salonnières'* dedication to cultivating human potential appears highly relevant today. Our cityscapes swarm with advertisements and motivational quotations that encourage us to improve ourselves by developing our capacities, whether it be through wellness programs, personal growth workshops, or meditation retreats. While the desire to improve is self-evident, it is crucial not to conflate the trends of the technological era with the historical conception of what cultivating potential means, since they are, in fundamental respects, diametrically opposed.

Cultivating potential, as Goethe and Schiller envisioned it, is a continuous exploration of the self, requiring a lifetime of assiduous commitment, a perpetual re-evaluation of how we have grown and which areas we must develop. This philosophy demands that we explore the worlds within, methodically determining where our latent possibilities lie. There is no end to this goal and there are no short cuts or formulaic paths for achieving it.

The greatest deterrence to the achievement of potential, beyond inertia, is the pursuit of superficial ends. We should remain wary of attempts to neatly package "self-help" endeavours to make us feel good about ourselves all the while our fundamental being remains unchanged. Developing potential cannot occur simply by buying motivational courses or following wellness trends. Nor can it be pursued with the indolence with which many contemporary self-improvement initiatives are approached. These singular, desultory activities will never be able to achieve the all-encompassing ends towards which this philosophy aspires. Indeed, it would be a travesty to conflate the often-superficial fashions of a given time with the demanding work of cultivating our inner life.

Emblematic of the superficial values that stunt our potential in the age of social media is the ubiquitous act of obsessively taking pictures of ourselves. While some may suggest that this social phenomenon is essentially harmless, its pervasiveness reveals that we prioritise physical appearance over the development of inner capacities. This should be a warning that our very conception of human worth has been perverted. In privileging the artificial projection of surface-level values, in any scenario, no matter how trivial it may seem, we risk pursuing ends that are personally fruitless and socially divisive.

Our culture encourages us to become shallow and self-involved so that we are no longer embarrassed about posting images of luxury holidays, gym-honed bodies, or diamond engagement rings on social media platforms. If we are embarrassed, we justify it with a misquoted Rumi line or an empty inspirational saying to force misappropriated meaning onto that which is fundamentally meaninglessness. Narcissists who make their money and gain influence out of actively encouraging economic, social, and physical inequalities are, for some inexplicable reason, lauded by a society purportedly concerned with social justice and equality. But logic and consistency no longer matter in our current desperate attempts to be noticed.

The myth of Narcissus aptly reveals the dehumanising dangers of extreme self-absorption. Narcissus, who is so obsessed with himself that he cannot bear to be torn away from his own reflection, eventually retreats to a state of nature, transforming into a flower. Like Goethe's plant metaphor, this myth illustrates that radical self-obsession ultimately stunts personal growth. The modern Narcissus who feels the need to take pictures of themself and express self-love on Twitter will similarly not have the capacity or fortitude to develop as a human being; personal weaknesses are obfuscated by a distorted perception of self.

In practicing this philosophy, we must resist the urge to partake in the inauthentic and self-aggrandising aspects of social media culture that distract us from the pursuit of more meaningful ends. If instead we value people reaching their full potential, then we cease to indulge our own narcissistic displays and refrain from adulating those of others. If our lives revolve around ephemeral pursuits such as power, fame, and physical appearances, or are controlled by other people's perceptions of us, then we must shift our priorities. Beautiful souls gravitate towards activities that are enduring and cannot be taken away from them: those that relate to the intellect and the spirit.

In order to overcome transient distractions to realise our potential, we must work diligently. Intrinsic to the cultivation of potential is a notion of relentless inner activity. Action constitutes the condition of the soul and determines its future flourishing. Accordingly, the soul is not an immutable entity but a malleable force susceptible to continuous change and development.

Cultivating a beautiful soul might appear like an all-consuming task, one which we no longer have the time to engage in as did the salon participants of centuries past. When we imagine what it was like to practice this philosophy, we might conjure images of people reclining in opulent living rooms, frittering the day away as they engage in esoteric conversations. Between our busy careers and familial responsibilities, who really has a moment to question the condition of their soul?

The problem, however, is not that we do not have time, but that we choose not to give priority to these ends. An excessively instrumental approach to time management often prevents us from partaking in pursuits of the mind. Any moment that is not spent on immediately advancing our wealth and social standing, or on idle forms of entertainment after an arduous day, is considered inessential. We spend countless hours scrolling through our social media newsfeeds but reading to enrich our intellect is perceived as a luxury. We must shift our priorities in order to acknowledge the value of rigorous personal development.

Self-cultivation relates to all the most important aspects of life. Fulfilling professional duties and familial responsibilities requires considering what they mean and how best to perform them. Improving character and worldly actions entails examining the ways in which behaviours can be improved. Every human activity—from personal relationships to career aspirations, cultural inspirations, and the general trajectory of our lives—immeasurably benefits from the intellectual clarity which this philosophy brings us. Cultivating a more beautiful soul may very well be the worthiest investment of our time.

When the philosophy of the Beautiful Soul was developed, activities undertaken outside of career aspirations were considered an essential aspect of personhood and an integral part of daily life. Engaging in conversation within a salon was not an idle social pastime but rather a scrupulous attempt at painstaking intellectual work. Although questioning the meaning of life or the nature of the human condition might sound too abstract to deem a valuable use of time in our contemporary world, such questions were previously considered a fundamental aspect of being alive, which everyone, not just philosophers should pursue.

Within my salons, I have found that the regularity of engagement plays a crucial role in the success of these events and the meaning that people derive from them. If potential is not cultivated systematically, and advancing the self is not in some way institutionalised, it becomes an unserious enterprise, one which fails to achieve results. Today, for instance, it is common to take language courses for a few months before abandoning them or attend a lecture series as a New Year's resolution that only lasts a few weeks. Salons, by contrast, are perceived by participants as an integral part of life. Even in times when social activities entail capriciously floating from one event to another to suit personal schedules and individual needs, the salon garners greater commitment because of its continuity. This sense of commitment is commensurate with the strength of the community and with the benefits received by helping individuals achieve their full intellectual potential.

Like the ideal salon participant, the practitioner of this philosophy must be conscious of its tenets and active in fulfilling its stringent demands. Every waking moment should, in theory, be an attempt to represent its ends. The all-encompassing significance of this philosophy makes it achievable because it is the very reason for being, not just a casual endeavour disconnected from daily life. Like breathing, practicing this concept becomes an intuitive, subconscious dimension of lived experience.

Pragmatically, the self-cultivated individual will regularly reflect upon the achievement of their full potential. If the activities that they engage in do not elevate their spirit or enrich their being, they must question their reasons for pursuing them and make changes to the way they live. The long periods consumed by indolence or distraction will be reclaimed to maximise the value of their finite time on earth. Unlike the quotidian activities of modern life which are, overall, either strategically useful but personally unfulfilling, or profoundly consumption oriented, beautiful souls give priority to pursuits that are intellectually, aesthetically, and morally rewarding.

CHAPTER 6

On Developing a Beautiful Character

T HE moral necessity of developing one's intellectual potential is principally directed at the cultivation of a beautiful and noble character. Indeed, beauty of soul is often equated with a state of perfect virtue and epitomised by a goodness of heart.[87]

The concern for virtue within this theory first emerged after the translation into German of Shaftesbury's *The Judgment of Hercules* in 1712.[88] In the drawing by Paolo de Matteis, which Shaftesbury examines in his work, Hercules sits between the figures of pleasure and virtue. On the right, pleasure reclines partially nude with the symbols of enjoyment around her. On the left, virtue points to the fortress of morality which stands in the distance. Hercules, torn between the two, is turned towards virtue as she speaks, a harbinger of his eventual choice. In making his decision, the theorists of the Beautiful Soul maintained that a process of *Bildung* is taking place within Hercules.[89] Like the fortress, the benefits of cultivation lie in the distance, while earthly pleasures promise immediate, yet unsustainable satisfaction. Ultimately, virtue proves the worthier pursuit, and the choice of the virtuous path represents the aim of this philosophy.

The virtues that the theorists of the Beautiful Soul were principally concerned with advocating were those formulated by the ancient Greeks and by the Prussians during the reign of

Frederick William I (1688-1740) — notably, courage, determination, humility, loyalty, reliability, sincerity, and a sense of service. One can find in the literature on the Beautiful Soul references to the self-cultivated person that touch upon the virtues of antiquity: prudence and fortitude, *agathos* defined by wisdom, bravery, justice, and the even more extensive list found in Aristotle's *Nicomachean Ethics*.[90] Drawing on these influences, Schiller claims that a beautiful soul will find pleasure in exercising justice, charity, temperance, fortitude, and fidelity as well as beneficence, moderation, constancy, and good faith.[91]

According to Aristotle, who inspired this philosophy's conception of virtue, the different virtues that we pursue will require an appropriate balance. For example, sociality in excess is obsequiousness. In deficit, it is cantankerousness. The ideal state of equilibrium is friendship. With regards to confidence, rashness is the extreme, while cowardice is the deficient state, and courage is the perfect mean. Finally, in temperament, irascibility is the negative excess, lack of spirit is the deficiency, and patience is the middle course.

Plato's *Phaedo*, which identifies courage and temperance as the virtues that constitute the Beautiful Soul, and his *Symposium*, were particularly influential works in these discussions, especially Diotima's "beauty of soul" dialogue in the *Symposium*. Here Diotima differentiates between those who are pregnant in the body and those pregnant in the soul and suggests that those with beautiful souls engender wisdom and virtue.[92] In her example, a poet outwardly expresses his inward state through his poetry.

Likewise, virtue is the external consequence of one's internal development, the natural product of a cultivated soul. As Goethe's maxim goes, "A man's manners are the mirror in which he shows his portrait."[93] The more fertile the inner world becomes, the more fruit it outwardly bears. Diotima's metaphor of birth is fitting because it captures the organic expression of an internal process that frames cultivation, not as a solipsistic pursuit without real world consequences, but as one able to beget a set of virtues that are socially significant.

Given the Greek influence on the virtues that the theorists of the Beautiful Soul advocated, we might classify these virtues according to the Platonic triad. Beauty is communicated through prudence, humility, sincerity, and most importantly, temperance and the harmonious balance of character traits. Truth is conceived as the logical exercise of rational faculties which involve wisdom, the courage to stand for what is correct, and the determination to pursue knowledge for its own sake. Goodness is found in a strong sense of justice, the exercise of kindness and benevolence, the capacity to feel compassion for others, and the loyalty and devotion necessary to respect another person's dignity and worth.

We may consider virtues that fall under the Platonic category of the Good, especially kindness and empathy, to be the cardinal virtues of this philosophy, since they are most often associated with fictional depictions of beautiful souls. According to standard interpretations, beautiful souls perform acts of charity: they resolutely work towards the wellbeing of their friends and family; and they unquestioningly help those around them in need, especially the poor and suffering. Their goodness is the mother of all virtues. Without it, virtues such as prudence and bravery can easily become occluded by poor intent or take a false turn. As Schiller writes, "virtue itself only becomes beautiful through kindness."[94] Beautiful souls perform benevolent actions, not from rigid adherence to moral law, but rather because they are inspired to do so because of their fundamental kindness and empathy. The propensity to be kind is the product of personal volition as well as their natural inclination towards the Good.

In "On Grace and Dignity" Schiller defines a beautiful soul from this perspective, in a subtle yet significant disagreement with Kant on the nature of moral responsibility. Kant makes a distinction between duty and inclination, favouring duty and pure practical reason, arguing that inclination cannot possess the features of morality. Schiller, in contrast, reasserts the primacy of inclination with his contention that virtue is "an inclination for duty." An ideal state of virtue (one which defines the Beautiful Soul) embodies the harmony of reason and sensibility, duty and inclination. Here, Schiller bridges the gap that Kant leaves open between moral law and individual inclination, with his concept of grace as "moveable beauty"—a beauty which is "not given by nature but produced by the subject itself."[95]

Unlike a person who maintains strict obedience to those moral commitments that the Kantian perspective prioritises, a beautiful soul "carries out humankind's most exacting duties with such ease that they might simply be the actions of its inner instinct."[96] Schiller compares an individual rigidly adhering to morality to a student learning to draw; he creates unsubtle lines while diligently practicing the craft as he has been instructed. While the noble soul, on the other hand, "is like a painting of Titian; all the harsh outlines are effaced, which does not prevent the whole face being more true, lifelike and harmonious."[97] Like the painter whose merit can be seen in the fineness of his work, one can tell if the soul has been beautified by the ease with which it approaches its moral responsibilities. As Schiller writes, "an ideal person leading a truly good life would be one who spontaneously wanted to do what reason demands, that is, whose actions were in unforced harmony with the demands of reason."[98]

Schiller offers an illuminating parable describing distinct kinds of virtuous actions, one that captures the instinctiveness of moral propensity: a man lies on the ground after having been brutally attacked by robbers and is left without his possessions or his clothing. He asks the first traveller he sees for help. The traveller agrees to come to his assistance but admits that his naked, wounded appearance revolts him and demands that he asks for nothing more. The second traveller who passes feels that he needs to fulfil his duty to help when asked but demands that he be compensated monetarily for his time and effort. The third traveller listens to the poor man's story, but he is sick himself and hesitates to put the wellbeing of another at his own expense, although, in the end, to honour his sense of duty, he offers his coat. Then two men approach and it is revealed that they are sworn enemies of the wounded man. He expects only hatred and revenge from them, but instead they offer their clothing. Moved by this gesture, the wounded man expresses his gratitude and asks for their forgiveness. But they coldly reply that his transgressions are not forgiven: their acts of charity are nothing more than a demonstration of their own generosity towards a wretched man. Finally, the fifth traveller approaches with a heavy load. Disappointed by the state of humanity, the wounded man does not ask for help. But on his own volition the traveller puts down his load. He tells the wounded man to climb onto his back so that he can take him to safety. The wounded man asks him what will become of his load, to which the traveller replies that he does not know but it concerns him little, for giving a sick man help is more important than material goods.

In Schiller's interpretation of this parable, the first traveller makes a decision that demands no personal suffering and sets strict constraints on his generosity. The second is merely useful but not moral because he expects a benefit for himself out of his charitable act. The third man is moral in that he agrees to follow a prescribed duty, but his reluctance to act reveals a state of vacillation. The two enemies assault the dignity of the wounded man seeking self-aggrandisement which sullies the goodness of their act. All, in the end, help the wounded man; some offer to do so at their own expense, but only the fifth traveller does so without solicitation or consideration of the ramifications of his actions for himself. He ignores his own needs and thereby fulfils his duty "with the ease of someone acting out of mere instinct." His actions, Schiller concludes, are morally beautiful.

Beautiful souls, then, perform duties in this selfless and instinctual way. Their morality is as natural to them as breathing, without a trace of affectation, self-interest, or irresolution. The facility with which a beautiful soul unites duty and inclination through spiritual grace makes their entire character, not just their particular actions, moral. Even if the wounded man had benefitted from the first four travellers' charity, this charity would not reveal a beauty of soul because these actions were distorted by an underlying instrumentality.[99]

Implicit to this understanding of virtue as a natural inclination is a state of innocence and simplicity. Like a child's visceral understanding of morality, virtue should come instinctually. In "On Simple and Sentimental Poetry" Schiller describes this natural state with two examples. The first example is that of the child who, upon hearing of a person dying of hunger, offers his purse to relieve him of his misery. The child reflects a state of innocence in which goodness is not confused by calculation or artificiality. The second example is that of a good-hearted man who blindly divulges secrets to a deceitful friend. While his actions may be injudicious, they demonstrate his unconditional trust, which is pure and true.

Both examples appear naïve in a society that elides the simplicity of moral responsibilities; yet it is this naiveté that elicits our love and admiration. The mendacious social façade of the artificial person is exposed by the innocence of the child, or by the adult who has retained childlike simplicity. Yet even the most artificial people will respond to the child's goodwill with kindness because it is genuine. As Schiller remarks on the expressions of a child, "They make us smile because they are in opposition to received manners; but men would always agree in the bottom of their hearts that the child is right."[100] Beautiful souls, then, are those who, in their simplicity, exhibit the features of the young and return humanity to its pure, ideal form.[101]

Schiller is sceptical of those for whom virtue does not come naturally. He questions if they can really be said to be virtuous when they cannot even trust themselves.[102] If the feelings around moral duties are suppressed or not present, the virtue appears to be less pure and true and, despite a favourable outcome, the individual is considered a weaker moral agent. This does not mean that Kantian obedience to duty cannot become an inclination as well. Through *Bildung*, a predilection towards virtue might form so that Schiller's scepticism can be overcome. However, a *feeling* for morality is just as important to cultivate as any particular moral outcome.

Schiller concedes that the truest and most beautiful expression of virtue is an aspiration and not always a reality. Sometimes we will fail to achieve virtue when our sensibility conflicts with the moral law. In "On the Sublime" Schiller imagines a man who delights in practicing virtues and "all the duties whose accomplishment is prescribed to him by circumstance are only a play to him, and I admit that fortune favours him in such wise that none of the actions which his good heart may demand of him will be hard to him."[103] Although Schiller says that this man is charming because we find a pleasing harmony between his instinct and the prescriptions of reason, Schiller questions whether he could really be called a virtuous man. This is because we do not know the purity of his actions since they have never been challenged and he has not been confronted with the possibility of acting in any other way.

Schiller goes on to imagine the misfortunes that befall this man whose virtue is in question. "He is deprived of his possessions; his reputation is destroyed; he is chained to his bed by sickness and suffering; he is robbed by death of all those he loves; he is forsaken in his distress by all in whom he had trusted."[104] In this terrible situation Schiller encourages us to investigate whether the same virtues would manifest as those that did in times of happiness and prosperity. He posits that:

> If he is found to be absolutely the same as before, if his poverty has not deteriorated his benevolence, or ingratitude his kindly offices of good-will, or bodily suffering his equanimity, or adversity his joy in the happiness of others; if his change of fortune is perceptible in externals, but not in his habits, in the matter, but not in the form of his conduct; then, doubtless, his virtue could not be explained by any reason drawn from the physical order...[105]

Schiller concludes that, in this case, the man perceives and acts above the constraints and possibilities of the material world and beyond his very nature since his inclination towards virtue never waivers. In this ultimate victory of moral being over physical necessity, the man transcends all fortune and circumstance and enters the realm of the ideal. This state of virtue, while undeniably difficult to reach, is the aspiration of any cultivated individual.

Schiller's perspective has implications for the Beautiful Soul in several important ways. The conception of virtue to which he directs his readers is unconditional, less fickle than "situational moralities" that rely on specific outcomes, rather than on the spirit from which those outcomes are derived. Unlike pure duty, which risks rigidity, Schiller's perspective depicts virtue as an end which can pleasurably coincide with one's cultivated nature. As Schiller warns us, "the idea of duty is delivered in Kantian moral philosophy with a severity that frightens away all the Graces, and that could easily tempt a weak understanding to seek moral perfection along the path of a gloomy and monkish asceticism."[106]

By contrast, Schiller's optimistic approach makes pursuing virtue more desirable and so ultimately proves more effective in following moral law. As Schiller argues, the moral perfection of humankind should not require protracted struggle, and, even if there is initial struggle, it can ultimately be overcome through the refinement of attitudes.

This perspective is also persuasive in granting people agency by assuming that they are capable of beautiful feelings and need not subserviently adhere to abstract principles in order to perform moral actions. Through cultivation, inclinations can develop, and instincts can evolve to such an extent that they transcend moral prescriptions.

Agency and autonomy, therefore, distinguish the Beautiful Soul. This complete state of virtue is subjectively derived: in fact, it must be if it is to produce the free, unmediated moral inclinations that Schiller envisions. Although there are certain virtues often associated with a beautiful soul, there is no model or set of principles that a person is required to maintain. Indeed, these thinkers were adamant in their desire not to overly define a beautiful soul or to prescribe a canonical set of virtues to follow.

Of course, there are some virtues, such as kindness, that a beautiful soul cannot be without. However, the establishment of a more extensive list of virtues is subjective and their harmonisation within each person is thought to be unique. Furthermore, the path to virtuous self-realisation cannot be exogenously imposed; areas of personal weakness become apparent in the process of self-cultivation. It is the responsibility of the individual, in a highly personal act, to determine which virtues to adopt, and to interpret what these virtues mean to their own lived experience.

Part of the reason why this is so important is that if the individual has not internalised a set of values for themself, they will not truly grasp the nature of morality. If they only aspire to practice certain prescribed moral principles, rather than to attain a state of morality, then ultimately their performance may devolve into an imperfect condition to which, according to Schiller, even the most refined people are susceptible.[107] In other words, if the approach to virtue is mechanical, then virtue can easily become confused with, or distorted into, vice. A person might perform good acts, but that does not mean that the person is intrinsically good. So, to propagate actions or codes of conduct would largely miss the point. The truest dispositions towards virtue must be subjectively conceived and organically *felt*.

The Berlin *salonnières* saw virtue as an essential dimension of human potential to cultivate within their salons. But, in this spirit of subjective inquiry, they did not blindly accept a set of classical virtues without interrogating their nature, validity, and ultimately redefining them for themselves. Varnhagen was wary of duties and obligations that are fulfilled out of subservience to a moral order without critical inquiry: "Fulfilment of duty is often nothing else than a form of punctiliousness and officiousness!"[108] She resisted adopting virtues that are followed out of religious fear or thoughtless conformity to accepted codes of behaviour. She believed that virtuousness comes out of the self-determined, conscious recognition of one's moral duties, advocating a kind of intellectual autonomy that aligns closely with the ethos of this philosophy.

In a letter to her friend and salon participant, the diplomat Georg Wilhelm Bokelmann (1779-1847), Varnhagen argues that a person must never blindly assume that a system of morality is correct, or depend solely on custom to guide practice: lack of critical thinking can be a threat to morality itself. The individual must remain mentally engaged, constantly questioning the moral frameworks that they follow and must always prioritise truth over convention.[109] To Varnhagen, a virtuous person is one who is profoundly conscious of the ethical stances that they take and the moral decisions that they make.

Varnhagen had strong views on the virtues required for the practice of the Beautiful Soul. She asserted that courage, as well as honesty and truthfulness, are supremely important in understanding one's essential nature and the pursuit of what one believes to be just: "When one is honest in one's thoughts, one is true. And only in truth is health to be found."[110] Without these three integral virtues, she thought it impossible to arrive at the deeper forms of self-awareness that represent true moral consciousness. "Some people have too little understanding to find the truth within them, others no courage to acknowledge it, and the great majority neither courage nor understanding, but they wander and lie and grope or stagnate through life even to the grave."[111] She also believed that it is important to practice self-discipline, loyalty, duty, and thoughtfulness in relationships, but she perpetually re-evaluated what these virtues mean in different contexts and the problems they may pose in certain situations.[112]

Varnhagen considered the period of one's youth to be "the most virtuous, most beautiful, and easiest to set on fire" because young people have the courage to discover their best nature and the purity not to allow cynicism or bitterness to impede sound moral judgements.[113] A large percentage of salon participants were in their early to mid-twenties, when their minds were especially malleable and open to moral development.[114] For those older adults who participated in salons, Varnhagen suggested that they turn to the young to learn how to be virtuous, for, unlike the youth for whom virtue comes more easily, experience thwarts its manifestation later in life. Without critical interrogation, that which was once virtuous can become distorted or misrepresented in practice. To live virtuously with age therefore means to ennoble experience with logical reflection. This task is one which the salon was naturally suited to facilitate through the rational inquiry, emotional sensitivity, and openness to ideas that defined salon conversations and kept even the older participants mentally young.[115]

Like Varnhagen, Henriette Herz was committed to the practice of the virtues associated with the Beautiful Soul. She displayed this dedication in her establishment of a *Tugendbund*, a society of virtue, whose members and mission were shared with her salons.[116] This society promoted friendship and learning as well as mutual moral and spiritual education. The *Tugendbund* had its own statutes that intended to further enlightenment in Germany and to promote mutual *Bildung*.[117] Its aim was moral improvement through the questioning and practice of the virtues that the secret society determined were integral to the concept's tradition.

This society believed that by establishing intimate relationships of the mind, each member would be able to sense the essential dimensions of other people's characters which would, in turn, strengthen compassion and the ability to live congenially with others.[118] In the intellectual gatherings that Herz organised, the Humboldt brothers, among other prominent intellectuals of the Beautiful Soul, found a "virtuous union," the "exercise of working love," which in this case meant cultivating feeling and a moral inclination towards goodness. The society was believed to be the lifeblood of sensitivity, the most meticulous and comprehensive enactment of the virtues that the theorists of the Beautiful Soul espoused.[119]

The purpose of the *Tugendbund* was to develop a set of coherent and comprehensive virtues in a small, enlightened community before propagating them among the larger population to ensure that these virtues were fair and feasible. Herz's sense of obligation extended from the conception of virtues to their wider dissemination which she believed could benefit all members of society. In her autobiography she recounts educating Jewish beggar children in the virtuous principles of her secret society so that they, too, could advance from this common set of values.[120] The Berlin *salonnières* shared in their belief that virtue is the common language of humanity, the only true metric to judge a person's worth, and the means by which one may improve society.

The *salonnières'* personal practice and dissemination of the values they propounded gained them the appellation of the most virtuous women in the German speaking world. What was even more impressive to their contemporaries was that they appeared to do so at a time when it was not fashionable to be virtuous. Although the specific virtues that the *salonnières* embodied differed, they shared the quality of compassion. One might interpret this virtue to be a part of the Judeo-Christian tradition rather than the expression of the ideals of the Beautiful Soul. However, salon participants attributed the qualities that they observed in the *salonnières* to their *Bildung* education.

Humboldt, for example, believed that it was Herz's goodness, derived from cultivation in the tradition of *Bildung*, that gave her the capacity to assimilate into German culture; he implicitly associated her virtuousness with *Bildung*.[121] The painter Louise Seidler (1786-1866) praised Herz for her kindness, saying: "The magic of her beauty and simplicity enveloped her whole being; she was distinguished by her genuinely feminine goodness of heart. Completely modest, she seldom revealed her many talents, especially her great gift of languages."[122]

Kindness and compassion were foundational virtues to the establishment of salons because they allowed the *salonnières* to understand other human beings and to constructively facilitate communication and favourable social dynamics. Varnhagen was especially remembered for her extraordinary empathy, sensitivity, and impartiality, which played a critical role in her eminence as a *salonnière*.[123] At the same time, she was so sensitive that she found it to be a burden that hindered her capacity to live freely. She came to believe that the extremity of her virtue turned into a vice:

> These two qualities of mine are: too much gratitude
> and too much consideration for human feelings. I
> would sooner reach for my own heart…and hurt
> it than offend another person or even see an
> offended one. And I am too grateful because I
> always fared badly and always immediately think of
> helping and forgiving; and also because I alone
> always helped; …like a plant which grows toward
> the earth: the most beautiful qualities turn into the
> most hideous.[124]

Varhagen's concern for others was, indeed, at times of pathological proportions: her empathy was constantly sharpened by repression imposed by her overbearing father and the patriarchal expectation that she have physical charm, when in reality it was her brilliance that distinguished her from other women of her time.[125] She understood her empathy to be destructive because it was born from her own suffering: "Through my too great consideration…I therefore am really destroying myself, who strong in many ways, was intended for other things by carelessly prodigal nature. So it is! Thus I must continue to die: I have already died many times…"[126]

Yet, despite the personal pain that her profound sensitivity caused her, it was also a rare gift that ensured her success as a *salonnière*. She was highly attuned to people's feelings so that her salon participants felt included and respected in her presence. Her magnified receptivity to emotions allowed her to empathise with different types of people and to understand their innermost nature.

Varnhagen acknowledged that her celebrated "social gifts were nothing but kindness."[127] She also understood that her extreme sensitivity had the consequence of making her particularly receptive to her sensory faculties as well as to the new ideas and cultural products debated in the salon: "From my youth up my inner life has been rich and in accordance with truth. Nature acted keenly and truly upon keen organs; it has given me a firm, sensitive heart which always duly put life into all other organs."[128] The psychological prowess that Varnhagen and Herz possessed made them ideal arbiters of ideas and emotions in the intense social dynamic of the salon. The very nature of the institution depended on a facilitator sensitive to the subtleties of human feeling, one who cared enough about the condition of others to facilitate the group dynamic. A finely honed empathy was particularly germane to the position of *salonnière*.[129]

An essential dimension of this role was to employ empathy to cultivate virtues in salon participants and to establish positive forms of social exchange.[130] The *salonnières* revealed the best qualities of their guests and made everyone feel like a valued member of the community. They exercised skill in directing discourse without dominating the conversation and never allowed themselves, or a single salon participant, to be the centre of attention. They paid each person an equal measure of respect and consideration.[131] An anonymous visitor to Varnhagen's salon best described the sense of purpose that she bestowed to all:

> A kind as well as lightning quick grasp of human nature gave her the ease with which she could quickly find the favourable side of every person, which she then promptly brought to light and animated, while the less favourable side automatically remained in the shadow. In this way, she had a personal relation with each individual... Here then

was a true coming together no…empty form…ever did anyone, man or woman feel like an empty social decoration, a lifeless salon caryatid; whereas, in other circles, I have often seen how, because they have nothing in common with their host, even outstanding persons served as mere room fillers…[132]

In this refined display of sensitivity and benevolence, the *salonnières* acted as models of the social graces, and inspired these virtues in others. But, in order to assist in moral development, they also understood that they had a duty to compassionately identify the less cultivated character traits of each participant and to diplomatically challenge their limitations through conversation.

In a skilful, structured analysis of beliefs and ideas, the *salonnières* encouraged participants to overcome their intellectual shortcomings and to strive towards moral betterment in the carefully curated environment that they had created. To identify character flaws and to pare them away was a feat of great virtuosity, a delicate art in the navigation of human emotions that could only be accomplished by a particularly sensitive *salonnière*.

This delicate role of interpersonal diplomacy demanded that the *salonnières thoroughly* appraise salon participants in order to hold them accountable. Their judgements were made on the substance of the soul and the moral merit they had attained.[133] *Salonnières* learned not to show signs of deprecation or unconstructive criticality that would diminish the confidence of their salon participants. In their interpretation of this philosophy, anyone had the capacity to improve their character, and so, everyone, especially those deficient in virtue, needed their support.

This proffered charitability and generosity of perception solidified the *salonnières*' status as moral pedagogues whom their participants could trust, revealing themselves without fear of judgement. The French aristocrat and writer, the Marquis de Custine (1790-1857) said of Varnhagen, "she had the mind of a sage and the heart of an apostle..."[134] while the diplomat and writer Friedrich von Gentz (1764-1832), called her "the first being in this world," "teacher," "oracle" and "friend."[135]

Varnhagen admitted that while her credulity had its benefits, once again the extremity with which she practiced this virtue became a vice. "People had only 'to weep and wish' to make her believe them capable of the nobility they desired!"[136] Varnhagen was easily disappointed when her salon participants did not live up to her high expectations. Nevertheless, it was also the extremity of this virtue that made her a successful *salonnière* since her conviction in humankind imparted the capacity to extract the finest qualities out of those whose lives she touched.

When entering a salon, participants understood that they were submitting to the guidance of the *salonnière,* in matters not only of the mind but of the soul—a dimension unique to the German case. The integrative duality of mind and spirit emphasises the imperative of the Beautiful Soul to cultivate both intellectual and moral-aesthetic faculties. A purely intellectual approach to cultivation would not achieve the broader moral demands that the philosophy required. This is significant in understanding the influences of this concept on the *salonnières'* activities. For while it may appear that the purpose of the salon was either intellectual or social, this was not the case. Rather, sociability through enlightened conversation was the means by which to cultivate the virtues and a sense of moral responsibility that represented the primary ends of the salon.

Although reaching new knowledge was an important dimension of these discursive spaces, the *way* in which new knowledge and sociability was gained was most significant. Discussing a new work of literature, reading a poem, or investigating a scientific theory was futile if it was not expressed with the nobility of spirit and sensitivity required to reach a refined standard of human conduct. Cultivating a gracious and humane *way of being* was given priority over specific intellectual outcomes, and the success of a salon was determined by the spirit of the conversation.

To understand this *way of being,* one must appreciate the cardinal virtues that became the focus of self-cultivation within the salon. The virtues that the *salonnières* cultivated were, like Herz's society of virtue, meant to act as a dynamic model to be propagated outside of the circles in which they were born. The ideal participant was a person who was intellectually curious, cultured, and kind. They possessed an innate love of learning, exhibited a reflective intelligence, and offered new ideas that were pleasing and well communicated to the group. They held principled opinions, but also demonstrated the utmost consideration towards the views of others and were willing to change their perspective if proven wrong. To be a good listener was as important as being a good orator, for this allowed more people to take part in the conversation and to learn from one another.

Erudition, wit, inventiveness and originality of thought were encouraged because they demonstrated an assiduous commitment to intellectual development and, moreover, brought others pleasure.[137] Platitudes, unimaginative procla-mations, and conventional forms of idle conversation revealed an undeveloped inner world and a lack of capacity to cultivate the intellect and imagination.

Careful preparation for a salon was praised because this signified a thoughtfulness and commitment towards the group that was more valuable than erudition alone. The manner in which ideas were expressed was of great importance, for, even if an idea was interesting and original, it would lose force if it were communicated with pride or arrogance. These vices signalled the wrong motivation for participating in a space created for the purposes of self-betterment, not self-adulation; vanity had no place in an institution that gave priority to expressions of modesty and humility.

Because the *salonnières* required participants to adhere to a principle of sincerity when participating in this community, self-love was tempered, at least within the framework of the salon. Subtleties in considerate forms of communication were valued because they were indicative of the greater cardinal virtues of kindness, empathy, and forbearance that the *salonnières* were ultimately concerned with instilling in their constituents. Utmost respect and graciousness were expected, and the *salonnières'* role was to elicit these positive qualities in salon participants, teaching civility and intellectual bravery, while tempering animosity that might arise in conversations.[138]

In encouraging empathy and tolerance, the *salonnières* shifted the hierarchy of values in sociability from those factors out of the individual's control (gender, social rank, and to a large extent talent and wealth) to virtues that are, in theory, universal and within every person's power to exercise. In doing so, they affirmed the ethos of self-determination necessary for the cultivation of a beautiful soul.

Their predilection for virtues that could be cultivated was expressed by Karl Varnhagen's articulation of them: "Where

79

we are separated by talents and nature, we are united by friendship, understanding, forbearance, justice, loyalty, honesty, true cultivation."[139] Camaraderie was established by working towards a shared system of values. This collective goal bonded participants in a formative and lifelong process that garnered commitment to the group and a deep respect for its structures.[140]

Virtues were methodically practiced in the salon through a culture of *politesse* and carefully delineated rules of social etiquette. The German *salonnières* adopted this culture from the French, with whom they shared the conviction that a culture of politeness would serve the ideals of the Enlightenment.[141] *Salonnières* considered it their responsibility to create rules for civility that would shape social interactions. Their system of etiquette made conscientious behaviour explicit so that kindness could prevail.[142] In a letter from 1840, the poet Heinrich Heine (1797-1856), who was a young participant in Varnhagen's second salon, lamented the loss of her subtle rules of civility and understanding after her death:

> We, we understood each other by simple glances, we looked at each other and knew our innermost concerns—this language of the eyes will soon be lost, and the written monuments that we leave behind, for example Rahel's letters, will be nothing for those who are born after us but indecipherable hieroglyphs—I know this, and I think of this with each new person departing, and returning home.[143]

His remarks demonstrate how significant these rules were to the institution of the salon and how easily they could be lost without this structure. They were a beautiful game of understanding, a ritual of togetherness that held the group together.

Politeness was important because it maintained social harmony so that even the most contentious issues could be discussed with respect and the boundaries of knowledge could be breached without causing irreparable hostilities or animosity among the group. The *salonnières* firmly believed that tolerance of contrasting ideologies is necessary in a healthy and dynamic society. Environments where everyone agrees with one another are potentially dangerous because they can easily lead to indoctrination and the treacherous irrationality that comes from not holding an opinion for oneself. The *salonnières*, therefore, welcomed free speech; they embraced disparate perspectives, for this, after all, was the very purpose of their salons. However, difference could become divisive if people were aggressive and let self-regarding hysteria cloud their civility. A culture of politeness was essential because it allowed for the expression of diverse ideas by easing the tensions that might arise from rudeness through perceptions of otherness or misunderstanding.

The *salonnières* used their shrewd judgment and social skills to anticipate problems and overcome tensions.[144] Varnhagen was remembered for her distinct ability to engage everyone in the conversation so that all felt listened to and included. She would employ her humour and intelligence to smooth antagonism and to sustain the conversation when there were uncomfortable pauses or when someone said something that caused division.[145] She artfully moderated debate while gracefully enabling different ideas to coexist.

The *salonnières* distinguished their salons from other intellectual spaces of the time through this institutionalised refinement of social graces. For the Berlin *salonnières,* who differed in this regard from the French, an ennobled state of communication did not end with a culture of *politesse* but continued into deeper terrains of ethical responsibility and moral perfection.[146] This commitment to moral ideals was embedded within the practical content and structure of the salons.

Today, the most important dimension of the philosophy of the Beautiful Soul that we can enact in our own lives, as the *salonnières* and their salon participants did in the past, is the cultivation of our character through the practice of virtues. Unfortunately, in the modern world we seem to have lost sight of the importance of the classical virtues which once acted as the foundation of social progress. In a society obsessed with the beauty of bodies we rarely consider how to improve the beauty of our souls. In a culture consumed with the relentless pursuit of power, sex, and money, we forget the importance of beauty, goodness, and truth. Classical virtues have been degraded or lost entirely so that we no longer find the inspiration to maintain even the most basic standards of decency.

We have lowered our expectations of human behaviour so far that to be ignoble, unvirtuous, greedy, accusatory, and self-obsessed is considered normal. Character flaws such as betrayal and dishonesty have become more accepted. Spouses are unfaithful to their partners and romantic suitors dehumanise the conveyer belt of individuals whom they date. Loss of the ideal in the domestic domain has had its rippling effects in our society. We have devolved from the assumption that a political leader should embody courage, integrity, and moral strength to accept instead overt displays of self-aggrandisement, pettiness, and an unbridled lust for power.

Cynicism is understandable when the politicians who are

supposed to represent the people fail to hide their self-seeking ends and their ties to special interests. Public figures no longer command our respect or embody qualities that we could admire or seek to emulate. World leaders, who are supposed to act as paragons of human decency, engage in overt flaunting of personal vanities, perpetuating cycles of superficiality and inequity.

In a world in which the most bellicose political candidates receive the most airtime and the most aggressive voices on social media attract the most "views," virtues appear as weaknesses rather than as strengths. Within a culture that incentivises aggression and the self above all else, patience, humility, and kindness appear archaic and naïve. Since there are few people to admire or cultural norms to guide us, we find it easier to replicate the negative attributes of those who have hurt or disappointed us than to embody that which we wish to see in others.

Yet virtues are the handmaiden of morality and without them we cannot act as ethical beings. To forego the pursuit of these timeless qualities of character means to be incapable of acting as moral agents. Like a body that is not used so that the muscles begin to atrophy, a character that is not improved will eventually deteriorate. The virtues necessary to overcome the deep schisms within our societies, such as empathy, humility, and forgiveness, are precisely the ones that appear the most undeveloped. Their revival becomes an urgent concern of our age.

Practicing the Beautiful Soul today entails recapturing the beautiful ideals and timeless virtues which represent the best aspects of our humanity. Instead of justifying an imperfect present condition out of cynicism or apathy, this philosophy encourages us to acknowledge that we can change for the better, asserting that it is both within our power, and our ultimate responsibility, to improve our character. We erroneously believe that it is normal when people change for the worse and entirely natural when our character degrades with age. But rarely do we believe that positive change is always possible, even though theoretically, with more knowledge and life experience, we should only become better people. In practicing this philosophy, we overcome this counterproductive mentality.

The theorists of the Beautiful Soul argued that we must approach the present from the perspective of how we would judge ourselves if we were on our death bed. If the characteristics that we exhibit and the activities that we pursue are not in keeping with the positive values for which we wish to be remembered, then we must reimagine and reconstruct how we live today.

Although it may be momentarily satisfying to blame other people or an imperfect world for the problems we experience in life, the inclination to deflect responsibility goes against our own real self-interest and ultimately holds us back. If a person is vain, egotistical, mean-spirited, or ungenerous, then evidently these undesirable qualities will make them a less desirable colleague, romantic partner, parent, or friend. We all have character weaknesses that we should aspire to improve. We can experience great joy in actively attempting to transcend our flaws so that we may develop into a better version of ourselves.

Because of a lack of self-awareness and unwillingness to acknowledge personal shortcomings, people go to great lengths to improve their circumstances while never actually addressing the underlying problem. They believe that they will have a happier family life if they take an expensive holiday, but then when they are on the holiday they bicker, complain about small inconveniences, and destroy all the pleasure that they could have derived from the experience. Instead of wasting their time and money on distractions, they could have worked on becoming a more loving and generous family member.

Likewise, people are encouraged to spend countless hours trying to make themselves physically desirable by obsessing over their clothing, body type, makeup, and beauty treatments while doing nothing to improve the most attractive part of themselves: their character. Instead of spending time on surface-level ends, they could have aspired to become kinder and more considerate, which, unlike physical appearances, will sustain a relationship in the long term.

The philosophy of the Beautiful Soul demonstrates that the benefits of self-improvement for our careers, friendships, family life, and romantic relationships are infinite. We must not leave our character, which defines who we are and determines so much of what we do, up to chance. Our character is constantly evolving and at any point we can change for the better. By deciding to improve, we actively take the direction of our lives into our own hands. We alone are responsible for the beauty of our souls. A sense of responsibility gives us the agency to shape our life course and achieve the future that we envision for ourselves.

But, in order to improve our character, we must first understand which virtues we wish to pursue to represent our personal value system. Since our society no longer prioritises virtue, we rarely consider which qualities to cultivate in a sustained or systematic way. A framework of virtues to live by gives our pursuit of self-cultivation clarity and structure.

This framework is not intended to be confining; indeed, it

should be liberating. It can be imagined as the technical foundation that any visual artist or musician needs to master before they can achieve creative genius. Some of the main, universal virtues in the literature on the Beautiful Soul that we can interpret for ourselves today are goodness, kindness, empathy, generosity, justice, loyalty, courage, fairness, humility, curiosity, and wisdom.

Although a self-cultivated person maintains a virtuous nature, they are by no means naïve, obliviously sailing through life, ignorant of the unsavoury dimensions of the human condition. Despite the deceit and corruption that they may experience and observe in the world around them, they will maintain a youthful candour and embody a particular type of innocence that is born from the spirit, not from a lack of experience. They triumph over bitterness by *choosing* to preserve a good and compassionate nature.

By practicing the Beautiful Soul, we experience an intense joy in living, passion, curiosity, a sense of possibility, and an openness to people that is characteristic of youth, which we intensify with the wisdom, humility, and maturity that comes with age.

As we have seen, from Schiller's perspective, the most important attribute of the Beautiful Soul is goodness. There is no way of practicing this philosophy without aspiring to cultivate a good heart. Indeed, the simplest definition of a beautiful soul is a person who is good. The goodness that a beautiful soul exhibits will relate to every other quality that they possess. If goodness is not at the core of their nature, then other virtues are markedly diminished. So, for example, courage is a worthy virtue to pursue, but if it is undertaken in the name of an unjust cause, then it will not bring us any closer to the ideal of a Beautiful Soul. Cleverness is undoubtedly a virtuous quality, but if it is overwhelmed by an unkind, judgmental nature, then there is little merit in its possession. Some may claim that goodness is not something that you can cultivate: you either are good or you are not. But the philosophy of the Beautiful Soul argues that every quality that exists must be maintained; every quality that does not yet exist can be practiced and eventually will transform into an intrinsic state.

Although deeply sympathetic to human suffering, the theorists of this philosophy dissuaded people from using difficult circumstances as an excuse to avoid character development. They demonstrated that there is great power in the ability to self-actualise and transcend circumstantial constraints. By exercising our capacity to determine who we wish to be, regardless of the misfortunes that may befall us or the injustices that we may experience, we express our innate freedom and embody the inherent dignity in our humanity.

In enacting the Beautiful Soul in this self-determined way, it is important to remember Schiller's example of the man whose character must be put to the test. Although we may believe that we possess a virtue, we cannot claim to exhibit it if we have never encountered challenging life circumstances. Most of us assume that we will behave nobly. We imagine that we will act like Mamoudou Gassama, "the real spiderman," who scaled four stories to save a child dangling from a building in Paris. But we never truly know what our response will be until an extreme situation arises that tests our virtue. We cannot assume we possess a strong character until we are placed in circumstances that challenge our core sense of self.

The Beautiful Soul encourages us to question our assumptions and consider how we would behave in certain situations before they occur so that, when the time comes, we may rise to the challenge. We do not want to be proven weak in the critical moment when our character is tested. Therefore, we must never grow too comfortable with a conception of who we are and what qualities we embody, continually striving to reassess the condition of our soul.

As the *salonnières* demonstrated, the sincerest attempt to develop a beautiful character occurs when we internalise virtues. Beyond the most basic virtues, there is no formula for the perfect set of characteristics that a person should exhibit since every individual is unique. To adopt a "one- size-fits-all" approach would undermine the nuance and personal specificity of this philosophy. The Beautiful Soul is compelling because it embraces our uniqueness while simultaneously offering a universal framework for self-cultivation.

In determining the virtues we most value and the way in which they should manifest, this philosophy encourages us to observe the positive qualities in others and systematically consider how we would cultivate them. Goethe and Schiller looked for "living models of beautiful souls." Their studies of these people informed the development of the fictional characters in their plays and literary works and their own pursuits of self-cultivation.

Goethe, for example, was profoundly inspired by his close friend Charlotte von Stein (1742-1827.) He wrote, "It would be a wonderful spectacle to see how the world is reflected in this soul. She sees the world as it is, and yet through the medium of love. Thus, gentleness is the general impression."[147] Contemplating the character of people who embodied an inner beauty thus informed his own pursuit of self-cultivation.

The modern practitioner of the Beautiful Soul would likewise find inspiration in the beautiful characteristics of friends, family members, mentors, and even of fictional examples in films and literature. In practicing this philosophy, they would consider why these qualities are admirable and how they manifest, assembling these virtues into a portrait of a beautiful soul.

I, for example, would say that my ideal person is kind, good, sweet-natured, develops their own opinions, is intellectually ambitious, and remains joyful and optimistic. This image is based on an amalgamation of qualities that my husband, parents, and salon participants possess.

If I ask myself what manifestations of goodness I admire, I might determine that I respect someone who performs benevolent deeds for no ulterior motive or who defends the good even when it is unpopular. The type of person I am imagining would stand up to a bully on the playground as a child, distinguishing themself from those who encouraged the bully or were too cowardly to act against them. As an adult, I respect a person who cares about social justice causes before they come into fashion and does not blindly follow what others say. They actively choose to develop their own moral compass. By reflecting in this way, I realise that my sense of goodness is intimately interconnected to a notion of authenticity and intellectual bravery.

This clarification allows me to refine the idea of a beautiful soul that I aspire to become in my own life. If, for example, I find myself helping an elderly woman carry her groceries and I realise that my intention was to impress my friend with this display of benevolence, I would compare this imperfect act of charity with my own definition of goodness to realise the underlying flaw in my action. The Beautiful Soul argues that we cannot develop ourselves if we have not first determined what qualities we value and the spirit in which they should be expressed.

In creating our conception of an ideal beautiful soul, we contemplate virtue on both a theoretical and a subjective level. Our insights into our own life experiences can be extraordinarily constructive and give us a more nuanced understanding of a virtue because it has been lived. Maintaining some level of objectivity is important in practicing this philosophy, however, in order not to delude ourselves into believing that certain behaviours are acceptable simply because they fit into the narrative of our lives.

In a salon on "Jealousy," one of the participants revealed that she had an unfaithful partner, and this inevitably informed her understanding of loyalty. She assumed that she no longer valued this quality because it seemed impossible to achieve based on her own experiences. She deceived herself into believing that fidelity is not a realistic virtue to expect and diluted her definition of it to fit the imperfect reality that she had come to know. Consequently, she ended up in relationships with people who did not share her true value system and thus perpetuated a cycle of disloyalty that she could have prevented.

We often justify our experiences at the expense of preserving ideals because this is the most convenient course of action. We must, therefore, maintain a level of objectivity in the assessment of our character and consider our values independent from what we assume is inevitable so that we do not create a diminished conception of human nature that becomes a self-fulfilling prophecy.

Once we are more aware of the virtues that we wish to pursue, this philosophy demands that we honestly assess our character strengths—but most importantly our weaknesses—in relation to this ideal image. Within the nineteenth century salons, admitting to one's flaws was actively encouraged and considered a normal part of the process of becoming culti-vated. However, this imperative may be more difficult to pursue today since our global culture dissuades us from acknowledging our flaws. It is a natural human tendency to affirm one's present condition rather than to find the motiva-tion to improve ourselves. One often hears excuses like "I have always been a quick-tempered person" or "I am naturally judgmental" which justify remaining in an imperfect state. Character flaws and poor life decisions are thus recast as necessary evils or even strengths.

Modern day self-help mantras reinforce the inclination towards moral and intellectual inertia by encouraging us to "love our flaws" and "embrace our imperfections." Failure to achieve goals or behave decently is described in positive terms and publicised for all the world to see. The cult of excessive self-love is a pernicious example of this trend. When we open our social media apps, we are sure to be subjected to a deluge of self-conscious displays in which people showcase their wealth, flaunt their physical attributes, and boast about their accomplishments. Not only have these puerile demonstrations become acceptable, but they are also actively encouraged by our society. Contrary to their intention, they expose deep insecurities: evidently authentic self-worth should not need to be broadcast for validation by others. Unselfconscious arro-gance and risible vanity no longer are considered a sign of sociopathy. Self-obsession is the malady of our times, expos-ing the immaturity of the modern psyche.

While it is easier to affirm a current mode of being than to relentlessly strive towards self-improvement, growing as an individual is evidently more valuable than justifying character weaknesses and remaining stationary out of apathy. We all know that deceiving ourselves into believing that we are perfect might make us superficially feel better but does nothing for our actual self-advancement. Creating a beautiful personality requires humility and hard work.

Since character weaknesses are revealed in interpersonal relationships, the salon was the perfect environment for self-assessment and to consider every idea one held from a different perspective. Any faults or inconsistencies in character or concepts were interrogated and challenged. The modern practitioner of this philosophy would likewise engage in discourse with others, to listen to disparate perspectives, even those that do not align with their value system in order to challenge their beliefs. Like the Socratic method employed within the salons, which uses questioning to arrive at greater self-knowledge, the modern practitioner of the Beautiful Soul relentlessly re-evaluates their understanding of the world and the validity of their views by engaging in practices that challenge their assumptions.

Although having the humility to be willing to listen and learn from others is fundamental to character development, this philosophy would caution us against relying too heavily on other people to form an accurate assessment of ourselves. Some people may have ulterior motives, or, despite best intentions, their perception of us may be just as skewed as our perception of ourselves. We often come to conclusions about people without full knowledge of who they are based on passing impressions that are not entirely accurate or completely arbitrary. How could we ever truly comprehend another person's nature when we only have decontextualised glimpses of them and will never gain full access to their personal history or life experiences? So much is lost in translation when verbalising our inner world for others to analyse. Only we have lived our own life and can fully understand both the ultimate beauty and most problematic aspects of our nature.

Salons were essential spaces for self-improvement because participants did not rely on individual opinions that could be flawed or misguided. Rather *collective* knowledge was brought to bear on the pursuit of personal development. Multiple perspectives given from a diverse audience meant that people had a wider breadth of knowledge to draw from when determining how to improve themselves. Like personal liberties which are, by and large, most respected in those democratic societies where different ideas can be expressed and free speech is tolerated, cultivating character potential is best suited to environments in which multiple frames of reference are undogmatically advanced.

As the *salonnières* understood, conquering the inclination to indulge inferior character states often requires the support of a distinct community that motivates people to commit themselves to this difficult, but ultimately fulfilling end. Social structures are essential to overcome the deleterious character traits that impede personal growth. These communities also serve the function of revealing the areas in which we need to improve ourselves, which may only become apparent when we engage in meaningful conversations and interactions with others.

Within my own salons, I have regularly witnessed the importance of community to character development. I have seen how people become more aware of their flaws when they find themselves within a community that demands intellectual and moral betterment. Since they are not shamed into acknowledging their weaknesses, but instead encouraged and inspired to improve, they find here the inner motivation and desire necessary to advance themselves.

I, for one, am a passionate person by nature, especially when I discuss topics that I believe are important. Through salon discourse I became aware that passion, if not bridled by reason, can appear unbalanced and obfuscate even the best ideas. By conversing within the salon, I learned to temper my passion so that I could form a cogent argument and was able to approach issues with greater nuance and subtlety. I preserved my passionate disposition while refining the way in which this passion was conveyed. I composed compelling points that lent substance to my perspectives and intensified my engagement with the ideas themselves. This process occurred organically; I naturally desired to improve this character weakness because I saw how preferable it is when people rationally communicate ideas by observing effective discourse within the salon. Placing ourselves in communities such as the salon that challenge us to examine our character traits makes self-improvement an organic process.

The philosophy of the Beautiful Soul suggests that before we can improve ourselves, we must first attempt to deeply understand the nature of our flaws and develop a greater self-awareness in order to assess the validity of the beliefs that inform our character. If we try to improve what we think is wrong with our character without fully comprehending where our faults lie, then we will never address the source of the problem.

The modern practitioner of this philosophy will thoroughly analyse their character weaknesses, questioning why they fail to exhibit certain virtues or allow undesirable personality traits to exist unchallenged. They will incorporate a constant questioning of their being into their daily life, habitually asking themself, "Is this the most beautiful personality trait that I can exhibit?" or, "Is this the most beautiful action that I can perform in this situation?" They will be honest in their self-assessment and thus make character development a normalised part of everyday existence.

At the same time, they will not become overly self-critical. Obsessing over past behaviour or harbouring excessive guilt is not constructive. Weaknesses are acknowledged within this philosophical tradition, not to make people feel ashamed of their flaws, but because this knowledge is necessary in order to achieve higher levels of self-realisation. Likewise, beautiful souls will admit to their shortcomings, but this does not mean that they allow people to take advantage of their humility. Their virtue is grounded in strength, not weakness. They do not engage in exaggerated displays of meekness or obsequiousness, which are just other forms of character weakness, not an admirable display of virtue.

Just as the practitioner of the Beautiful Soul is not self-critical to a detrimental degree, they are also not excessively critical of others. They expect that people will behave decently. But they do not use their own self-cultivation as a reason to be judgmental. They are generous in their opinions of others and acknowledge when past negative impressions are wrong.

In practicing the virtue ethics of the Beautiful Soul, we must therefore be forgiving of our own flaws and other people's weaknesses, focusing on future improvements instead of past misdeeds. An enlightened society is one in which people are inspired to act virtuously because this has been made inherently desirable through social and cultural norms; morality is not enforced by self-inflicted or public shaming.

Once the practitioner of the Beautiful Soul has made a fair character assessment in relation to their ideal, the path to self-cultivation is evident. Ignoble character traits are often just bad habits, not necessarily fundamental states of being. Echoing

Greek virtue ethics, this philosophy suggests that the more an individual performs beautiful character traits, the more satisfaction she derives from seeing herself transform into a noble-spirited person and the more likely she is to naturally perform the given virtue. The most difficult part of cultivating oneself is the initial action towards this end. But once this step has been taken, the pursuit of virtue becomes intuitive.

In habitually enacting virtues, the practitioner of the Beautiful Soul will ensure that their approach is consistent and generalisable. To be patient does not mean simply behaving patiently with my partner but not with my friends. It would mean practicing patience in every aspect of my life. Some people adopt the attitude that it is acceptable to be unkind to their parents because they will love them anyway, or to be ungenerous to a stranger because they will never see them again. But virtues that are reserved for only certain people and performed in specific circumstances are not true virtues. The practice of a virtue must extend to every relationship and situation, no matter how insignificant it may seem.

When I go to the marketplace, I must ask myself if I am treating the vendors with the respect that they merit or if I have allowed my frustrations waiting in line and the accumulation of daily irritations to prevent me from behaving civilly. Within a professional setting, am I preserving my dignity in the face of the smallness of other people's actions, or have I allowed petty office disputes to perpetuate cycles of gossip? In relationships, have I overcome my ego so that I can relate to my partner, or has bickering over trivial matters, brought about from a lack of generosity within my own soul, prohibited me from finding happiness? Although the ideals of self-cultivation appear lofty, they ultimately manifest in the humblest forms of comportment in daily life.

A person who has cultivated their character in the way that this philosophy demands is not necessarily a world leader forging grand policy decisions on an international scale. They could equally be the local community member who performs simple acts of kindness intuitively. It is often the immediate, interpersonal cases that reveal the depths of a person's character. What is most important is that a person acts with empathy in their relationships with others. Behaving with a nobility of soul in varied situations, no matter how small or insignificant they may seem, is the sign of a truly cultivated individual.

In enacting this philosophy, we perpetually hold ourselves accountable to embody the character traits that we determined were valuable. Perhaps, for instance, I value truthfulness and I commit myself to this end. In most of my life I exhibit this virtue. However, there may be a case in which I lie because the situation seems insignificant and it would be inconvenient to tell the truth, or I lie so as not to hurt a person's feelings. Although my reasons may be understandable, and perhaps even preferable than the alternative, I must not act against the virtue lightly or dismiss my action as a single instance of an indulged character weakness. Defying virtuous qualities must be taken seriously and possess a sense of gravity.

No laws or norms exist, beyond social encouragement, to ensure that we exhibit virtues, nor should there be laws since this would infringe upon individual liberties and quickly become coercive. However, if we do not experience some societal pressure to display noble characteristics, we can easily deviate from our ideal. The pursuit of a beautiful personality must be approached as a lifelong, self-directed commitment. Cultivating virtues should be accompanied by the cultivation of a corresponding sense of duty and determination to adhere to virtue.

This rigorous process of developing our character entails perpetually re-evaluating our attainment of a virtue and revising the idealised qualities of a beautiful soul as new knowledge and life experiences are incorporated into our greater understanding of the world. The theorists of this philosophy were fully aware of the perils of a belief system that is impervious to change. They understood that rigid mentalities lead to ignorance, dogmatism, and myopic thinking. People who never reconsider their opinions do not demonstrate strength nor even an admirable commitment to their view. Instead, they reveal that they have remained intellectually stagnant. Like life itself, which is in a state of constant metamorphosis, our beliefs should evolve to incorporate the wisdom that we have gained.

Although cultivating a beautiful soul is a life-long commitment that requires dedication and continuous inner activity, it should ultimately be approached with elation and a sense of creative possibility. The original eighteenth century practitioners of the Beautiful Soul imagined themselves as artists, sculpting away the impurities in their soul to create something beautiful. In the same way, we may think about sculpting a more beautiful character as a wholly creative undertaking. Conceptualising character development in this way makes the art of self-cultivation a tangible process, one that each of us can creatively adopt in the development of a more beautiful soul.

CHAPTER 7

On Overcoming Utilitarianism and the Pursuit of Meaningful Work

THE practitioner of the Beautiful Soul pursues meaningful work and cultivates intellectual interests. In creating a life course that is personally fulfilling, this philosophy cautions against utilitarianism. Schiller warns of the "bread and butter man," the individual who focuses only on his career without making conceptual links between distinct subjects and so remains blind to the deeper significance of his existence.[148] Novalis likewise describes the prosaic person who destroys all beauty and meaning with the predictability of their routines and the vacuous nature of their means to uninspired ends. With great foresight, he depicted the course that humanity would follow in observing what was already taking place on the individual level:

> Philistines lead only a daily life. The chief means appears to be their only end. They do everything for the sake of their earthly life, as it seems and must seem from their behaviour. They mingle poetry with their lives only according to need because they have grown used to a little distraction from their daily routine. Usually this diversion happens every seven days and could be called a poetic weekly fever. On Sundays work ceases; they live a little better than usual and this festivity ends

99

with a deeper sleep; but only so that on Monday everything can resume a brisker pace. Their *parties de plaisir* must be conventional, habitual and fashionable; but even their pleasures are worked through like everything else, laboriously and formally.[149]

The person that Novalis sombrely portrays embodies the inhuman regimentation of existence and the soulless path of convention that has become a feature of modern life. With their mindless schedules of labour and their simulated allotments of pleasure, they stifle true productivity and suffocate the very poetry that they seek to consume. How can any great ideas, brilliant innovations, or astute observations be discovered by this modern person who circles mindlessly in their self-erected cage, never stopping to witness the tragedy of their own imprisonment?

The theorists of the Beautiful Soul did not negate the importance of applying oneself. They were rather concerned with the rigid mentalities that arise from specialisation and the prosaicness of a society that gives highest priority to material realities at the expense of the unquantifiable dimensions of culture, the arts, and sciences. Goethe and Schiller believed that the predicament which plagues the modern age is the blind pursuit of profit and efficiency at the expense of Beauty, Goodness and Truth.[150] They argued that a re-conception of human worth that advances more elevated forms of being, rather than the quotidian concern for functional outcomes, is necessary before any moral-aesthetic education can be undertaken. They advocated an intellectual engagement that can extrapolate, making connections across multiple domains, such that subjective knowledge may disclose objective values and touch upon other epistemic foundations and disciplinary truths. As Schiller observes:

> If nature has endowed him with the gifts for plastic art, he will study the structure of man with the scalpel of the anatomist; he will descend into the lowest depths to be true in representing surfaces, and he will question the whole race in order to be just to the individual. If he is born to be a poet, he examines humanity in his own heart to understand the infinite variety of scenes in which it acts on the vast theatre of the world. He subjects imagination and its exuberant fruitfulness to the discipline of taste, and charges the understanding to mark out in its cool wisdom the banks that should confine the raging waters of inspiration.[151]

The self-cultivated individual, then, is receptive to everything from philosophy and literature to theatre, medicine, the visual arts and sciences. They understand that knowledge has no boundaries, and that curiosity need not be relegated to a single area of interest. Humboldt argues that "an interesting man, is interesting in all situations and all activities, though he only attains the most matured and graceful consummation of his activity when his way of life is harmoniously in keeping with his character."[152] The practitioner of this philosophy maintains a focus, while remaining well-versed in many schools of thought and ways of seeing. They retain an intellectual suppleness and openness to new impressions.

Part of what it means to overcome utilitarianism is to perform activities for their own sake. In viewing *Bildung* from a contemporary perspective we might interpret it simply to mean education in an instrumental sense, but this does not capture the spirit of the word. Self-cultivation is not a practical end *per se*, such as a student who seeks university education to gain a prestigious job, or a painter who learns the techniques of his *métier* merely to sell his work. Although cultivation might include these ends, it cannot be reduced to them. Rather, it is a commitment to a nobler way of thinking and being which comes, in part, from doing things for no reason other than a commitment to the end itself.

Actions of a beautiful soul that were often cited in the eighteenth century were, for instance, a good deed that is performed without the public knowing and pursued for no other purpose than to do good; an instrument that is played without the intent to receive accolades from an audience; or a subject that is mastered without seeking adulation for one's erudition. As Schleiermacher comments in his *Monologues*, self-cultivation must be pursued without consideration of how one's thoughts and actions will be perceived, for "I have neither time nor inclination to trouble myself about this. In this short life I have to move on and, as far as possible, perfect my individual nature through new thoughts and deeds."[153]

In removing oneself from external forms of validation, the individual is both freed to follow the true course necessary for their personal development and to overcome appearances. In so doing, they move beyond evanescent pursuits and feckless social expectations derived from fashionable preferences and transitory circumstances that have little significance for the ultimate ends of human worth. Beautiful souls are not swayed by external judgement nor are they seduced by fame or recognition. Those who undertake a moral-aesthetic education for self-seeking reasons are thought not to be truly educated in the most profound sense. The person who craves immediate gratification and social admiration loses the motivation and qualities necessary to perfect their soul.

The theorists of the Beautiful Soul decried the distortion of its noble ends by the elite's vanity, false erudition, and self-aggrandisement. They consistently valued an authentic spirit over action whose intention was misplaced. As Schiller remarks:

> The civilised classes present to us the still more repugnant spectacle of indolence, and a depravity of character which is all the more shocking since culture itself is the source of it. I forget which ancient or modern philosopher made the remark that what is more noble is in its corruption the more abominable; but it is equally true in the moral sphere. The child of nature, when he breaks loose, becomes a maniac, the disciple of art an abandoned wretch. The intellectual enlightenment on which the refined ranks of society, not without justification, pride themselves, reveals on the whole an influence upon the disposition so little ennobling that it rather furnishes maxims to confirm depravity.[154]

A high value was placed on authenticity to avoid hypocrisy and keep this philosophy true to its ideological ends. In an example Schiller gives following Kant's observations, he argues that we cannot delight in a bird's song if we learn that it is produced by human imitation, for it will not accord with its own laws, and it is in this concordance that we find pleasure, because the effect is moral. If something we think is beautiful and true turns out to be artificial, we are sorely disappointed.

103

Simply put, a person who artificially follows the principles of this philosophy out of disingenuous motivations, cannot possess a beautiful soul because their actions do not harmonise with their nature. A beautiful soul, then, overcomes utilitarianism by pursuing activities for their own sake.

The theorists of the Beautiful Soul embodied this non-utilitarian ethos in their own lived experiences. Goethe, for example, was not only a philosopher, poet, and playwright but also a scientist. His poetic mind informed his scientific mind by making conceptual connections between the two.[155] Schiller, who was a physician and playwright in addition to being a historian and philosopher, spanned disciplines and integrated seemingly disparate subject matters. In a letter to Goethe on April 7, 1797, Schiller refers to a Hebrew dialogue on love that combines mythologies, chemistry, and astronomy, making "ingenious comparisons of the planets with human limbs." He recounts his delight in reading this text and writes that he intends to give the "astrological material a poetic dignity."[156] These theorists derived great meaning from exploring different disciplinary systems and cultural approaches to knowledge which they drew from and creatively elaborated upon in surprising ways. Even if their philosophical observations are generally more acute than their scientific ones, their philosophy undoubtedly benefited from the breadth of their interests and their sensitivity to the world around them.

The transdisciplinary curiosity that these thinkers maintained is precisely the spirit in which their philosophy is intended to be undertaken. Like Schiller and Goethe, Humboldt spanned many disciplines as a diplomat, philosopher, linguist, and educational theorist. But beyond his own career, his wide-ranging approach to learning is reflected in his ideas on *Bildung*, especially his passion for the integration of the arts and sciences within educational models. In his "Theory of *Bildung*" he states:

> It is the ultimate task of our existence to achieve as much substance as possible for the concept of humanity in our person, both during the span of our life and beyond it, through the traces we leave by means of our vital activity… by the linking of the self to the world to achieve the most general, most animated, and most unrestrained interplay.[157]

Like seeing the pattern within a constellation, Humboldt believed that creating links between different disciplines forms more complex systems of understanding and a denser network of relationships that facilitates answering essential questions with a measure of objectivity. In his conception, before a person specialises, it is the responsibility of the State to transform them into a well-rounded individual through a liberal education. This is the only way that they can reasonably fulfil their responsibilities as a citizen and exercise their agency as a member of a rational and enlightened society. He argues:

> There are undeniably certain kinds of knowledge that must be of a general nature and, more importantly, a certain cultivation of the mind and character that nobody can afford to be without. People obviously cannot be good craft workers, merchants, soldiers or businessmen unless, regardless of their occupation, they are good, upstanding and – according to their condition – well-informed human beings and citizens. If this basis is laid

through schooling, vocational skills are easily
acquired later on, and a person is always free to
move from one occupation to another, as so often
happens in life.[158]

However, despite the successes of Humboldt's educational
model and the extent to which he realised these ambitions, the
goal of a well-formed citizen, versed in a wider range of
subjects, contrasted sharply with the direction that society was
headed at a historical moment when Germany, and the rest of
Europe, was on the brink of unprecedented industrial change.
These thinkers anticipated the dangers of industrialisation and
the detrimental effects that an ethic of extreme pragmatism has
on the human soul. They observed how quickly people can be
turned into automatons fulfilling functions that are economically
efficient but degrade the scope of human faculties and the
integrity of moral ends. As Schiller states in his *Aesthetic Letters*:

Eternally chained to only one single little fragment
of the whole, Man himself grew to be only a
fragment; with the monotonous noise of the wheel,
he drives everlastingly in his ears, he never develops
the harmony of his being, and instead of imprinting
humanity upon his nature he becomes merely the
imprint of his occupation, of his science.[159]

The fragmentation to which Schiller refers reduces people
to a tool in an economic system, no longer capable of a full
expression of their humanity but limited to a singular, method-
ical task. The pettiness of necessity robs the individual of their
dignity. Schiller aptly captures the wide-reaching consequences of this obsession with pragmatism:

But today necessity is master and bends a degraded humanity beneath its tyrannous yoke. Utility is the great idol of the age, to which all powers must do service and all talents swear allegiance. In these clumsy scales the spiritual service of art has no weight; deprived of all encouragement, she flees from the noisy mart of our century. The very spirit of philo-sophical enquiry seizes one province after another from the imagination, and the frontiers of art are contracted as the boundaries of science are enlarged.[160]

And yet, despite the dismal nature of an overly functional society, there is still hope. This process of self-improvement offers an alternative to the fragmentation of modern life, elevating the individual to something greater than the sum of their economic value. Beauty and its contemplation assist in the process of breaking away from the yoke of utility and envisioning more illuminated ends since it is, by definition, independent of practical purpose. As Schiller says, we call something beautiful "if we do not need to be helped by the idea to see the form, if the form is free and purposeless and comes from itself, and all the parts seem to limit themselves from within themselves."[161] Beautiful souls, therefore, surpass a strictly utilitarian conception of value. They defy the dehumanisation of homogenisation using the breadth of their learning and the depth of their curiosity.

The philosophy of the Beautiful Soul can be understood as one of the first theoretical critiques of capitalism and industri-alisation. The issues its proponents anticipated became only more pronounced in the centuries that were to come, and their socio-economic insights are perhaps more relevant today than they ever were when they were first written.

In adopting the Beautiful Soul's non-utilitarian premise, the *salonnières* prided themselves on acting without an explicitly instrumental purpose. Their distaste for the banality and limitations of pragmatic activities was part of a mentality among the intellectual elite in Germany that discouraged utilitarian approaches to knowledge. They believed in the primacy of ideas without the need to demonstrate quantifiable ends.[162] They considered it profane to think about the strategic aims of the arts and culture.

Varnhagen captured this sentiment when responding to David Veit, who considered the possibility of becoming a doctor: she said that she could not imagine him becoming anything specific.[163] The *salonnières* did not oppose the need for a vocation, but rather contested the idea of identifying a person solely with a particular profession. This, they believed, reduced the integrity of their being to one single end. Varnhagen adamantly contended that ideas and sociability should be pursued for their own sake, a view reflected in her observations on pedagogical practice. Although she encouraged the practical application of knowledge, she also believed that it should derive from a natural, unforced urge and exist as an end in itself. She saw little purpose in imposing education on those who felt no desire to learn. She rejected the idea that pursuits of the mind need an instrumental outcome to legitimise their worth.[164]

Schleiermacher, who was a close friend and regular participant in the salons of Varnhagen and Herz, as well as a theorist of *Bildung*, developed his rules of sociability based on the model of the salons. He theorised an ideal of discourse that emphasised the unification of the fragmented parts of the individual which modern life had caused. He argued that conversation should be liberated from function and "free sociability, neither bound nor determined by any external purpose."[165] He was referring to the relationship to knowledge that he witnessed in the salons when he remarked:

> The most versatile is one who is at the same time the most polymath and original, one who is prepared to engage in any subject matter, even the most trivial and unfamiliar, and still know how to express his own uniqueness in a variety of ways.[166]

He acknowledged that the *salonnières* had perfected this ideal of sociability, and with it addressed the modern ill associated with the individual being, as Schiller lamented, reduced to "nothing more than the imprint of his occupation or of his specialised knowledge."[167]

The dismissal of utilitarian calculus was, in part, because the *salonnières* were interested in a range of different subjects as reflected in the often-interdisciplinary content of their salons. As polymaths whose education was rigorous and extensive, they saw purpose in spanning many art forms and intellectual disciplines. Although the *salonnières* were, for the most part, particularly interested in ancient Greek and Romantic literature and music, they did not limit themselves to these areas; they were well-versed in myriad subject matters and read the latest works in the arts, politics, philosophy, and the sciences, while encouraging their participants to do the same. The intellectual variety of their readings inspired the multifaceted subject matter of their salons. The freedom with which they approached ideas and disciplines led to rich and inventive connections between subjects.

The *salonnières'* erudition reflected the central purposes of the salon: to engage in subject matters that extended beyond single specialties or vocations. Musicians would take part in literary affairs; scientists would discuss philosophical questions; and poets would listen to music in the salon. To be a cultivated person meant to be curious in the most general sense.

In the joint salon of Henriette and Marcus Herz, for example, after some participants discussed the work of early Romantic writers in the room governed by Henriette, and others discussed questions of science and reason in the room governed by Marcus, the group came together to share ideas raised in their conversations, thereby forming bridges between the arts and sciences.[168] Their salon was a representation of the great breadth of questions discussed and the possibilities associated with interdisciplinary perspectives. Salons were simultaneously traditional in their subject matter, posing questions from antiquity, and at the forefront of new intellectual and artistic movements and scientific discoveries that engaged broadly with novel ideas of their time.

The *salonnières* circumvented the limitations of singular disciplines by avoiding topics that were explicitly politicised or required an immediate response. They imbued every question raised with meaning and metaphor, a philosophical abstractness and a poetry that eschewed instrumentality. The topics discussed could have political or pragmatic dimensions, not simply entail abstract literary or philosophical reflections; but they were not burdened by the obligation to arrive at a particular solution. They afforded participants the liberty to creatively explore ideas unhindered by expediency or instrumentality. This multidimensional approach to learning differed fundamentally from clubs and associations that focused on one area of interest or study. Unlike these clubs, the salon required a certain intellectual suppleness and willingness to make oneself endlessly receptive to new forms of knowledge. This meant exploring questions that elevated the conversations beyond the concerns of a specific group of people at a particular moment in time; to examine issues that, in theory at least, were universally significant. As Schleiermacher wrote, "no topic should be broached that is not a part of the common sphere of interest."[169]

The *salonnières* accompanied their efforts to avoid utilitarian subject matters by suppressing the participation of those individuals who took part in the salon overtly for self-promotion or for a strategic benefit. This was difficult to police, especially when the salon adhered to a principle of continual openness to those who sought admission. However, by articulating the importance of living without self-seeking utilitarianism, instrumentality became unfashionable. Varnhagen exclaimed: "I kill pedantry within a radius of thirty miles, I am such a poison tree for it."[170]

This did not mean, however, that salon culture did not practically benefit those individuals who participated. The careers of the artists, intellectuals, and musicians who shared their work was unquestionably advanced and the *salonnières* acted as patrons for aspiring creatives in need. The unspoken rule of the salon was that one could derive practical benefit on the condition that one made a reciprocal intellectual contribution and that the motivation for one's participation was not self-promotion, but a true concern for the values at hand. This culture of "purposeful purposelessness" had the beneficial effect of allowing the expression of ideas that might otherwise be considered irrelevant, fostering a vibrant diversity of thought. Ironically this did more to achieve pragmatic, tangible ends, such as the production of influential intellectual works, than a culture attenuated by the preoccupation with self-advancement which prioritised career success over true creativity.

The spectre of extreme utilitarianism expressed by the *salonnières* materialised after their deaths on an unprecedented scale. Their foresight into the direction society was headed, once again, proved astonishingly prescient. Since the rise of industrialisation people have increasingly narrowed their horizons to specific careers and interests that fit within the limited parameters of a capitalistic, market-driven lifestyle. The ideal of the Renaissance man, deeply passionate about a wide range of issues and talented in many different areas, pursuing knowledge for its own sake and for its contribution to society, seems sorrowfully distant.

Modern existence entails functionalising our decisions to maximise utility within a global economic system in which we are inescapably enmeshed. Shrewd economic calculations have changed mentalities to such a degree that almost every pursuit appears to be performed for some other commercial end. We advance our careers, not for the love of the work itself, but for the money we can earn. We "network" with people, not for the value of interacting with those whom we are genuinely interested in, but for the social capital it can bring us. We run marathons, not for the pleasure of running, but to display our driven personality, fearing that we may not keep pace with others. We attend art events, not to learn and be moved by sensory impressions, but to broadcast our erudition and cultural acumen.

The hyper-functionalization of our lives has contributed to the crisis of values that marks our times. When more and more activities are undertaken solely to maximise influence and wealth, it becomes easy to lose a more valuable sense of meaning as we seek instrumental goals that may never materialise or make us happy in the end. To live according to the philosophy of the Beautiful Soul means to expand our

112

conception of what being human means, overcoming a sterile vision that reduces the full promise of our humanity.

In my salons I have attempted to revive the non-utilitarian ethos and polymathic curiosity that the *salonnières* instilled in their salon participants. I founded my salons upon the principle that anyone can, and should, discuss almost anything, even topics in which they have little expertise. Universal aspects of the human condition that each person intuitively understands or has experienced in some way provide rich material for a vibrant conversation. I do not need to be a philosopher who specialises in love to discuss what love means to me. I do not need to be a clinical psychologist to explore the complexity of emotional states that I myself have experienced. Nor is it necessary that I am a climate scientist to question the future of environmental policies. Although the discussion of such issues undoubtedly benefits from the opinion of someone who has specialised knowledge, it is by no means required for rich conversations. Everyone, when probed, has a perspective that might animate the topic at hand.

The most rewarding conversations within my salons have occurred when people in many fields with different frames of knowledge discuss the same issue, and by doing so expand their distinct perceptions. A scientist might have an entirely different perspective from an artist or an engineer, and this richness in disciplinary training and distinct life courses animates the conversation. In a salon on "Genetic Editing," for example, a physician focused on the possibilities associated with overcoming previously incurable genetic diseases while a sociologist discussed the dangers implicit in selecting desirable traits and its implications for exacerbating inequality. Both perspectives were legitimate and brought different analytical and philosophical approaches to a pressing social issue.

The practitioner of this philosophy will cultivate the curiosity necessary to converse about a wide range of topics and seek different viewpoints to approach an idea from multiple frames of reference. This interdisciplinary emphasis proves socially advantageous since it contributes to a more thoughtful, well-rounded populace better equipped to make informed contributions to the public sphere. Since we ordinarily spend time with individuals who share similar careers or worldviews, there is a danger that we will never experience these enlightening exchanges, narrowing our conversations to what we already know or have been conditioned to believe. Engaging in meaningful conversations in which diverse perspectives are explored proves critical in overcoming mere instrumentality in our relations with others and upholding our democratic responsibilities.

In addition to partaking in more interdisciplinary conversations, the main area of modern life that could be de-instrumentalised is our careers. Since work defines so much of who we are by virtue of the time we dedicate to it, the Beautiful Soul encourages us to exert our energies in the service of greater goals which fulfil us personally and make a positive contribution to society. Increasingly, more people need not follow a predetermined familial path, or be tied to a set of professions constrained by their socio-economic positions. Unfortunately, at a time when more people than ever before have the possibility of engaging in work that truly interests them, few actualise their potential to forge the fulfilling career and life-course that they envision.

One of my salon participants entered the salon at a time when he was unhappy with his career. Like many urban people from relatively advantaged socio-economic positions, he pursued a career in finance that brought him little personal meaning. He described his occupation as drudgery, a "futile pursuit," yet he felt "bound by golden handcuffs," an expression so commonly used among affluent millennials. He wanted to understand different dimensions of himself, to overcome his acute sense of emptiness and apathy.

Slowly, through salon conversations, he was able to discover more about his interests beyond a career path he had assumed he must take. He came to comprehend that his lucrative occupation underscored his ultimate servitude to forces that he fundamentally opposed. He began pursuing activities that brought him meaning and surrounded himself with people who shared similar values. His desire to evolve, and his commitment to a community which could help him in this endeavour, was the beginning of his journey towards intellectual liberation and professional emancipation.

Like my salon participant, many people convince themselves that they have no other option than to pursue a career about which they are not passionate, when many options are, in fact, fully available to them. Even if they are not wealthy, they have some basic financial safety net that mitigates the existential fear of being unable to provide for their families. When probed, it often becomes clear that it is easier to take what they consider to be the safe, normal route than to strive for the life that would make them truly happy.

But what happens if in the pursuit of utilitarian ends a person never finds meaning? What if they become jaded in the process or caught up in a rat race in which they never really wanted to take part in the first place? How much will they have to sacrifice in the process? Their youth, their happiness, their hope, their sense of possibility? The most promising years of their life will have been plagued by discontent. Once one takes a divergent path, it is difficult for even the most driven people to find their way back. Often as soon as a dream is deferred, it is lost.

The philosophy of the Beautiful Soul encourages us to acknowledge that we cannot justify remaining miserable on the assumption that we can buy our happiness or freedom later. Nor should we pursue ends that are not intrinsically valuable in the hope that we might eventually do something meaningful. Not only is it a shame to squander one's existence on a career that is not suited to one's nature, but it is also an insult to those who lack the luxury of doing what would make them happy. To waste one's good fortune and potential out of fear or apathy is, according to Goethe and Schiller, irresponsible and unjust.

In the pursuit of meaningful work, one must not deceive oneself into believing that one's career path is worthwhile. Even the professions most lauded by society can often be purposeless. Rarely do we stop to ponder the true value of our decisions, many of which we might have been told are "prestigious" or are given a high social value by arbitrary standards, but, upon interrogation, are exposed for their ultimate futility. Our society has developed such a distorted perception of success that, today, to create the next app that makes having sex easier or streamlines the purchase of junk food is deemed "changing the world for the better." Meanwhile, municipal workers who keep our cities running or manual laborers who provide food for our tables are rarely valued for their tangible contributions to society.

People assume that becoming the CEO of a large company will make them happy, even if the actual work is tedious and the product the company offers does nothing to serve humanity. Eulogies will never be written to express gratitude to an individual who increased the worldwide consumption of sugary drinks by ten percent. A life wasted compromising personal happiness to achieve such meaningless goals is a tragedy. If we want to live well, we cannot disconnect the meaning of our work from the meaning of our lives.

This philosophy forces us to be brutally honest with ourselves and to choose a profession that holds *true* meaning, one that advances ends of a higher value. It requires us to grapple with fundamental questions such as, "Is my work personally fulfilling?" "Does it contribute to humanity?" "Is this truly what I want to be remembered for when I die?" It allows for no self-delusions or compromise.

Adopting the Beautiful Soul does not necessarily mean changing paths if we are content with our profession or we do not have the ability to transition to another job. Instead, it entails trying to find a deeper relevance in our work. If I am a physicist, maintaining a myopic view of what physics entails by remaining purely in the realm of mathematical equations will diminish the meaning I might derive from my profession. To see the beauty in the composition of the universe, which my work helps reveal, immeasurably enhances the scientific task at hand, giving an unquantifiable value to a specific scientific undertaking. If I am a teacher, to forget the fact that I shape the lives of human beings and the state of the future world that they will occupy will detract from the importance of my endeavours. But if I grasp the rippling effect that my lessons may have in changing the course of a life for the better, then my efforts will constitute a monumental undertaking. If I work in sanitation, conceding that my profession is somehow insignificant because it is not appreciated in the artificial monetary calculation of value inherent in a capitalistic society, effectively does me a disservice. But if I understand that this work prevents millions of residents from contracting diseases, I give great significance to an essential job.

Of course, as Goethe and Schiller warned, in a post-industrial society there is some work that is by its very nature, so fragmented and disconnected from a higher purpose that it is impossible to imaginatively perceive its significance. The classic Marxist example is a factory worker who undertakes the monotonous task of making a tiny screw for a large machine, never witnessing the end or value of their labour. Unfortunately, many modern jobs are fundamentally useless and alienating: they do not help anyone, they do not advance new knowledge, they do not achieve greater human understanding or social progress. In our globalised economy many of these jobs are also actively destructive to other people, animals, or the environment.

The philosophy of the Beautiful Soul argues that since the most important goal in life is to be a good person, then strategic ends, such as excess wealth, do not actually serve our self-interest if they counteract this most fundamental aim. Beautiful souls do not perform unbeautiful actions simply because they can cognitively distance themselves from them. Their actions correspond with their value system. They have the strength of character to be honest with themselves about the *true* nature of their work. The empathy and aesthetic sensitivity that they are required to exercise in cultivating a beautiful personality is employed to clearly envision the implications of their career decisions and to hold themselves accountable. Furthermore, counterbalancing destructive work by donating to charity would not relieve beautiful souls of their moral duties since, according to this philosophy, the *means* to an end are as important as the end itself.

Ideally the practitioner of the Beautiful Soul would be able to say that their work fulfils them personally and makes some positive contribution to the arts, sciences, culture, society, politics, animals, or the environment. But even if one pursues a career that is meaningful and interesting, it is only truly purposeful if the spirit in which it is performed is beautiful. Many people hold fascinating jobs that they render banal because they themselves are not personally inspired. There are heads of human rights organisations who engage in this work mostly because it is advantageous for their careers, not because they are particularly passionate about helping people. There are musicians who approach music with a pedestrian mentality, focusing only on technique instead of artistry. The spirit of the work and the passion with which it is pursued is critical.

Unfortunately, the term "finding one's passion" has become so overused that it is no longer a courageous or ultimately meaningful pursuit. Instead, it has become a highly commodified, hackneyed endeavour that expresses little more than the vacuous jargon of multi-national corporations and technology firms. A standard set of idols, typically celebrities within tech industries, are lionised as individuals who followed their passions and, in so doing, purportedly achieved great things. But such visions are confined to a small number of industries and offer a limited set of mostly economic values.

Instead of leading to personal emancipation, following one's passions often results in taking the opposite path of mass conformity, subscribing to a pre-determined definition of what success means. This definition may apply to some but not to all and by adopting it we risk choosing careers that are fundamentally discordant with our nature and capacities. We must therefore explicitly distinguish our own approach to passions from any pre-established societal norms or expectations.

Those who do not concretely know where their passions lie might be presented with a paradox of choice. Suffocated by the wealth of possibilities available to them, they may never fully commit themselves to anything. From infinite choice, the seeds of discontentment are sown. Choosing a particular life path necessarily reduces the infinite possibilities of self that are available. As Schiller declares "When one note on an instrument is touched, among all those that it virtually offers, this note alone is real. When man is actually modified, the infinite possibility of all his modifications is limited to this single mode of existence."[171] However, this singular choice is by no means contrary to this philosophy's conception of humankind as creatures of limitless possibility. Rather, it allows the individual to concentrate on a particular domain of practice, and thereby maximise their prospects in a way that would be impossible for a person who flounders in the realm of infinite possibility. The aspects of one's personhood that are nurtured in the act of making a choice and maintaining this commitment can be extrapolated to other areas of life; thus, cultivating the particular is the pathway towards the infinite.[172]

To strive towards the highest degree of potential in one's given *métier* is immensely more valuable, both to oneself and to society, than extending one's energies across different domains. If a venture or life course is undertaken in the true spirit of the Beautiful Soul, then it will transcend its own limitations. What matters is not the number of interests pursued, but rather, the quality with which those undertaken are pursued.

Of course, not all paths followed will be correct. Self-cultivation requires a trial-and-error process in which one accepts that one may take wrong steps, but that ultimately this process will lead to greater knowledge about one's life purpose. The Beautiful Soul encourages us to judge ourselves not on the success that we may experience in our career, which is often dependent upon factors outside of our control, but on the decision to create a meaningful life by committing ourselves to a passion.

CHAPTER 8

On Freedom and Intellectual Autonomy

THE theorists of the Beautiful Soul advanced a complex notion of subjectivity and individual freedom, but they did so explicitly for the purpose of promoting universal ends that attend to the social collective. This subjective-universal relationship reflected a precise moment in history: the transitional period between the Enlightenment, focused primarily on universal values, and Romanticism, grounded in a strong conception of individual agency. The Beautiful Soul was a compelling theory to people of the time because it balanced and integrated these two distinct schools of thought. Freedom became the cornerstone of this concept in the early nineteenth century, distinguishing it from its ancient formulations.

According to this philosophy, freedom is necessarily creative. Novalis argues that "All education (*Bildung*) leads to nothing else than what one can call freedom, although this should not designate a mere concept but the creative ground of all existence."[173] The conception of freedom as creativity expands the definition of freedom itself, demonstrating that it is not something that is assumed, but rather actively cultivated. Schlegel's very definition of *Bildung* is "the development of independence."[174] Humboldt likewise wrote to Georg Forster (1754-1794), the naturalist and revolutionary, on November 1, 1792 that "the cause of freedom, or rather of one's own energy, has to be the cause of every cultivated man."[175]

Freedom does not simply mean exerting one's will on the world independent of external constraints.[176] Instead it means possessing the intellectual capacity to imaginatively determine precisely who one is, in all one's specificity, and what one wants to become. Before freedom can be granted or taken away, it first must be determined where one's freedom lies. Equally, in preserving this freedom, it is as important to question personally imposed limitations as those externally enforced. Cultivating oneself is the only way to determine the wider spectrum of one's liberties, beyond the most basic and intuitive ones.

Subjectivity is embedded within this notion of freedom. As Schlegel says "all independence is original, and all originality is moral, the originality of the whole person. Without it there is no energy of reason or beauty of soul."[177] Goethe argues that "every man must think after his own fashion; for on his own path he finds a truth, or a kind of truth, which helps him through life."[178]

Intellectual freedom through personal development is vital because it is a necessary safeguard against oppression. The theorists of the Beautiful Soul directly responded to Kant's essay "What is Enlightenment?" (1784) when they argued this point. In this essay, Kant asserts that "Enlightenment is man's emergence from his self-incurred immaturity."[179] He challenges the individual to recognise the power of their intellect and to break away from the ignorance born from received dogma through the cultivation of their mind. Kant argues that this ignorance is self-imposed:

> Laziness and cowardice are the reasons why such
> a large part of mankind gladly remain minors all
> their lives, long after nature has freed them from

external guidance. They are the reasons why it is so easy for others to set themselves up as guardians. It is so comfortable to be a minor. If I have a book that thinks for me, a pastor who acts as my conscience, a physician who prescribes my diet, and so on—then I have no need to exert myself.[180]

The Beautiful Soul is naturally suited to address this obstacle to Enlightenment because of its emphasis on the intellectual development of the self. In Kantian terms, it challenges the individual to "Dare to Know," *Sapere Aude!* Its theorists firmly believed that people should think critically, never blindly accepting orthodoxy. Humboldt, especially, cautions that people must act on their own subjective judgments, for, the more they conform to norms or become part of larger associations, the more they risk becoming the instrument of external power interests.[181]

However, just like conformity which can lead to tyranny and oppression, liberty can become a threat to society if the individual's conception of it is still in development. As Schiller remarks:

The gift of liberal principles becomes a piece of treachery to the whole, when it is associated with a still nature; the law of conformity becomes tyranny towards the individual when it is combined with an already prevailing weakness and physical limitation, and so extinguishes the last glimmering sparks of spontaneity and individuality.[182]

Therefore, a measure of autonomous, internal liberty must be exercised in the process of self-cultivating before the expression of external liberty can follow. People earn the right to exert themselves through rational reflection, critical thinking, and intellectual activity.

The challenge that Schiller identifies is that most people do not desire to undertake the laborious exercise of employing their rationality. It is easier to be led than to think in an autonomous capacity. As Schiller declares:

> The greater part of humanity is too much harassed and fatigued by the struggle with want, to rally itself for a new and sterner struggle with error. Content if they themselves escape the hard labour of thought, men gladly resign to others the guardianship of their ideas, and if it happens that higher needs are stirred in them, they embrace with eager faith the formulas which State and priesthood hold in readiness for such an occasion.[183]

Despite this dispiriting challenge, people are encouraged to overcome the seduction of political and moral lethargy; they are urged to live "a more active kind of citizenship" through self-cultivation.[184]

Living an active intellectual life does not mean that the individual necessarily must be at odds with the ideologies and institutions of their time. Rather, they must be cautious of their influences and, most importantly, maintain a definitive measure of control over themselves. This is a moderate approach to the ideal of citizenship, not a gratuitously reactionary one. Schiller reflects:

> Live with your century, but do not be its creature; render to your contemporaries what they need, not

what they praise. Without sharing their guilt, share
with noble resignation their penalties, and bow with
freedom beneath the yoke which they can as ill
dispense with as they can bear it.[185]

Part of the way in which the individual maintains control
over the institutions and associations which bind them is
through spontaneous action. For Humboldt, spontaneous
action is a necessary condition of liberty and a sacred right of
the individual to sustain personal dignity. Without this liberating possibility, progress can be undone by the ignorance that
breeds in the stagnant waters of total conformity and likewise
in the tumultuous tides of mob mentalities. Any steps forward
can quickly be taken back, and history fulfils the dispiriting
prophecy of repeating itself. Once again, these thinkers cited
the devastation of the Terror that had taken place in France,
which was born from admirable republican principles and
sacred universal ends that were shattered in their enactment
by an angry, amorphous mob.

However, the theorists of the Beautiful Soul were social
optimists. They believed that the history of humanity is, or at
least could become, a positive trajectory. The practice of this
philosophy would ultimately lead to the complete freedom of
the individual's inner world and become the crucible of
progress.[186] The Beautiful Soul became associated with the
struggle against oppression upon which "the whole greatness
of mankind ultimately depends."[187] In humanity's gradual
evolution through *Bildung*, freedom would manifest itself not
only in the minds of individuals, but also in the institutions
and associations that these individuals occupy, thereby paving
the way for human progress.

The subjectivity that this concept advances is, even for

today, deeply progressive since most ideologies depend either explicitly or implicitly on individuals' conforming— before or after giving consent. In contrast, the Beautiful Soul is intended to be a liberating doctrine of personal action that can flourish independent of the judgement or authority of others. It is this optimism in individuals' abilities, paired with an acute perception of the problems that must be overcome in the face of political discord, that makes this theory simultaneously idealistic and pragmatic.

The conceptual development of freedom and spontaneity are intimately connected to the aesthetic dimension of the Beautiful Soul since beauty, according to this philosophy, is free and as such can assist in freeing the mind and spirit. Schiller's animal metaphors are relevant to this discussion. In his *Kallias Letters,* he argues that we would not call the workhorse free or beautiful because it treads along tiredly, "its movement no longer springs from its nature." Robbed of its natural motion by the drudgery of the wagon it must bear, gravity pulls it down. The stallion, on the other hand, who lithely trots through the fields, is free. By actualising the possibilities of his nature through graceful movement, he attains beauty.

Schiller argues that beauty and freedom overcome heaviness, which is why, for example, when we attempt to describe Psyche's freedom, we depict her with butterfly wings.[188] We can apply this metaphor to human life and argue that the individual who is forced into conformity, who figuratively bears weights that hold them down, will never fully realise their natural faculties. Beautiful souls, by definition, must be intellectually free, with a lightness of being that moves them beyond enslavement to the will of others. They live, according to Schiller, with grace, the "beauty of form under freedom's influence" and this grace is derived from their "personal merit" because they have acquired it through the force of their own volition.[189]

The theorists of the Beautiful Soul did not believe that the grace of freedom negates the seriousness of one's communal responsibilities or infringes upon the liberty of others. Emphasis on the individual is not intended to remove a person from the world but rather to integrate them into the full breadth of human experience. According to Schiller, personal freedom springs from "the beauty of social relations" and vice versa.[190] The first law of gentility is to "have consideration for the freedom of others" and the second is to "show your freedom."[191] Schiller represents this interplay of the individual and the collective will through his image of a well-choreographed English dance:

> The spectator in the gallery sees countless movements which cross each other colourfully and change their direction wilfully but *never collide*. Everything has been arranged such that the first has already made room for the second before he arrives, everything comes together so skilfully and yet so artlessly that both seem merely to be following their own mind and still never get in the way of the other. This is the most fitting picture of maintained personal freedom and the spared freedom of the other.[192]

This depiction of dancers who respect their own freedom by gracefully moving in resonance with the freedom of those around them is a far cry from the exertion of brutish individual force with which freedom so often has come to be associated.

The Beautiful Soul offers a refined understanding of human liberty, one which subtly considers the positions of others while never negating one's own. Individual rights are only true liberties when they are pursued in reference to the collective wellbeing upon which the individual undeniably depends. While this nuanced conception of subjectivity is more complex, it is possible to achieve accord in even the most contentious matters with the artful diplomacy that beautiful souls will have cultivated in the very exercise of their inner freedom.

Regarding the personal freedom that was practiced within the salons, it was ultimately the role of the individual to determine what they believed and to forge their own character according to the principle of self-direction. Respecting and fostering the subjectivity of each participant was integral to the intellectual freedom that the salon championed. Affirming the validity of each person's unique perspective came naturally to the *salonnières*, who were themselves a creation of their own vibrant imaginations, whose startling originality was often lauded within the intellectual circles of their time.

The *salonnières* differed dramatically from each other in fundamental respects and were not shy to express their originality.[193] Each *salonnière* was remembered for qualities that were unique to her personality and her salon was constructed around these differences. Varnhagen was believed to be the most intellectual and soulful; Schlegel was considered the bohemian and the most influential in Romantic circles; Herz was the beauty and the muse of the greatest thinkers.[194] Herz was praised for her openness to new influences. Her "greatest originality," according to Goethe, resided in her freedom from bias which made her endlessly receptive to new experiences and her ability to understand things in relation to one another.[195] Varnhagen, by contrast, was reputed to have an original, unconventional intelligence, and a particularly passionate nature.[196] She was not afraid to wear her eccentricities on her sleeve and even described herself as unique: "I am as unique as the greatest being on this earth…the greatest artist, philosopher or poet is not above me. We are made of the same element."[197] Varnhagen understood this uniqueness, not as an indication of an exceptional nature, but as an example of what all people could be by following this philosophy.[198] She was often compared to Philine in Goethe's Wilhelm Meister because of their shared unconventionality and affirmation of the principle of *Bildung,* namely to exist with fearless intellectual autonomy.[199]

The originality that the *salonnières* possessed and the fascination of their personalities, motivated an intellectual elite to associate with them and to frequent their salons.[200] The Austrian poet Franz Grillparzer (1791-1872) described the power of Varnhagen's enchanting presence, even during the second stage of her salons when her health had diminished considerably:

> Then the aging woman, who has perhaps never been pretty and was now bent over by illness, who resembled a fairy, if not a witch, began to speak and I was enchanted. My tiredness disappeared or rather, gave way to intoxication. She spoke and spoke until almost midnight, and I no longer know whether they chased me away or I left on my own. Never in my life have I heard anyone speak more interestingly or better.[201]

Salon culture depended on charismatic *salonnières* who attracted loyal participants with the striking originality of their ideas and their ways of being that liberated those in their presence from the suffocating tedium of everyday life. Like a political or religious leader, their success depended on a magnetism that transcended their personhood; they became the vessel for the hopes of others. This cult of personality coalesced the disparate actors and activities of the salon.

Individuality was an attribute that the *salonnières* naturally expressed but also encouraged in their salon participants. "The charm of the early Berlin salons was that nothing really mattered but personality and the uniqueness of character, talent, and expression. Such uniqueness, which alone made possible an almost unbounded communication and unrestricted intimacy, could be replaced neither by rank, money, success, nor literary fame."[202] Eccentricities were actively cultivated and idiosyncrasies in personality were an important part of the success of a salon, rendering it entertaining, engaging, and real.[203] The diversity and uniqueness of the personalities made the salon a particularly exciting space in which discourse went far beyond the pedantic frivolities of polite society and entered deeper terrains of self-discovery.

Displays of individuality were valued not only because they made discourse interesting, but also because they revealed the essence of a person, which was crucial to a philosophy grounded in the cultivation of character. *Salonnières* could not assist in this cultivation if the participant's current state of being was occluded. The true nature of each guest must be revealed and understood before it could be improved. Salons offered the rare visionaries of the time a place to congregate where their uniqueness was not repressed but embraced. They facilitated self-expression that dared to venture outside the realm of what was, to imagine instead what could be.[204] As social pariahs who had experienced the injustice of being

131

ostracised because of their Jewish identity, the *salonnières* made an explicit statement with their deviation from the norm to demonstrate the possibilities of a more diverse and creative intellectual environment.

The uniqueness exhibited by the habitués of the salon also represented a certain level of emancipation.[205] It implied that the individual had exercised the autonomy necessary to find their true self. This quality ensured that those present were not reinforcing old dogmas or entrenched political alliances. Rather, they were thinking for themselves and solidifying the salon's status as a critical space for rational decision making. In acknowledging the importance of personhood, the *salonnières* successfully responded to the Kantian imperative to further the historical process of Enlightenment through rational action, helping others autonomously determine who they were and who they wished to become.

The freedom that the theorists of the Beautiful Soul and the *salonnières* were advocating was in fundamental respects opposed to colloquial understandings of freedom today. Freedom in a contemporary context often entails the aggressive defence of the self, an assumed license to act however we please and to assert our "liberties" whatever the consequences for others. The underlying message is one in which validating my rights almost necessarily infringes upon the rights of others. The aesthetic of these modern-day displays is often inherently antagonistic, no longer beautiful and graceful, but violent and divisive. Whether it is the freedom to work for a company that infringes upon the rights of others in order to maximise one's chances for economic gain, or the freedom to express opinions in virulent virtual posts with sanctimonious rage, this contemporary truculent approach to asserting our liberties is deeply misguided.

Further reinforcing the difference between historical and modern conceptions of freedom, rights-based rhetoric has focused on the notion of individual liberties instead of collective responsibilities. We instinctually consider our personal needs over those of our communities. Individualism has become so deeply entrenched that declarations defining human rights, regarded as inherently sacrosanct, are in fact grounded in fundamentally individualistic assumptions.

The theorists of the Beautiful Soul, by contrast, consistently refer to a collective *humanity* in their writing. Self-cultivation is undertaken in the service of humankind, not merely for individual gratification. Although they believed that individuals would personally benefit from this philosophy, their ends were always directed at society. This difference might seem significant solely in terms of language, but conceptual shifts can create fundamental changes to the ends that are pursued and, moreover, the means by which those ends are achieved. A philosophy of self-cultivation intended to improve humanity could easily be distorted to serve purely selfish needs, if this difference is not consciously perceived and reconciled.

Perhaps most dangerous to the realisation of this collective conception of freedom, partisan assertions of personal liberties often lack clarity and coherence. Instead of a logical set of principles, their tenets become a hodgepodge of individual desires. Without a communal ethos embedded within the concept of personal rights, and a systematic and informed understanding of what constitutes those rights, we remain far from actualising the enlightened vision of freedom that this philosophy sought to achieve.

With respect to the freedom associated with originality and self-expression, the *salonnières* would have undoubtedly been dismayed to witness the epidemic of conformity today. There is something deeply worrying about the fact that we can almost certainly predict what the stranger next to us might say or spends their time doing, and so easily resort to pedestrian conversations that fluctuate among a limited number of topics. The lack of originality with which we live, and the repetitive nature of everyday actions, unveil the uncomfortable reality that we are overly reliant on social conventions, and thus more vulnerable to indoctrination.

Practicing intellectual freedom entails undertaking the wonderfully creative task of determining who one is and how one wants to present oneself in order to represent this inner state. To be a liberated person means to question if the activities we are engaged in truly represent our individuality or are simply ones that we think we should pursue because they fit within the expectations of our social position. In the best of all worlds, our character will be so wholly novel that it is difficult to easily categorise or predetermine. Our identity will be an assemblage of qualities to which there is no necessary logic or classification. Like spontaneous action, such randomness and unpredictability in one's interests suggests intellectual emancipation. This philosophy grants us the freedom to determine who we are, independent of what others assume, in the most radical and expansive sense.

Salons seem to naturally attract a mélange of genuinely interesting people. There have been habitués of my salons who are philosophical opera composers, writers of metaphysical poetry, post-modern film directors, and polymathic concert artists. The speakers have included an acclaimed opera singer, an arctic explorer, a moral philosopher, a transhumanist scientist, a maximum-security prison guard, and one of the world's most notorious art forgers. The people who are truly free in their interests naturally gravitate to the salon environment. As crucibles for exploring alternative realities, salons appeal to those interested in cultivating different dimensions of their lives by remaining open to new knowledge and experiences.

The salon provides these participants with the support and sense of solidarity necessary to discover themselves, facilitating a freedom in thought that is reciprocated. Although the proclivities of salon participants differ vastly, their intense curiosity acts as a unifying principle. The most original dimensions of themselves are cultivated in an environment that celebrates this uniqueness. In ascertaining where one's true interests lie, finding a community which fosters personal exploration is indispensable to intellectual liberation.

Practicing the freedom implicit to this philosophical tradition within a salon, entails overcoming the cult of extreme individualism, considering one's decisions and viewpoints in relation to the social whole. By maintaining a concern for the collective, we are better able to understand what it means to be free as individuals who also depend upon a collective to thrive. The practitioner of this philosophy will not reflexively reject what others consider to be their personal liberties. If, for instance, they are vehemently opposed to assisted suicide, they will nevertheless listen attentively to the perspective of someone who has a debilitating disease and believes that dying is their fundamental right and the only path to escape their misery. They understand that freedoms are negotiated within a public sphere and must be continuously recalibrated to fit collective social needs.

Above all, beautiful souls will develop their own opinions, overcoming the inclination to blindly follow others and prescriptively adopt existing social norms. Unfortunately, the human proclivity to follow convention often results in conformity being dangerously conflated with morality. Even if the outcome is good, the uncritical acceptance of a dominant ideology still presents a serious threat because it means that we could equally be swayed by negative forces instead of autonomously exercising our independent critical faculties.

The Jewish *salonnières* seemed to prophesise the tragedies that befell modernity when they warned about the dangers associated with masses of people indiscriminately following ideas that enabled the rise of fascism a century later. We look back on the terrible tragedies of past centuries with horror, yet we continue to fall into similar traps of uncritical acquiescence to the ideologies of the day. When morality becomes an ever-changing fashion statement and a mark of affiliation, not a profound philosophical inquiry that can be substantiated with thoughtful reflection, it is most in peril. Adopting a set of political trends that are shared by many does not mean that we are acting as moral agents. Whether it is following the fascist ideologies of the twentieth century or "cancelling" people in the twenty-first century, time and time again over the course of human history Schiller's words ring painfully true that "the voice of the majority is no proof of justice."[206]

Unfortunately, today we appear far from developing our own moral compass in an age in which the internet has amplified the catastrophic inclination to blindly follow what others say. Social media platforms capitalise on the perilous human tendency to succumb to mob mentalities and blindly parrot popular views. With "like" buttons and other similar functions on these applications, the conditions are irrevocably created for uncritical acquiescence to ideologies that eliminate all nuance or subtlety in thought. Indulging the desire for gossip and destructive displays of drama, the most provocative, biased, and incendiary content becomes "viral," warping public opinion and promulgating irrational views like wildfire. Shock factor, entertainment value, and self-indulgence are privileged over truth, reason, and moral integrity.

No longer do we have philosophers and poets shaping public opinion by virtue of their extensive knowledge. Instagram influencers, whose claim to fame is posting provocative photos of themselves, have somehow been given the critical role of informing our views on society and politics. Film stars are given special access to discuss their opinions on education or prison reform with heads of state. Minor celebrity figures are offered platforms to debate their uninformed geo-political perspectives, changing the national debate and even influencing elections.

A decline in the integrity and seriousness of whom we engage with to inform our opinions undermines the "marketplace" of ideas and represents a serious threat to a meaningful public sphere. A loss of credible experts informing public perceptions means that we remain largely ignorant on issues about which we have a responsibility to be informed. We follow fashions instead of seriously considering our social and political ideas from multiple, unbiased perspectives.

To practice the Beautiful Soul today we must intelligently inform ourselves about a wide range of issues from experts who are truly knowledgeable and then develop our own opinions so that we are not overly influenced by others. We should approach issues by examining multiple perspectives and forming an opinion that is independent and rational. In doing so, we engage with as many perspectives as possible, especially those with which we might disagree, seeking the lineaments of wider consensus. This approach, while less satisfying than indulging a desire for histrionic public displays, ultimately does more to advance the issues we care about than professing unsubstantiated opinions that lack nuance or objectivity. To be well-versed should be seen as a civic duty, since democracy depends upon people rationally comprehending issues to achieve desirable outcomes.

To be an intellectually liberated person, we must overcome the dangerous inclination to fall prey to mob mentalities. We should remain open to changing our views but not be easily coerced, manipulated, or susceptible to whatever ideology is socially accepted even if it is wrong or morally questionable. This is especially true of our political views. Whether I am liberal or conservative, I will not blindly follow party dictates. No single political orientation could ever encompass the depths of who I am or align with all my values. To artificially box ourselves into political, social, or cultural groups means that we have not considered what we care about or are not courageous enough to uphold our fundamental beliefs. We have uncritically accepted what we have been told and are dangerously susceptible to indoctrination.

According to this philosophy, we are in peril when individuals are unwilling to listen to challenges to their opinions, are unable to critique themselves, or refuse to admit when the opposing side is correct or has been successful. Of course, people often agree with popular ideologies without posing counter arguments so that they can more easily assimilate into a social group. But we can still exist within groups without having to affirm everything that they say or represent and if the group is productive and not coercive, our divergent opinions will be properly respected.

Beautiful souls maintain criticality so as not to be indoctrinated. They possess the rare quality of being able to admit when they are wrong. They are confident about the opinions that they have carefully developed and have faith in what they believe. However, they are not overly zealous, arrogant, or incapable of listening to other perspectives. They are intellectually and emotionally mature enough to sacrifice the comfort of maintaining a position that they do not have to question in order to attain greater knowledge and a commitment to the truth. Although they might feel a sense of solidarity with certain groups, beautiful souls are not defined by them. They are fair and flexible, yet principled, independent, and uncoerced.

CHAPTER 9

On Advancing the Good

T HE cultivation of individual qualities is ultimately directed towards the collective good. If every person is more virtuous and intellectually free then naturally, only positive outcomes will arise for society. Concern for the individual is simultaneously a concern for the wellbeing of a community comprised of all those individuals. Cultivating citizens who are morally and intellectually sound is the most effective way to improve the world, especially when one acknowledges the fact that individual decisions can have far larger social and political consequences. The character features that the proponents of the Beautiful Soul sought to develop were the foundation for shared ends and a common set of values that Goethe and Schiller believed could only be attained through the practice of this philosophy.

As a testament to the power of this concept, in the late eighteenth and early nineteenth centuries, The Beautiful Soul became the very symbol of morality and the ethical ideal, the cornerstone of philosophical thought and popular discourse on the good:

> By the end of the 1780s, particularly, but by no means solely, in the German-speaking states, the discourse generated by the concept of moral beauty had been completely absorbed, and largely

accepted, by the learned and laymen alike. The 'beautiful soul'- the '*Schöne Seele*' and the '*belle âme*'- appeared in countless works and contexts: in philosophical essays and private letters, in novels, poems, and plays, and if Lavater would have had his way, in the streets and salons of Europe as well.[207]

The phenomenal rapidity of the Beautiful Soul's traction as *the preeminent* moral ideal in late eighteenth century Europe was astounding. It crossed cultural, gender-based, socio-economic, and ideological divides. This concept had a universal appeal precisely because of its resoluteness on moral issues and its affirmation of a good that rested not upon subjective, or culturally specific ends, but upon universal Platonic values. It maintained integrity through its ethical clarity, seeking nothing less than a totalised state of perfected decency.

Goethe and Schiller adamantly affirmed that an objective Good exists towards which people are naturally inclined. Schiller went as far as to say that every individual, without exception, always prefers good over evil, simply because it is good. He explains that conflict occurs only between that which is good and that which is agreeable, namely, the difference between reason and desire. This conflict, he argues, can be overcome either when reason is strengthened or the inclination towards temptation is broken. He advocates the second possibility because it bolsters the will and is most compatible with a moral character.[208] The point, however, is that a lack of goodness is not caused by a desire for evil, but rather by weakness, which, unlike an intrinsic condition, might ultimately be overcome.

Unlike frail mortals who need socially imposed value

structures to uphold their sense of decency, the idealised figure of the Beautiful Soul maintains the good even in dystopic settings where all morality appears to be absent. This unconditional good, which acts as the inspiration for those in pursuit of self-cultivation, is conceived in two interrelated senses.

The first use of the term is that of an empirically demonstrable social good—the enlightenment of inner faculties as a means of bringing about a consonance of people. In this regard, one of the foremost attributes of a beautiful soul is a strong sense of fairness and justice.[209] The desire to stand for what is right, even if it is not fashionable to do so, is the impetus for their actions and a quality that they sustain regardless of whether it brings any personal advantage. A beautiful soul reflects on the world from more objective perspectives and considers the needs of others as if they were their own. They choose the path of empathy, offering everyone the respect that they deserve without falling prey to righteousness or self-flattery. To be good is not an act of charity or a source of admiration, but rather a natural disposition, one that demands no praise or encouragement.

The second sense of the good is of a more abstract nature: as an object of philosophical inquiry that carries ethical and political significance. A beautiful soul, in this sense, is preoccupied with the development of more perfect normative principles that eventually bring humanity closer to uncovering moral truths. Though they are concerned with their immediate reality, and the quality of the social relationships which comprise it, their ambition to achieve the good extends far beyond these limited parameters. They do not focus on one or two issues but are interested in larger structures and complete systems, interrogating the fundamental assumptions that govern society. In identifying problems and contradictions that inhibit goodness from manifesting, they can propose reforms and in doing so contribute to society on a far larger scale.

Although each beautiful soul is unique, what they represent is universal—and it is in this universality that the theory can derive wider value for its moral ends. The theorists of the Beautiful Soul fervently defended the existence of a metaphysical Good against those who denied the reality of such a universal value. They also maintained a conviction that those elements of one's moral being that the individual has endeavoured to cultivate will forever endure. This is perhaps as close to a matter of faith as this philosophy espouses. Goethe reflected in a conversation with Eckermann on May 2, 1824:

> At the age of seventy-five...one must, of course, think frequently of death. But this thought never gives me the least uneasiness- I am so fully convinced that the soul is indestructible, and that its activity will continue through eternity. It is like the sun, which seems to our earthly eyes to set in night, but is in reality gone to diffuse its light elsewhere.[210]

His perspective on the eternal nature of the soul makes cultivating a beautiful soul even more significant. Nevertheless, even if the perpetuity of the soul is not true and an abstract Good does not exist, this would not detract from the goodness that is created in its pursuit. Its belief, not its objective reality, provides the clarity and motivation necessary to create this goodness in the world.

Furthermore, a sense that morality is not merely subjective and ephemeral but rather has a universal value is not a necessary precondition to the practice of this philosophy. The nihilist can still pursue the Beautiful Soul. However, it does make this theory more widely attractive to those who wish to believe in something larger than themselves; it provides greater incentive to maintain one's moral nature if one assumes the existence of an objective Good that exceeds the narrow confines of physical reality.

Advancing the Good is, then, both an individual and collective process. This process contributes to the construction of a shared moral framework that is continuously refined as knowledge is acquired through personal experience, existential questioning, and shared intellectual reasoning. The belief in a transcendental Good, and notions about the eternal condition of the soul, replaced religious thought, and thus in this period the Beautiful Soul evolved into a secular alternative to religion.

Even though the Judeo-Christian tradition is not fully compatible with the humanistic, secular ideas upon which the Beautiful Soul is based, there is still the need for some form of spiritual meaning to remain embedded within the concept— whose origin, after all, was theological. The Beautiful Soul, therefore, superseded its pedagogical ends and became an entire belief system. Schlegel commented on the almost accidental religious aspect of this philosophy when he said, "Your goal is art and science, your life love and culture (*Bildung*). Without knowing it, you are on the way to religion. Recognise this and you will be sure of achieving your goal."[211]

Because the Beautiful Soul references the non-physical and eternal, it can answer fundamental eschatological questions relating to life after death. Yet, unlike many religious belief systems (of which Goethe and Schiller were particularly critical), the experience of eternity is not dominated by a powerful and fear inspiring God. Instead of an anthropomorphised figure, God evolves into the trinity of the Platonic forms and priests are replaced by poets, "the priests of the beautiful."[212] Artists and intellectuals, the bearers of culture, are thought to be the educators and the agents of morality who, by virtue of creating aesthetic experience, can bring individuals closer to these forms. They fill the void of meaning that the religious figures left open when they were dismantled by modern thought, reawakening humanity to the beauty and mystery of the world.

Schiller encouraged people not to despair that modern society had become demystified in the evolution of rationality because each person could restore a "unity" within themself and in doing so, discover the divine. The individual in pursuit of the Beautiful Soul re-establishes the ultimate ideal, "a kind of unity of unity" that Schiller envisions, by becoming receptive to all that is beautiful, good, and true and by re-enchanting the world through their poetic perception of it.[213] They cultivate their faculties as if it is a spiritual exercise, a kind of secular prayer. The religious dimension of the Beautiful Soul is, essentially, the sustained contemplation of the universe in all its unity, poetry, and moral force.[214]

The metaphysical significance of this concept saves it from being construed merely as a practical exercise with no larger philosophical ambitions. Equally, its pragmatic dimensions rescue it from the other extreme of being an abstract ideal with no empirical application. Unlike classical religions, it actively evolves, never becoming a permanent system of fixed and inflexible rules of conduct that are impervious to change. It is specific enough to be binding and character building, but at the same time, abstract enough to permit reflection upon the human condition writ large, and thereby to remain relevant in an ever-evolving social milieu. The Beautiful Soul is the humanist alternative to religion for those in pursuit of Beauty, Goodness, and Truth.

The discussion of the good, in relation to this philosophy, is inextricably linked to a concern for one's fellow human beings and an interest in sharing the fruits of self-cultivation while acknowledging that all people are worthy and capable of this pursuit. Practice of the Beautiful Soul's conception of the good is predicated upon an egalitarian impulse and the supposition that anyone can become a part of its tradition, a member of this progressive ideology that is meritocratic and inclusionary.[215]Although this principle of equality is affirmed consistently throughout the literature, it is often assumed that the Beautiful Soul was an elitist concept. This false perception, grounded upon the modern prejudice that "high culture" is implicitly exclusionary, should be disabused.

Self-cultivation is undeniably more accessible to the middle and upper classes who have the time and energy to cultivate their minds through philosophy, literature, and music. More-over, the *Bildungsbürgertum,* an educated middle class that emerged in the mid eighteenth century, tried to isolate them-selves from other social classes and legitimise their privileged position through their practice of *Bildung.*[216] This would appear to negate the egalitarian principle and demonstrates that a philosophy based on specific cultural practices can easily become fraught with social divisions and assertions of moral superiority. Although I do not wish to contest the elitism of the *Bildungsbürgertum*, given that it was embedded in many social circles and an undeniable facet of their *Bildung* practice, it is essential to distinguish the theory from its specific practice by certain groups of people who superficially appropriated its aims.

In its classic formulations, the concept is, in fact, radically egalitarian. It strongly affirms the French Revolution's princi-ples of liberty and fraternity, encourages tolerance and advances equality. The Beautiful Soul not only reflected burgeoning notions on equality, but it also galvanised interest in the novel political dimensions of its formulation as a complete (inner and outer) emancipation through personal practice. Throughout its principal theorists' philosophical essays, there are consistent assertions that anyone, no matter what their class or social status, can develop their faculties and, in the process, come closer to this ideal. At the time, the mere assertion of such a total equality was a revolutionary stance.

By the principles of this philosophy, everyone has an intellect and a sense of morality that is capable of development, and this is the only condition that is required for its practice. The Beautiful Soul does not depend upon social status, inheritance, physical appearance, or inherent states of being, but rather is formed through a strong work ethic, diligence, good deeds, and personal commitment available to all. The Beautiful Soul is not something that can be materially acquired, nor is it the product of chance: its attainment is entirely dependent upon the internal faculties invested in a person at birth.[217] Since even the act of thinking beautifully is a pathway towards self-cultivation, all can pursue it, even those who do not have the time or resources to engage with culture and the arts. At its most basic, the Beautiful Soul is nothing more than an enlightened way of being which can be cultivated by everyone from the actor, the labourer, and the bricklayer to the prince, the poet, and the politician. It can be formed in every context from the garden, the studio, and the art museum to the kitchen, the hay field, and the concert hall. Universal reach and applicability are a central fixture of this philosophy.

But even though the Beautiful Soul requires no material resources to pursue, many of its theorists were still deeply

147

concerned with the conditions of the poor and the accessibility of the concept to the working classes, a testament to the extent to which they sought its universal implementation. Although formal education and access to cultural products is not the sole means by which to enrich the soul, they can substantively assist in the process. If most people are excluded from these experiences, it narrows their intellectual prospects. The theorists of the Beautiful Soul were some of the first to acknowledge the class-based problems of poverty, unemployment, and inhumane working conditions that a society on the verge of massive industrialisation faced.[218] They were ahead of their time in attempting to make sense of and address these perils to human survival and prosperity.

Beyond expressing the urgency of addressing basic needs, Schiller was aware of the conditions of the poor and the problems associated with a lack of time and cultural resources that impeded their ability to flourish. One of the greatest obstacles to *Bildung* and the enlightenment it represented, he believed, came from the impoverished conditions of peasants.[219] He vehemently criticised class structures and argued that the state must improve the material condition of the poor so that they be afforded the same opportunities to self-cultivate as more affluent members of society. "First the spirit must be liberated from the yoke of necessity before one can lead it to the freedom of reason."[220] From Schiller's perspective, for people to liberate themselves intellectually, they must first be liberated physically from those bonds that constrain their ability to exercise their mind. Thus, the responsibility lies first with the state to ease economic inequalities. Once basic economic security is achieved, it becomes the responsibility of the individual to liberate themself through self-cultivation.

For an elite endowed with sufficient resources to act freely, their own cultivation will include the exercise of benevolence. As a result, an equitable economic state of affairs will come about sooner than if those in power ignore the social problems that others face and are unwilling to assist in the amelioration of their condition. One of the aims of a *Bildung* education is to ensure that humankind constantly holds within itself "the consciousness of all humanity."[221] With this consciousness, whoever is in the better position will use their advantage to benefit others and to resolve the structural problems at hand. Therefore, even if the Beautiful Soul first begins with an elite, it will have positive economic effects for the working classes who will eventually be able to self-cultivate with fewer resource constraints. However, this is by no means a "trickle down philosophy." Its power lies in the fact that, if practiced on a broad scale, the core philosophical precepts will lead to mutually considerate behaviour, yet the only person whom one needs to rely upon to enjoy its benefits is oneself, and everyone, not just a privileged few, are included in its formulation.

This perspective challenges narratives which frame the Beautiful Soul as elitist.[222] These narratives are, ironically, often infused with elitism themselves, implicitly assuming that the working classes are not truly capable of or interested in self-cultivation. It exposes implicit class bias by those who ironically view themselves as progressive. What is so compelling about this standpoint on social equality is that it acknowledges the serious economic limitations placed on the poor and considers ways to address this problem, but it also includes all of humanity into its system with the implicit assumption that everyone has the competency to achieve its goals. This is not a feigned ideology of equality, but one that is truly progressive.

Furthermore, it gives no special advantages to any one group. False piety or obsequiousness is frowned upon, and acts of charity undertaken from self-love are considered distasteful. A truly cultivated person will treat a prince or a pauper in the same way. The prince will not be flattered by the sycophant in order to receive social favours and the pauper will not be insincerely pandered to in order to display virtue; such actions would do nothing more than reinforce pre-existing hierarchies. No one gains favours from false means and everyone is treated with equal respect and dignity.

In this philosophy social hierarchies and the rigidities of class systems are critiqued, and a judgement of worth based on merit is encouraged. Schiller's play, *The Robbers*, for example, is a criticism of class structures and economic inequalities, while Goethe's characters often express opposition to social schisms and they maintain friendships with people of different statuses. In Goethe's *The Sorrows of Young Werther* (1774) Werther, the protagonist states:

> I have often noticed that people of some standing always keep coldly aloof from the common folk, as if they believe they would lose if they approached them...I maintain that he who supposes he must keep his distance from what they call the rabble, to preserve the respect due to him, is as much to blame as a coward who hides from his enemy for fear of being beaten.[223]

Here, social distance is rejected and the man in favour of hierarchies is likened to a coward. By contrast, the type of heterogeneous relationships that a cultivated person might foster are depicted in *Wilhelm Meister* in which Wilhelm, along his *Bildung* journey, develops meaningful friendships across all classes from orphans, impoverished actors, and destitute musicians to noble ladies and distinguished scholars. He learns from many different types of people, all of whom help him grow and elicit various positive aspects of his character. His diverse friendships and social interactions are portrayed as equal in value, and never as self-congratulatory acts of benevolence towards social inferiors. His forays into new social spheres and his desire to engage in mutual education represents what it means to be truly cultivated.

This exploration of equality and inclusion merits further investigation in its relationship to gender politics. Like most philosophical theories of the time, *Bildung* was predominately directed towards male subjects. This issue has already been thoroughly explored by scholars and there have been multiple attempts at feminist rewritings of *Bildung* and the *Bildungsroman*.[224] Nevertheless, dismissing the concept as fundamentally sexist or ultimately unconcerned with female narratives would be too facile a conclusion. *Bildung* was principally a male-undertaking, but the idealised end, the figure of *die schöne Seele,* is female, both linguistically in the article *die*, and in her depiction in literature. The feminine is glorified in the concept's formulation; it was commonly believed that women are naturally more sociable and artful, in other words, better suited to perfect their souls. As Humboldt comments:

> Woman is, strictly speaking, nearer to the ideal human nature than man; and whilst it is true that she more rarely reaches it, it may only be that it is more difficult to ascend by the steep, immediate path than by the winding one. Now, how much

such a being—so sensitive, yet so complete in herself, who therefore responds to everything with her whole being—must be disturbed by external disharmony, is incalculable. Hence the infinite social consequences of the culture of the female character.[225]

Although I am aware of the argument that misogyny may be embedded in the archetype of the muse, I would differ from much of the existing literature on the subject. I suggest in the alternative that the Beautiful Soul's very representation as an ideal, feminine form, and the stereotypical female qualities that permeated many of the subjective characteristics of *Bildung*, demonstrate more favourable attitudes towards women through a willingness to adopt the feminine in male narratives, at least in theoretical and literary terms. In giving sentiment (stereotypically associated with the feminine) equal status with reason (stereotypically considered male), a significant paradigm shift in gender dynamics of the time occurred. This could be interpreted as a reflection of more progressive views on the status of women in society.

Humboldt spent much time balancing "feminine" and "masculine" forces and showing their different but equal qualities and mutual interdependence.[226] In Goethe's work, there is a certain fluidity of gender norms in which "if, on one side, Goethe's beautiful souls are women, on the other one must note that these women do not have all the physical attributes of a 'woman' just like Wilhelm himself seems to be quite effeminate at times."[227] The gender dynamics are undoubtedly complex and although historical details, such as the fact that Humboldt and Goethe were greatly influenced by women in their formulation of the concept, might be revealing, they do not necessarily bring a deeper understanding of the concept itself. The basic characteristics of *Bildung* do, however, demonstrate that this philosophy, through its harmonisation of "male" and "female" qualities with unclear divisions between the two, could be applied independent of gender norms.

From another perspective, the Beautiful Soul might be critiqued as an elitist proposition reserved for the very few because, like genius or exceptional artistic abilities, not everyone has the intellectual or moral capacities to attain such a lofty and demanding goal. Although not everyone will become a more beautiful soul, this does not mean the quest is not worthy of pursuit—especially when the faculties of self-reflection that it requires are, in fact, available to all.

Although this philosophy could not immediately resolve larger social inequalities, this does not diminish from its egalitarian tenets and its aspirations to promote universal equality. Furthermore, Humboldt's educational model is a trenchant example of a concrete, practical achievement that this concept inspired. Paired with the salon's documented historical practice of egalitarianism, there is sufficient evidence to suggest that, contrary to certain portrayals, the Beautiful Soul was the most progressive doctrine of its time, both in theory and in application.

The dialectic between the subjective and collective nature of self-cultivation, in which the self is perfected for the sake of a more enlightened humanity, was negotiated in the salon through this concern for equality and commitment to the Good. The *salonnières* were believed to be the personification of goodness and the "mouthpiece of eternal justice."[228] They shared an intense devotion to help others and a resolute desire to contribute to the betterment of society. Schlegel was known to be thoroughly outraged whenever she saw injustice.[229] She often considered the position of the poor and did everything that she could to alleviate their suffering. In 1793, for example, she started a school for impoverished children and had plans to establish an orphanage.[230]

For Varnhagen, no dogma, patriotism, power, or social pressures were believed to be able to corrupt her sense of justice.[231] She had an immoveable sense of right and wrong and a steadfast conviction in the Good. One personal anecdote reveals this sense of moral conviction. During the time of the Wars of Liberation in 1813, Varnhagen saw the opportunity to volunteer as a true blessing and delighted in discovering her talents in aiding the wounded, sick, and poor.[232] She wrote "Making a business of doing good is my only amusement, consolation and source of strength!" and "…nothing interests me deeply but that which may make the earth better for us, the earth itself and our actions upon it."[233] In one of her many aphorisms Varnhagen describes her inability to grasp cruelty:

> We hate in a character everything we don't under-
> stand; the immoral is really incomprehensible as
> well. It is incomprehensible why a person would
> want to cause another disagreeable sensations: since
> he must surely desire agreeable ones for himself.
> But it is completely understandable that we want
> to do good to another: we desire for the other
> person that which we want for ourselves. Malice,
> which isn't revenge—the latter derives from a sense
> of justice—is completely incomprehensible.[234]

Her sense of what was just was so intuitive that she could not understand the motivations of those who willingly sought to cause injury. Malevolence was a foreign concept that she struggled to comprehend.

Varnhagen often expressed profound concern about injustices related to the conditions of the lower classes:

> I also considered the whole mass of human culture,
> and whether its quintessence, the highest delight
> of noble richly gifted persons in each other, and
> every other bright and lofty element in life, is worth
> all the suffering and misery of those whom it has
> required for centuries as its manure.[235]

But she believed that ultimately everyone could benefit from and take part in the intellectual and cultural resources reserved to the upper classes. This perspective stemmed from conviction in the meritocratic foundations of the Beautiful Soul. Without considering the economic feasibility of such an idea, the sentiment was a powerful one for the time.

It is easy to critique the *salonnières* for holding strong views on social justice while catering to an intellectual elite in their salons, but such a conclusion would be a mistake. Their intellectual activities did not diminish from their humanitarian endeavours; in fact, they strengthened them. Self-cultivation and cultural production were viewed as the vanguard of human progress that would address the social ills afflicting humankind. It was logical that the *salonnières* would choose to cultivate humane values and cultured forms of association among the elite who held the power to improve the conditions of others. If fairer and more benevolent perspectives emerged in these circles, then they could positively shape policies and institutions that affected all people's lives, especially the poor.

The *salonnières* were greatly admired for their seemingly

endless devotion to social justice and the personal sacrifices that they made to advance the utopian worlds of their salons. They were thought to be generous in almost all aspects of their lives, with their ideas and actions, their time and their emotions, their home and financial resources, their patronage and charitable activities. They kept their salons open for decades and committed themselves to the personal relationships that they established because they wanted to maintain a vision of reality that aligned with their sense of the Good. Each salon participant was a case study in the different manifestations of inequity, unfairness, and prejudice that the *salonnières* could redress, and, in the process, resolve larger socio-political problems.

Their concern for justice was, in part, informed by their moral indignation at being treated unfairly as women and Jews. They turned to *Bildung* to find personal agency in changing an unjust world.[236] However, the *salonnières* wanted to create a more humane reality— not only for themselves and the people with whom they were identified, but for humanity. They believed that they were part of the human race, not simply members of a circumscribed social class. They were far too ambitious, and charged with a sense of duty, to limit their activities to anything other than all of humankind. Furthermore, their understanding of justice was not bound to a single, politicised issue. Rather, it was an all-encompassing pursuit. They attempted to act in every circumstance with the reflection, fairness, and objectivity necessary to arrive at the purest representation of the Good. Heinrich Heine captured the *salonnières*' sweeping and compulsive sense of responsibility when he remarked of Amalie Beer:

> No day passes without her helping the poor; it even appears as though she could not go to sleep without

> having done a noble deed. In the process she does
> not discriminate between religions giving to Jews,
> Christians, Turks, and even infidels of the worst
> kind.[237]

Like the blindfolded figure of Lady Justice, they believed in acting with impartial benevolence towards all.

The *salonnières* lived with exceptional compassion because they understood that a concern for an abstract universal Good began with a concern for those around them. In exercising empathy on the individual level, they believed that they could inspire improved forms of sociability, which would have far larger consequences for society. By bringing out the humanity in salon participants through their own displays of conscientious solicitude, they endeavoured to form individuals with a goodness that could be exercised in their various spheres of social influence; they understood that individual practice is how all larger social norms emerge.

Concern for the Good came not only through admirable actions in the salons, but also in the choice of subject matter. Varnhagen's passion for social justice was explored through discussion of the writings of Claude-Henri de Saint-Simon.[238] Often this took the form of a debate to refute moral scepticism. In one example, Varnhagen was wary of the Swiss political activist and writer Benjamin Constant (1767-1830) and his criticism of social progress. "Just because he is right in saying that life is full of contradictions and confusion," she said, did not negate the fact that "the craving for reason, goodness, and justice, which is inherent in us, is a pledge that in some way we shall attain them all."[239] Like the theorists of the Beautiful Soul, the *salonnières* were adamant in their belief that people are naturally inclined to the Good. This was foundational to their conviction that by practicing self-cultivation humans would improve, and that this could be achieved within their salons.

Some have interpreted the *salonnières'* altruism as acquiescence to gender norms.[240] But this interpretation wrongly reduces the *salonnières'* acts to the mere fulfilment of social expectations. In contrast, their magnanimity could be interpreted as the attainment of the Beautiful Soul's imperative to direct one's life towards the Good. Their dedication in this regard was not performed out of subservience to the men in their salons but rather came from an emancipatory conviction in their ideals. They displayed great autonomy in their belief that they could shape social behaviour and individual action, despite the limitations of their position. This interpretation fits with the *salonnières'* own understanding of their actions.

Furthermore, their charitableness was not without personal benefit. It contributed to the *salonnières'* rise in social status and enabled them to transcend some of the limitations imposed upon them by their religion and their gender. As Varnhagen conceded "no lady of her kind penetrated into the circle of the high nobility," and the position she achieved was "through many years of self-reliance in dignity and splendour, through great charity and social activities, allied with spiritual courage and notable wisdom of the world."[241]

To be good, as a reflection of a transcendental form, held spiritual significance and the *salonnières* practiced self-cultivation as if it were a religion. Schlegel explicitly expressed the belief that she belonged to the "religion of *Bildung,*" a sentiment that she nurtured within the salons and the circle of the early Romantic writers.[242] In her interpretation, which she jointly articulated with her husband Friedrich Schlegel, God is a transcendental Good and priests are poets. Human *Bil-*

dung's symmetry with natural *Bildung* informed her pantheistic spiritual views and she searched for expressions of divinity in nature and culture, respectively. In one instance, she likens God to the foam of ocean waves or a poet's creation of a verse.[243] The spirit of this humanist "religion in self-cultivation" is expressed in a passage of Friedrich Schlegel's *Dialogue on Poetry* (1800):

> There is and never has been for us humans any other object or source of activity and joy but that one poem of the godhead the earth, of which we, too, are part and flower. We are able to perceive the music of the universe and to understand the beauty of the poem because a part of the poet, a spark of his creative spirit, lives in us and never ceases to glow with secret force deep under the ashes of our self-induced unreason…poetry bursts forth spontaneously from the invisible primordial power of humankind when the warming ray of the divine sun shines on it and fertilizes it.[244]

Here we see that within poetry a natural divinity is found, and goodness emerges from the manifestation of this poetic impulse. Through the primordial expression of poetry, or *poiesis* in the more expansive sense, human *Bildung* and natural *Bildung* come together as one. Thus, to worship the God of *Bildung* (the form of the Good), is to turn to poetry and culture to contemplate nature and the universe in all its magnificence.

Dorothea Schlegel believed that artists bring divine inspiration and that musicians create work that is the purest expression of this infinite realm. From her perspective, religious doctrine would no longer be necessary if people listened to more music, especially Bach. In her *Bildungsroman Florentin*, the main character finds divinity in the priestess and musician's muse, Clementina. "Never had he understood the divinity of music as in front of this sight."[245] God is reached through music, and, in a reversal of traditional gender roles, Clementina is the bearer of divinity in her position as a musician.

Although divinity is represented on earth through music, Schlegel understood one's religious duties to be the practice of humanitarian actions. The demonstration of spiritual devotion is nothing other than improving the conditions of the poor, providing opportunities for all those in need, and helping others self-cultivate. This understanding of religion as humanitarian action was influenced by her father Moses Mendelssohn's ideas on *Humanitätsreligion*.[246] Her salon became a secular church of *Bildung* in which her guests could access the divine through communication (both verbal and musical) and cultivate the humanitarian impulse to live with piety through acts of altruism, compassion, and the development of an objective sense of justice through shared moral reasoning.

Like Schlegel, Varnhagen discovered the divine in art, most especially in poetry and literature. She turned to Goethe and professed his thought as a religion because he poetically captured the Good to which she aspired.[247] Varnhagen was enamoured with all of Goethe's writings, but unsurprisingly, *Wilhelm Meister* was her favourite since it was most closely connected to the Beautiful Soul's tradition.[248] Goethe had said that the soul that sees beauty may sometimes walk alone. This was something that Varnhagen intimately felt, and *Wilhelm Meister* comforted her in times of need when she saw all the beauty in the world but felt isolated from people who did not share her powers of Platonic perception. His novel imparted conviction in her ideals and the ability to speak when she was voiceless.[249] She read it as "one reads the Bible in misfortune."[250] In her words:

> A new volume of Goethe was a feast to me...a dearly loved, respected, honoured guest, opening new doors for me into a new life, unknown, but full of light. He accompanied me all through my life; I took seizing of his kingdom, he was my one, my truest friend, my rock, saving me from spending myself with ghosts; my superior and my consoling friend, for I knew the hell he knew, I grew up with him, and after a thousand separations I always found him again. I, who am no writer, can never express what he was to me![251]

For Varnhagen, the impetus for all noble actions was reflected in the pages of this *Bildungsroman* which became the secular religious text that accompanied her *Bildung* education and informed those who sought enrichment in her salons.

Instead of conforming to existing doctrines, the *salonnières* chose to form their own religion of human goodness in the Beautiful Soul, a religion which most closely represented their humanistic values. The eternity which they perceived in the Platonic unity and a soul of beauty was undoubtedly a spiritual belief, but one that they pragmatically achieved by advancing culture and benevolence within their salons.

The Berlin *salonnières* wholly embraced the Beautiful Soul's egalitarian ethic in its conception of the Good. They understood that the harmonious society towards which they strove must include all people. Exclusivity, rigid hierarchies, and class division would only lead to social discord. Advancing egalitarian principles, while helping every individual self-cultivate, proved instrumental in demonstrating the validity of the idea of the Beautiful Soul. The *salonnières* took inspiration from the later incarnations of this philosophy's principles, those that allowed for a freer flowing, inclusive interpretation of its tenets. They also contributed to the very construction of this egalitarian structure and articulated progressive views in their literary works.

In her novel *Florentin*, Dorothea Schlegel imagines a society in which traditional class hierarchies are overcome, the poor have better conditions, including increased access to health care and education, statute labour is abolished, and work hours are reduced so that every person can self-cultivate. In the story, the character of the Chief Cavalry Sergeant depicts a man who demonstrates a lack of concern for the welfare of the villagers who work his land. He assumes that he has greater knowledge than them and the humiliation he causes fuels social tensions:

> The Chief Cavalry Sergeant's improvements were usually aimed at making him richer, rather than, as he alleged, making his property truly conducive to the common welfare. And with all the precautions he took to educate his farmers, he never imagined that they were bright enough to understand his actual intention and for this very reason not only did they not promote it but worked against it in all imaginable ways. For these reasons he lived with eternal vexations and quarrels.[252]

By contrast, Schlegel's characters of the Count and Countess embody the new spirit of equality. The Countess asks the farmers who work her land what improvements are needed, because she understands that they know the land better than she ever could. She then finances their ideas and gives them their fair share of the profit. She also expresses concern for the villagers' welfare and takes measures to improve their conditions, including instituting a system of universal health care. More important than the ideas on labour, education, and heath care is Schlegel's emphasis on treating the working classes with dignity and appreciating their contributions to society. The Countess is acutely aware that her estate depends on those who work the land and her respect is reflected in her attitudes and actions.[253]

This *Bildungsroman* describes the ideal society that the *salonnières* envisioned clearly, stipulating their views on equality and elucidating the egalitarian structures upon which their salons were founded. The salon was the material realisation of this progressive value system. By unifying the disparate strands of German society through the Beautiful Soul, the *salonnières* challenged existing social positions and promoted a culture in which worth was determined by intellectual merit and moral decency. Members of different social classes took part in the salons, seeking friendships in a socially diverse milieu.[254] Everyone from the educated lower and middle classes to the aristocracy were welcomed into the homes of the *salonnières* in a spirit of respect and impartiality. Guests ranged in social standing and profession from impoverished tutors, unknown actors, and struggling writers, to princes, professors, and influential politicians.[255]

The *salonnières* were famous for disregarding their participants' social position, favouring the desirable character traits that they exhibited over their wealth or family standing. "It was as the saying went 'a case not of who one was, but what one was, in order to gain admission."[256] To foster an egalitarian environment, the *salonnières* had to overcome multiple barriers:

> The Jewish *salonnières* in Berlin presided over a socially, religiously, and gender-mixed coterie distinctive in Germany both at the time and across time. The stories about these salons suggested that these women had accomplished a triple feat by emancipating themselves from their traditional patriarchal families, helping to create high culture in a crucially creative era, and, in the process, forging bonds across classes, religious groups and the two sexes.[257]

The *salonnières'* remarkable feat contributed to a wider shift in German public discourse and, by the late eighteenth century, merit and talent were often privileged over circumstances of birth.[258] On the nature of this mixed society Brinckmann said of Varnhagen's salon that it was:

> [A] circle, to be admitted to which royal princes, foreign diplomats, artists, scholars, and business men of the first rank, countesses and actresses were all equally eager, and where each was worth no more, but at the same time no less, than the impression he himself produced by his cultured personality.[259]

The writer Bettina von Arnim (1785-1859) described the wonderfully heterogeneous mix of people that Varnhagen gathered in her salon when she wrote: "All sorts of passers-through, strangers, the Countess Henchel and daughter and sister. The Barnekows, Count Yorck, the Willisens, Hegel, Humboldt, Ranke. Why mention another forty names! Each contradicts the other."[260] Of all the personalities present, Varnhagen never granted preferential treatment to one. Whether it was a poor writer or a prince, she committed herself equally to them all. As the poet Clemens Brentano (1778-1842) remarked:

> ...That Prince Louis Ferdinand and Prince Radzi-
> will visit her causes much envy, but she doesn't care
> anymore than if they were lieutenants or students,
> if these had as much spirit and talent as those, they
> would be equally welcome to her.[261]

Varnhagen herself rejoiced at the diversity of her salon when she said, "All classes, all kinds of people talk to me."[262] She commented that "Noblemen I am often fond of, the nobility never."[263]

As we can infer from these accounts, the egalitarianism that the salon espoused is perhaps not how we understand egalitarianism today. The salons were mostly a place for the middle class and bourgeoisie to mingle with the aristocracy, and participants still came from the relatively limited circles of an intellectual elite. Furthermore, simply because people of different social statuses congregated in the same space did not mean that there was total equality in their interactions. But the fact that openness and egalitarianism were even aspirational principles was, in itself, revolutionary. That men submitted to the intellectual leadership of female *salonnières* and were willing to be associated with a space of relative diversity is extraordinary for the time.

Furthermore, countless examples demonstrate that a spirit of equality was indeed accomplished in fundamental ways, more than any other institution of the period.[264] The heterogeneity of the salon is one of the most widely discussed attributes in the literature, rendering it impossible to facilely dismiss them as elitist. The *salonnières'* great achievement was their ability to bring people together who would never normally meet, changing the ways they chose to associate with each other and the values to which they aspired. For the late eighteenth and early nineteenth centuries, the salon was radical in the degree of egalitarianism that it attained.

The social fluidity that occurred required that the *salonnières* establish the proper environment for respectful exchange. "Conversations inside the salon reflected a reciprocal, egalitarian model of communicative exchange that assumed a willingness to suspend whatever criteria of social distinction may have existed outside it."[265] Salons represented an unprecedented ideal of social interaction in which one was supposed to be judged, not by one's social standing, religion, or gender, but by the quality of one's character and the substance of one's ideas. The *salonnières* monitored class integration by establishing reciprocal relationships between themselves and their salon participants. They bonded very different people through the exercise of interpersonal skill and conversational tact developed through rigorous training and experience.[266]

The *salonnières* took pride in facilitating the integration of Catholics, Protestants, and Jews, along with distinct social classes, by gracefully facilitating these new encounters. One "…delighted in seating her Jewish and commoner guests next to prominent nobles at the tiny tables she preferred over the usual long ones."[267] The *salonnières* often reflected on the egalitarian dimensions of their work. Herz's autobiography emphasises that behaviours markedly changed, and the cultivated mind became a powerful equaliser unifying different people through mutual respect, humility, and courtesy.[268] She considered the larger consequences of the egalitarianism which was practiced in her space, commenting on the fact that "this spirit of equality penetrated the highest circles of Berlin society."[269]

The elite who chose to participate in these salons understood that they could no longer depend on the prerogatives of their position when the social values of the salon increasingly favoured the cultivation of latent potential, not manifest privilege. The *salonnières* encouraged their participants to act as individuals, not as members of a social class or religion.[270] Varnhagen's salon was described as "a socially neutral place where all classes met and where it was taken for granted that each person would be an individual."[271] This principle of conscious inclusiveness both advanced the social integration that was occurring and facilitated the process of self-cultivation by stripping the individual of a pre-determined identity that he or she had not worked to shape.

One might pose the question, why did the aristocracy choose to take part in a space that did not give deference to their social standing? Apart from a theory of pure pragmatism that proposes the elites attended the salons motivated by a desire to borrow money from wealthy Jews (which cannot stand on its own, given the precarious financial situation of some of the most prominent *salonnières*), no other major hypotheses exist on what cultural historians agree was a radical departure from the social hierarchies of the time. However, the Beautiful Soul's status as the philosophy upon which the Berlin salons were based itself offers an explanation. The salon's adoption of philosophical tenets widely accepted by aristocratic intellectuals because of their strong identification with German values made changes in social practice not only palatable, but relevant and desirable. Apart from the salon, no other private institution was able to enact the Beautiful Soul's popular philosophy. Aristocrats desired to secure their status among a new cultural elite emerging in the salons who were then transforming the intellectual landscape of their time. Nobles entered salons because they wished to be among the vanguard of German intellectualism. Their fondness for the *salonnières* and the depth of friendship that they received makes sense of the evident willingness to submit to their guidance and leadership.

Scholars such as Schleiermacher used the *salonnières'* example in their own work further disseminating ideas on egalitarianism. His Essay "On a Theory of Social Behaviour" (1799) captures what he found compelling about the social interactions, freed from a concern for rank or position, that he experienced in the salons of Herz and Varnhagen.[272] Schleiermacher was heavily influenced by Varnhagen's model for equality even though he had initial qualms about the mixed company that she kept. His friendship with her, and his participation in a space comprised of heterogeneous people, eventually changed his assumptions. Developing personal relationships was, from this perspective, the simplest way to overcome deeply engrained prejudices.

Although some of the influential elite's classist conceptions were changed in their interactions with the *salonnières* as they strove to adhere to a principle of egalitarianism within the salons, this did not mean that these pioneering women did not encounter profound difficulties in their efforts at social integration. Their role required great strength of character and the active exercise of tolerance. Fichte, for example, notoriously held anti-Semitic views, which he directed toward the Jewish *salonnières*. Yet Varnhagen, who admired his work on *Bildung,* welcomed him into her salons in which he rose from poverty, and from which he benefited both socially and professionally.[273] Such self-sacrifices that the *salonnières* willingly endured to advance their meritocratic philosophy illustrate their profound commitment to their beliefs, and the remarkable courage required to establish a space that rejected entrenched social divisions.

Ultimately their almost preternatural endurance ensured their success. "The Berlin salons were the fulfilment of the assimilationist dream in miniature."[274] They offered a radical opportunity to everyone involved to redefine their identity and to transgress rigid social norms that had effectively fragmented society. Although Jewish *salonnières* were accused of abandoning their culture by associating with Christian aristocrats, they undeniably advanced the position of Jews in Germany with their "nearly unlimited domination in the cultural arena."[275] There is scholarly consensus that "Jewish cultural influence in Germany has its beginnings in these salons."[276]

Another dimension of the egalitarianism fostered in the salon was the changing nature of gender dynamics. Although approximately two thirds of participants were men, female *salonnières* hosted the events, chose the topics, invited speakers, and moderated conversations.[277] The gender of the *salonnières* played an important, yet complicated role. Since it was common at this time to see women as "civilising" agents who were emotionally sensitive and whose responsibility it was to tame the unsavoury impulses of men, we can understand why it would be socially acceptable for the *salonnières* to cater to "polite society" in this way.[278] However, while their salons were stereotypically feminine in this sense, they were also stereotypically masculine in their intellectual rigour and the significant power and social influence that they exerted.

The salons represented an age of transition in the early nineteenth century in which masculine and feminine qualities were no longer distinctly separated but merged in new ways.[279] Strict gender expectations could be challenged through intellectual experimentation and the boundaries of social behaviour tested within a space that assigned value according to the characteristics of the Beautiful Soul, which the *salonnières* understood as including both men and women through amalgamating traditionally conceived female and masculine qualities. A universal conception of the Beautiful Soul allowed salon participants to explore aspects of themselves that had before been socially unavailable to them as males or females but were now integrated into this non-gendered conception of a cultivated person whose qualities transcended such essentialised partitions. This conception of the Beautiful Soul was specific to the salon. Outside of its perimeters during this period, *Bildung* was mostly directed at men and thus a consideration of the concept in relation to gender norms was less pronounced.

The *salonnières* were often seen as androgynous creatures, equally male as female. Friedrich von Gentz, for example, perceived himself and Varnhagen as exchanging gender roles. He stated, "You are an infinitely productive creature, I am an infinitely receptive one: you are a great man, I am the first among women."[280] He compared her erudition and lucidity to male capabilities, and his own sensitivity, and the authority that she held over him, to female properties in a way that was extraordinarily unusual for the time. Varnhagen's brother Ludwig Robert (1778-1832) also saw her masculine nature and coined the term "Schwester- Freund" (sister- (male) friend) and later Vater Freund und Schwester (father- (male) friend and sister).[281] Even with her husband Karl Varnhagen, the masculine and the feminine were blurred. Rahel called Karl the diminutive "Varnhägken" "Gustchen" and even the feminine form "Guste." She compared herself to a sturdy tree able to endure anything and her husband to a dainty bird or a flower.[282]

In part, these unusual changes in gender roles reflected the figure of the Beautiful Soul that the *salonnières* sought to emulate. In the literature, beautiful souls are feminine characters who are sensitive and empathetic, but also strong and independent, like Goethe's Iphigenia.[283] The *salonnières*, who were often unmarried, childless, or married for love late in life, identified with these characters who desired freedom and social influence. Above all, they did not want to fall into domestic roles that inhibited intellectual activity. They were eager to create careers for themselves and to become intellectuals in their own right. Some, such as Varnhagen and Schlegel, were adamant defenders of women's rights and saw their salons as an act of emancipation, freeing participants from the limitations of their gender.[284] Of course, they could never entirely liberate themselves. There was always a concern that they would become "unfeminine" or that they would make men too feminine, but the androgyny with which they experimented, and that others were eager to perceive in them, was remarkable.[285]

Furthermore, the gender fluidity that took place in the salon was conducive to enacting new, more expansive forms of *Bildung*. The positive qualities associated with each gender were reciprocally integrated to create a more perfect model of personhood. A male in the salon no longer was expected to be brutish and insensitive but could adopt the social refinement previously identified with the feminine. Likewise, a woman was not only lauded for her social sensitivity but was admired and praised for her intellectual brilliance, typically considered a quality that only a male could possess.

Thus, from class, racial, religious, and gender perspectives, the *salonnières* reconceived contemporary social norms, creating an institution of their own design with an ideological concern for inclusiveness.[286] They recognised that a fully integrated society would not immediately come into being. The changes they made in the ways that the middle class and the aristocracy interacted with each other were already radical for their time. They experienced an unforeseen degree of success in demonstrating the power of social contact to foster friendships that transformed deeply engrained biases. Egalitarianism in a more expansive sense was a long journey that began with the cultivation of the individual in a group and would eventually extend to wider circles of society. Across generations, they envisioned that their model for respectful exchange and a consideration of the condition of others could change the whole of society.

In practicing this philosophy in the modern age, its concern for social justice should appeal to us. Like other features of the Beautiful Soul, this concern is highly relevant today. We are fortunate to live in times when people are becoming more socially and environmentally aware. Yet, having granted that some positive developments have been made, we should not be blind to the problems at hand or absolve ourselves of responsibility in the pursuit of a good that has yet to be attained.

The problem remains that our engagement with social issues is often one-dimensional, hypocritical, and so highly politicised that it is fair to ask if it is truly justice we seek or our own self-interest. Information technologies have increased the visibility of salient social issues, yet we struggle to translate that world-wide visibility into tangible action. Although in theory more people have a voice than ever before, it is questionable if the relatively universal ability to write content online constitutes true participation in social issues. We may, instead, be partaking in a chaotic, unmediated space that proliferates misinformation, further impeding progress and, indeed, suppressing the voices of many people. To assume that writing a comment in the anarchical void of an unmoderated forum will give individuals a real say in their society or will make them part of a movement in any meaningful sense is dangerous. We can superficially quantify engagement, which might suggest progress, but it is uncertain what has ultimately been achieved by doing so.

Unfortunately, the individualism that has defined modern thought is amplified in the constitution of internet forums and the particular type of content that they elicit. Like most of our online pursuits, social goods have become an opportunity for self-promotion for which we receive the addictive rush of accolades from our equally self-indulgent Facebook friends. Manufactured moral outrage becomes a virulent weapon of the world wide web. The hysterical online mob gesticulates without facts, rational reflection, or the empathy intrinsic to morality. Ideologies of extremity flourish as substantive debate recedes before the onslaught of cynical self-promotion; all of this driven by the desire to be noticed by the habitués of social media. In its anonymity and lack of accountability, the internet fuels the worst human tendencies: igniting a hatred spawned from envy, misinformation, prejudice and wilful ignorance.

Within this context, people with disparate views rarely come together and discuss their differences with measured respect and civility. Conversations and political debates often take the form of a vicious tournament of provocation in which all senses of decorum and decency are lost. The inability to listen casts society into a state of chaos and aggravates hostilities until it becomes untenable to interact with anyone other than with likeminded people in one's immediate sphere. The amorphous, decontextualised public that comprises the internet cannot easily adhere to social norms that are neither expected nor enforced in the anarchic cyber realm. People can easily shield themselves behind an online alias and write the cruellest comments. The worst human qualities are encouraged by how the platforms we have created operate.

In physical space, uncorroborated provocations require further substantiation because they will be interrogated in a systematic way. In the virtual sphere, however, false ideas spread unchallenged without nuance, accountability, or profound reflection. There is also not the possibility for redemption. A comment made in physical space, however illogical or inaccurate it may be, does not linger forever like one posted in cyber space. People are therefore more willing to experiment with their ideas and listen to different perspectives without the fear that they will be unjustly humiliated. The possibility of learning from others and evolving from past mistakes increases.

Cancel culture is an example of an injustice committed in the name of justice which represents the dangerous self-centeredness characterising social engagement today. This odious social phenomenon entails publicly humiliating and socially ostracising individuals who are perceived to hold views or to have made comments to which others object. These online "moral crusaders" are extremely vocal about their opinions on Twitter, but they fail to exercise true empathy. They appear to forget that justice is not vindictive and small, it is courageous and all-embracing. They pursue it not for its own sake but for the sake of performatively displaying their "good deeds." They take distinct pleasure in accusing others of immorality and use the language of social justice to advance their instrumental desires. But the fairness and objective consideration that is required in the practice of justice appears absent in them; they are vacant vessels of self-righteousness gone awry. They unravel rational attempts at progress by instantiating extremity, all for the end of indulging their false humanitarianism and sense of superiority. The same human failings that facilitate cruelty and oppression, such as the disassociation from the feelings of others, are employed in their feckless pursuit of the "good."

This culture grossly mischaracterises and falsely accuses without proof, nuance, or validity. It silences dialogue, negates free speech, and denies differences in perspectives. To cancel someone is essentially to dehumanise them, to brand them with a scarlet letter, forcing them into social and professional ostracization. Such a brutal cultural mentality deployed through police state tactics acts as the dystopic antithesis to an Enlightenment philosophy like the Beautiful Soul. Stripping people of their humanity is a dangerous game to play, one that inevitably leads to deeper injustices and a virtual epidemic of cruelty. The frenzied "canceler" only stops accusing when the tables are turned, and others accuse them. The inevitable desire for revenge, the primordial mentality of an eye for an eye, can only end in social catastrophe.

Within this incendiary reality we are encouraged to assert ourselves at all costs even if it means hurting those around us. We protect ourselves by attacking, not by behaving with decency and expecting decency in return. In this Hobbesian war of all against all, brought about, not because of a necessary state of nature, but because we have chosen to live this way, it has become common to write social media diatribes without considering the implications for those we pit ourselves against, or to presumptuously comment on topics about which we have little knowledge, thereby proliferating misinformation. The internet does not reinforce the primacy of facts, nor does it adhere to structures of etiquette that sustain principles of kindness and sensitivity. To exercise a generosity of spirit is far from its *modus operandi*.

The glossy veneer of justice as appearance and rhetoric that hides the impoverished means by which it is pursued is then augmented on a global scale by the insincerity of so-called "corporate social responsibility." Large corporations tout their social justice programs and environmental advertisement campaigns while simultaneously engaging in profit maximising practices that exacerbate the problems they claim to combat. Some argue that, even if they disingenuously espouse progressive views, at least these corporations are exposing important social problems. But if we allow justice to become a commodity that can be bought and sold by multinational corporations, we risk degrading the concept beyond recognition. We must ask ourselves who is truly benefiting and where we will draw the line on such morally opaque practices.

The corporatisation of the good is symptomatic of the hyper-commodification and extreme individualism that drives our concern for social justice today. Whether it is by public shaming that shatters compassion, or by corporate campaigns that profit from other people's suffering, these duplicitous approaches to the good are indicative of a more fundamental problem. They suggest that our society is gravely ill and experiencing an impoverishment of the soul that renders social progress ultimately untenable. Individuals deprived of a strong sense of a communal spirit and the loss of robust values will not have the ethical training or strength of character to advocate for anything other than a false façade of the good.

In my salon on "Online Social Movements," participants concurred that many of the initial aims of modern social justice movements that were positive have become distorted by companies and individuals who exploit virtual forums to serve their own needs. Content that is thoughtful and productive is ultimately lost in a sea of self-promotion, intolerance, and irrationality. Part of the reason for the fragility and contradictions intrinsic to online movements is that participation requires no special effort and follows no protocol of good practice. People who are benighted and actively destructive are given the same access as those who are well-versed and well-intentioned. Online-inspired social movements lack a coherent leadership and accountability that is difficult to achieve in cyber space. Their aims are often undefined— or, if they are defined, there is no real way to implement them, so they either descend into accusations, contradictions, and lies or eventually dissolve. Salon participants agreed that prioritising the pursuit of social justice by taking concrete actions and assessing their effects in the material world is the only way to ensure systematic change and to monitor the methods by which this change is undertaken.

While the modern approaches for pursuing justice were criticised in that salon, in another salon on "The Future of Utopia" we explored a larger vision for a just society. The academic who framed the conversation spoke on past utopic visions from Plato to Hegel, Marx and Gandhi and then asked why our vision of the future seems modest by comparison. Salon participants discussed the possibilities and problems associated with envisioning utopias and described the features they believed were indispensable for a fair and just world.

Our principal conclusion was that contemporary society has been marked by small ideas. Academia itself is reflective of a wider societal trend towards idolising the insignificant. Today, scholars will not be taken seriously if they propose grand new theories. To achieve recognition, they are told to focus their scholarly attention on analysis of the increasingly arcane within their tightly circumscribed domain of expertise: the exegesis of minutiae becomes the gold standard of academic prowess. Political theorists and philosophers are expected to critique that which has already been said instead of creating something new. Likewise, the public is exhorted to behave "pragmatically" in order to fit within the framework of existing dominant ideologies, even if this framework is fundamentally flawed or inherently immoral.

By the end of this salon there was a consensus that fervour, hope, and well-reasoned optimism will need to be revived to enable new visions of the future, while at the same time ambitious ideas must be grounded in humane actions to come closer to achieving a just society. Such a vision resonates with the philosophy of the Beautiful Soul, which addresses the source of social problems by actively transforming individuals into compassionate moral agents.

In practicing this philosophy today, we must remember that behind online aliases lie real people, not characters in a virtual fantasy game that we can brutalise and dehumanise. Cultivating our ability to understand another person's position by returning to interactions in physical space is crucial. If we are not immediately confronted with the repercussions of our beliefs and actions, then we will not develop the compassion that underlies morality. To be a moral person requires that we condition ourselves to avoid the sterile immorality of the internet, to shrive ourselves of all those acts of aggression and ego-driven hysteria that have become commonplace. Perfecting compassionate faculties in our personal lives and within public forums is essential in achieving a more beautiful soul in the modern age.

Beyond practicing considerate behaviour in communicative exchanges, beautiful souls demonstrate their respect for others by striving towards equality in social relations. Like the Berlin *salonnières,* the practitioners of this philosophy will contribute to a more just and equitable world. Their aspiration would be a society in which people are freed from economic, social, or political oppression and are afforded basic opportunities. Eradicating human misery and contributing to solutions that offer more individuals the possibility to realise their potential and to flourish is a central concern for anyone practicing this philosophy.

Today, some of the goals of equality that the *salonnières* envisioned have been realised on a global scale. Varnhagen and Herz would be delighted to observe that their ideas on the essential equality of all human beings were not an unrealistic fantasy, but an achievable reality which has partially materialised in important areas, such as in voting rights. However, they would also be concerned about the extreme economic inequalities that continue to plague society and the areas in which social inequities persist.

Despite our progress on distinct fronts, global equality remains largely unattained. What is not an obstacle socially, remains an obstacle economically. The "American Dream" has now become the presumption in most of the West and much of the world; the idea that hard work promises financial success has proven to be a cruel deception, supported by a few tantalising cases that are the exception, not the rule. Although the capitalist success story is grounded in the assumption of equal access through individual initiative, it has dramatically increased inequality. Mass disparities between a handful of billionaires who hold most of the global wealth and the rest of the population have only intensified, propagated by false expectations that anyone can one day reach the summit of power and wealth.

These socio-economic disparities are as strong a deterrent for equality within social interactions as class prejudices were in centuries past. Although we might like to think that we maintain diverse relationships today, it remains rare for a banker to be friends with a petrol station worker or for a grocery store employee to be seated at the same dinner table with a high-powered lawyer. If such a relationship is established, it is often encumbered by self-congratulatory insincerity on the part of the person who believes they are performing an act of charity by engaging with different people, only reinforcing the most pernicious prejudices and social divisions.

The practitioner of the Beautiful Soul does not counteract the aim of equality with self-congratulation or obsequiousness, both of which reflect propensities derived from a false sense of superiority. They have internalised the value of equality, and this is reflected in the sincerity of their relationships with others. Whether it is by exercising considerate behaviour in social relations or forging diverse interactions unencumbered by dehumanising displays of feigned benevolence, beautiful souls treat others just as they would wish to be treated because they *truly* see them as their equals.

To overcome the debilitating social fractures that inhibit genuine human interactions today, we may study the *salonnières'* model to understand how best we can relate to others under imperfect social conditions. Instead of proselytising abstractly about social equality, this philosophy challenges us to create communities that include different types of people and to improve the ways that we interact with one another.

A critical insight of the *salonnières*, which we fail to realise today even though the possibilities for interacting with different types of people are far greater, is that true equality requires physical contact and sustained human connection. We cannot remain in our isolated social circles divided by socio-economic status or political views if we are to achieve a tangible measure of equality in our multicultural societies. Diversity of ideas, life circumstances, and backgrounds should not be gratuitously displayed, but integrated into the fabric of social life.

Fostering an egalitarian spirit is feasible in a salon because the emphasis is placed strictly on the conversation at hand. Rarely will participants speak about their careers or backgrounds, which are the first generic topics of conversation that people normally engage in, which either consciously or unconsciously divide them. Since the focus of a salon is on ideas which anyone can discuss, social bonds are more easily established. For this reason, everyone from financiers, aristocrats, and politicians to taxi drivers, genocide survivors, and social workers, have interacted in this space and found a productive common ground.

My disparate salon participants often become friends and learn intimate details about each other's views on everything from death to altruism, comedy, and architectural design. But only months later do they realise that they had never learned what the other person did for a living and still have no sense of their family background or social position. By the time they do learn this information it appears secondary, if not irrelevant, because so much has been discovered that is infinitely more valuable.

In salons on political issues such as "The Future of the European Union" it was the first time that many of my participants had discussed these topics with those on the opposite side of the debate. After hours of intense discussion, in which both sides were able to develop their arguments with a complexity that far surpassed that of a tweet, some realised that the views they held of their political adversaries were one-dimensional caricatures. They had demonised their opponents, unwittingly fuelling anger and prejudices that only diminished their ability to achieve concrete solutions. Humanising the opposing side and understanding the underlying reasons for their views allowed them to reach consensus on several issues. They practiced the compassion and civility necessary to a vibrant democracy which depends on people working together to achieve consensus. Often it is not the issues themselves that cause tension but the way they are perceived and presented. But by exercising mutual respect and privileging human decency, enough commonality can be found to make progress tenable.

There are, and will always be, those who act destructively within a salon, or in any other social community. This is the paradox of equality. Opening the salon to a general public can be problematic because if one individual is divisive, it poses a threat to the community. However, if the *salonnière* hand-picks salon participants, the salon's egalitarian spirit quickly devolves into an exclusive club, not a representative public sphere. Even if the *salonnière* chooses participants, it is impossible for her to anticipate what they will say or if they will prove to be a negative force. Fortunately, the people who do not affirm the spirit of a salon often stop participating because their need for self-validation is left unfulfilled. It is only those who actively wish to interact with different viewpoints and are open to genuine multifaceted conversations who remain.

In practicing the Beautiful Soul today, we would enact the qualities of the ideal salon participant by behaving tolerantly and embracing free speech, respecting differences of opinion, remaining open to changing our views when proven wrong, and incorporating compassion and forgiveness into our methods of conversation. We must accept that communication will never be perfect. People may say things that insult us, express views that we do not share, or force us to challenge our own assumptions. Part of what it means to become a cultivated person is to develop the strength of character to positively respond to such challenges because we acknowledge that remaining locked within our social media echo chamber is the greatest deterrent to a civil society.

The philosophy of the Beautiful Soul encourages us to approach human relations with generosity and optimism. It inspires us to assume that most people are capable of being good, and to bring out the goodness in them by behaving with goodness towards them. The practitioner of this philosophy will not extrapolate from past negative experiences by assuming that all people are ill-intentioned because some have hurt or betrayed them. They will not let their behaviour distort their beautiful worldview. They maintain hope in humanity, not because they have seen the good in all people, but because they have cultivated the goodness within themself and remain open to the possibility of goodness in others.

A beautiful soul's commitment to the good begins by turning inward and assessing the condition of their own nature before they question the ideas and actions of other people. Their pursuit of equality may take longer to come into fruition than a violent approach, but it is evidently just, enduring, and universally beneficial.

CHAPTER 10

On Becoming Cultured

A LIFE directed at contributing to the good is actualised in the realm of culture. Schlegel argued that the highest good and everything that is valuable to society is the advancement of culture through *Bildung*.[287] Culture is important to this tradition because it emphasises the universal nature of this concept and facilitates trans-generational creation in which one age builds upon the artistic and intellectual legacies of those past. In doing so, they contribute to a common quest for knowledge which the ambitious theorists of the Beautiful Soul believed every human being should participate in, out of a sense of collective responsibility and the desire to achieve personal flourishing for the benefit of society even beyond death. If one imagines the good that Mozart and Beethoven continue to do by virtue of the enduring nature of their musical contributions long after their demise, this perspective makes eminent sense.

This philosophy maintains that culture is a collective patrimony with tangible, objective importance. The arts and ideas are by no means superfluous, but rather, a most fundamental part of the human condition that holds universal value. The effort to perfect one's soul by becoming cultured and participating in the theatre, visual arts, music, literature and poetry, among other media is, then, not a transient pursuit, but rather a lasting source of material for the benefit of future generations. Culture gives the person who undertakes their moral-aesthetic development a collective purpose and application. Self-cultivation has a greater social value, one that exceeds the individual through the creations they put forth in the world.

Analogies drawn from aesthetic practices were often used to describe the Beautiful Soul, the most popular of which was the comparison to an orchestra. As the character Jarno in Goethe's *Wilhelm Meister* exhorts:

> Make yourself a first-rate violinist, and you may be sure that the conductor will gladly find a place for you in the orchestra. Make yourself competent in one thing, and see what position society will assign to you in the life of the whole.[288]

In playing an instrument, one exercises a certain level of autonomy and imagination. At the same time an orchestra, which represents a collective creation, cannot function if the individual musicians stray from their well-defined roles. The individual plays an instrument (pursues self-cultivation) for the sake of the orchestra (society), in a shared constructive project. Culture, in this sense, celebrates the union between the beautiful (the music) and the good (contributing to the commonweal) which is brought about from this individual-collective dynamic.

Like an instrument that is left un-played, beautiful souls placed in an environment shorn of cultural products cannot achieve their full potential. Reading evocative pieces of literature, partaking in stimulating conversations, or listening to moving musical compositions, while not the ends of the Beautiful Soul, are vehicles by which beautiful souls may be cultivated. If they do not receive this cultural stimulation, they will find it more difficult to refine their faculties and bring something of greater value into the world. The Beautiful Soul of *Wilhelm Meister* describes the depravity she feels living in a milieu with little sensitivity to culture or ideas and the detriment that this causes her:

> The hurry and the crowd I lived in dissipated my attention, and carried me along as in a rapid stream. These were the emptiest years of my life. All day long to speak of nothing, to have no solid thought, never to do anything but revel: such was my employment. On my beloved books I never once bestowed a thought. The people I lived among had not the slightest tinge of literature or science: they were German courtiers, a class of men at that time altogether destitute of culture.[289]

In a bureaucratic, materialistic society that busies itself with chasing trivial ends, the poetic soul who yearns for culture can be overcome with what Goethe describes in *Poetry and Truth* as *taedium vitae*, the weariness of living, derived from the emptiness of a social order bereft of artistic inspiration. If society values the wellbeing of its citizens and expects them to positively contribute to the collective, it must provide them with the cultural resources that stimulate the poetic force of their spirits and excite their imaginations, lifting them above the banalities of modern life. Championing the arts is not an unwarranted excess, but rather an investment in social stability. A rational society will readily seek to cultivate morally and aesthetically cultured citizens to achieve prosperity and cohesion. Making culture more accessible and placing a higher value on it, as Humboldt did with his public projects and models of education, is a pragmatic means to facilitate the maturation of an enlightened citizenship.

Within the Berlin salons, the advancement of culture offered a shared narrative and a common history that could unite participants with one another and with European society. The efforts that individuals made to cultivate themselves were bound to the collective will through culture. This inward process was justified and rendered relevant when the individual employed their moral-aesthetic education to produce something of collective significance in the setting of the salon.

The *salonnières* recognised the imperative of the Beautiful Soul to advance culture, sharing Moses Mendelssohn's conviction that this was the best means to achieve social progress. Their concept of culture was greatly influenced by Goethe who saw the individual as the bearer of culture.[290] They believed that human intercourse in salon conversations was the most important means to contribute to social progress because it integrated every individual into a shared creation, one that was constantly evolving and generated other cultural products.[291] Indeed, salons were traditionally at the heart of artistic movements, forging collaborations among the most important intellectuals and virtuosos of their day. Salon conversations established a forum for the collective production of a wider aesthetic and intellectual patrimony. We can trace many of the artistic and intellectual movements in Europe between the sixteenth and nineteenth centuries to a manifestation of salon culture. At this time, the salons most greatly influenced the development of Romanticism in the visual arts, literature, and music.

Musical analogies were drawn that compared the role of the *salonnière* to that of a conductor, acknowledging her commitment to cultural ends. These analogies were shared with the concept of the Beautiful Soul which, as we have seen, likened the pursuit of self-cultivation for the sake of society to an individual who plays an instrument in an orchestra. According to these analogies, the *salonnière* was sensitive to the character (instruments) of each of her salon participants (the musicians). Her responsibility was to conduct discourse (the musical score) in a way that encouraged the best perform-ance (attainment of the Beautiful Soul's notion of full poten-tial) for the purpose of a larger social good. In her capacity as conductor, the *salonnière* was able to facilitate the cultivation of each person which benefited them, but more importantly, produced something that collectively surpassed their individ-ual self. The use of the same analogy between philosophy and institution demonstrates that the *salonnières* were, in fact, tangibly enacting the Beautiful Soul, and doing so with exceptional success.

The *salonnières* understood, however, that their salons could only reach relatively few people and therefore their efforts to propagate this philosophy were limited.[292] They were aware that the power of the salon lay in its cultural symbolism. Broader influence could eventually come into being if they demonstrated the efficacy of their model. But since this would take time and they had only just set the historical process in motion, they emphasised cultural produc-tion within their salons in literary works, philosophical treatises, and musical compositions that engendered the spirit of this philosophy and were easily disseminated.

The *salonnières* were both the creators of culture (in producing their salons and in writing letters, novels, and musical compositions) and also cultural matriarchs (facilitating the production of cultural works by others through engagement in their salons). They shared a dedication to actively support the artistic projects of their time. By giving artists and intellectuals the opportunity to present their work before a sympathetic group of private individuals, the salon served the pragmatic function of allowing them to receive feedback before performing or publishing in front of a wider public. Over two thirds of the salon guests were active in the literary world, so the salons provided authors with a constructive environment to develop and revise their ideas.[293] They represented a new, material recognition of the fact that the value of a work is legitimised through public judgement and a collective process of creative exchange.[294] Within this vibrant milieu, musicians and writers found and fostered inspiration.[295]

Salonnières also acted as patrons of the arts, commissioning pieces of fiction or musical compositions to be premiered in these spaces. Some, such as Fanny Mendelssohn, who was a talented musician and composer, even used their salons to promote their own art as a form of aesthetic self-expression.[296] Promoting and creating cultural works represented a way for the Jewesses to shape German history, from which they had been excluded. If the *salonnières* produced (and were the reason for someone else producing) something of such universal significance that it would become a part of Germany's cultural heritage, then they would finally receive the recognition and inclusion that they deserved. Their approach was to perfect and to expand upon the aspects of German culture that they embraced. This prospect invariably influenced their activities, for they were careful to control the narrative of their legacy by monitoring the letters that were saved for posterity.[297]

Their efforts to preserve their ideas, especially as they related to the Beautiful Soul, as well as the happenings of their salons, illustrates their belief that their work could one day become an important part of the cultural patrimony and, most importantly, contribute to the trans-generational development of this philosophy. The *salonnières* aimed at nothing less than contributing to the future of humankind for generations to come. Since political policies change, social attitudes transform, and economic realities evolve, they believed that the only sphere with a lasting influence for the benefit of posterity was culture.

Today, "high culture" is no longer revered as it was in the time of the *salonnières*, nor does it maintain the same social influence. Despite the apparent elitist undertones of the term "high culture," I do not consider this a supercilious term, nor does it maintain a patronising hierarchy of superior or inferior artistic or intellectual creations. Rather, I define it simply as creative works that are produced, not merely for commercial or entertainment value (though they may include these ends) but whose aim is that knowledge or artistic expression which requires intellectual maturity and aesthetic cultivation to fully appreciate and understand.

Unfortunately, our current hyper-capitalist system does not adequately acknowledge the significance of creating works of art or literature that can be classified under this definition of high culture. If something does not demonstrably increase the GDP, then it is thought not to be worth the investment. This profit-driven mentality has led to the substantial defunding of the arts and to political restrictions placed upon subsidised public projects which severely stifle creativity. Globally, visual artists, writers, and musicians struggle to maintain their *metiér* under these hostile conditions.

A predominately materialistic perspective is detrimental to cultural advancement because it inhibits innovation. Universally recognised human achievements have never been pro-

190

duced merely by the shrewd calculation of anticipated profits. The value of that which is wholly original cannot be immediately ascertained or quantified. More important, the greatest contributions to society are not necessarily those which generate wealth. This utilitarian approach to culture restricts human achievement to the arbitrary parameters written by the economists' pen. Hearing a symphony as a child might leave an indelible impression that fundamentally shapes the course of a life for the better, but this outcome will never be captured in an Excel file. To try to place a numerical value on a theatre production or a work of art is a grotesque mis-valuation. In our age of feral capitalism, reasserting the primacy of culture to explore the human condition and to provide people with meaning is crucial. Revitalising the cultural sphere and making artistic and intellectual productions more accessible to a wider demographic are essential to this end.

First, however, we must revisit the underlying values and aesthetic with which culture is pursued. If our sense of cultural experience entails attending a multi-media exhibition curated with vivid graphics to fit increasingly short attention spans, our reaction to the artistic creation begins to resemble the products we consume at the shopping mall. If we cannot tear ourselves away from our cell phone screens as we watch a great play, undoubtedly the experience will have little effect on us. If we learn an instrument solely because it is socially prestigious, then it is unlikely that we will produce anything that holds a deeper value. The aesthetic with which culture is consumed, and the integrity of its expression, is just as important as the production of the cultural works themselves.

Today, celebrity culture and the entertainment industry have infiltrated culture and the arts. Reality television stars were, at first, acknowledged as superficial, then legitimised, and now they are embraced by serious cultural institutions with whom they collaborate for financial gain. This has led to the degradation of culture and the debasement of artistic and intellectual creations. The democratisation of high culture should not entail indulging in reduction to the lowest common denominator. If culture is sexualised, vulgarised, and commodified to attract more people to theatres and concert halls, we jeopardise the production and performance of art until its content is so diminished that it is ultimately meaningless. Culture can retain its integrity while its accessibility is promoted. Educating a wider public is an important step. To assume that most people are incapable of appreciating high art is an underestimation of the power of the human spirit to find the will to learn and to achieve great depth.

Participating in a salon, or a community like a salon, practically facilitates the advancement of culture, and the integrity that it maintains, because it offers the opportunity to communicatively exchange with others about cultural works. If culture is collective, it becomes even more significant; ideas are formed and meaning created through dialogical practice. A salon fulfils the function of comprehensively engaging with culture by providing a time and space in which to do so. It also makes the experience more enjoyable since it is sociable.

In one of my salons, an opera singer informally discussed his art with participants who were unversed in this area. The convergence of a desire on the part of salon participants to learn and a tenor who was passionate about his work inspired an impromptu analysis of opera recordings. The singer was able to express exactly what was so moving about the sound of a particular voice or the artistic liberties they took in a certain passage. He described why the technique of one singer was unique and emphasised the differences in interpretations of a given piece. This guidance, brought about naturally in an environment conducive to curiosity, was the greatest insight into an often-inaccessible art form and the beginning of a new passion for several of the people who were present. After explaining elements of his art, the tenor impulsively sang passages from arias to the great delight of the guests. The musically inspired evening exemplified the possibilities of a salon: to organically engage in mutual education, animatedly taking part in a cultural experience which is spontaneous and natural, not sterile and detached.

The greatest artists and thinkers crucially need a community of people to inform their practice. Rarely does creativity occur in isolation. Salons can provide the modern creator with the inspiration, motivation, and perspective necessary to advance their *métier*. In my own salons, poems and academic articles have been written, musical compositions created, concerts played, and ideas conceived because the structure of a salon is ripe for inspiration.

There is no reason to despair if the modern practitioner of this philosophy initially fails to comprehend the significance of an important work of art. It is only natural that our appreciation of truly nuanced artistic creations requires the refinement of faculties that take time to develop and mature. Like acquiring a palate for wine or a taste for the most sophisticated cuisine, this is not an inherent gift, but requires effort.

Today people might attend a ballet once a year or read a book on holiday, but it is rare for someone to engage with culture systematically as was done in the past. Consequently, most of us are largely ignorant about many art forms and topics of conversation. Practicing this philosophy necessitates absorbing a vast body of social and cultural knowledge, expanding our minds, wherever possible.

In becoming cultured, we would span the spectrum of intellectual and artistic creations. A sophisticated person might be knowledgeable about literature, but they will also be well versed in music and visual arts. They might harbour a special love for Russian film, but they will also be interested in Chinese painting and Japanese philosophy. Although they will have preferences and areas of expertise, they do not limit themself to one art form or cultural tradition. Instead, they draw inspiration from the finest creations of all cultural canons, expanding their mind by consuming the vast body of human knowledge that has been accumulated since the Ancient Sumerians, Persians, Egyptians, Chinese, and Greeks. They embrace the fruits of culture, which they earnestly share with the rest of humanity.

In practicing this philosophy, engaging with cultural productions becomes a priority. We must make the effort to understand art by educating ourselves instead of superficially checking cultural creations off a list of objects to be seen. Our aim should be to become truly cultured because we are genuinely interested in what we can learn, not to appear erudite or fit into an intellectual elite. Becoming fully cultivated demands a serious engagement with culture and an understanding of the spirit from which it is born. Once this perception has been formed our lives are irrevocably changed from having fully understood the great beauty of existence and the essence of the human experience captured in art.

CHAPTER 11

On Cultivating Beautiful Relationships

Like a musical instrument brought into consonance with an orchestra, the individual is meant to integrate themself into the fabric of society after first defining their identity and selfhood. To successfully engage in creating moral frameworks, laws, contracts, and forms of association that shape a more perfect reality, they must become part of a larger social whole. Although the Beautiful Soul focuses on individual self-cultivation, its underlying social philosophy depends on people working together, through the advancement of their individual faculties, to reach common goals.

Social harmony is not only a pragmatic necessity that is required to establish order, but it also creates the kinship derived from a sense of belonging. Although self-cultivation is a pursuit of individual subjects, the process is framed through the integrative dimensions of a collective cultural identity.[298] In the Beautiful Soul, harmony is a multidimensional process, starting first with the harmony of the self in balancing one's inner constitution, and then the harmonisation of this unified self with the social whole.

The first stage of harmonisation entails balancing the individual characteristics of the Beautiful Soul within, such as virtue, morality, and intellectual autonomy. An aesthetic education, in which individuals integrate these qualities, can produce harmoniousness across all human faculties.[299] Herder emphasised that *Bildung* is not an arbitrary set of disparate traits but a cohesive whole.[300] Harmony exists on the level of individual activity as well as in the totality of actions that come to define a person's life. Since beauty is defined by both Goethe and Schiller as harmonious, beautiful souls reach a state of perfect harmony by aesthetically balancing their faculties.[301]

If a person's character is not harmoniously balanced, the danger, according to Schiller, is that they will be blind to the harmony that exists in nature and in other people. Resentfulness, hostility, and cynicism will fester from internal imbalance.[302] However, if harmony occurs within, then, as Novalis suggests, the person appears at peace and their relationship with the outer world is beautiful and harmonious too.[303] Furthermore, if a person's internal world is in consonance, then this consonance is reflected in beautiful works. Schiller believed that the most ennobled music or the greatest statue, like those of antiquity, possess this unity of form which so pleases us with its calming, peaceful effect specifically because of the internal unity which it embodies.[304]

In reaching individual harmony through the balance of human faculties and the creation of harmonious works, Schiller believed that the soul of beauty is inclined towards enlightened sociability. Those who cultivate themselves can more easily feel the "electric charge" of community and thus intuit the slightest movements and subtlest needs of others.[305] This means that the second phase of harmonisation is born naturally from the successful realisation of the first. Individual harmonisation, which occurs through a moral-aesthetic education, creates a sociable nature which harmonises the individual with the rest of society.[306] Since self-cultivation is an all-encompassing pursuit representing the totality of what it means to be human, people will aspire to reach this concordance and then desire to share their "soul-awakening" experiences with others. The harmony of their own faculties can develop in a community—whose creation the very act of self-cultivation has inspired.[307]

The foundation of community in the Beautiful Soul is friendship, the basic unit of social cohesion. Friendship allows for the possibility that human ingenuity might emerge through the development of intimate relationships of the mind. A person can only become truly cultivated if they are able to look beyond themself, to readily learn from others and to take part in collective practice. As Schlegel remarks "Humanity cannot be inoculated, and virtue cannot be taught or learned, other than through friendship and love with capable and genuine people, and other than through contact with ourselves, with the divine within us."[308] Social encounters in which mutual understanding emerges prove valuable, since every person has a perspective that can inform the acquisition of knowledge. If these distinct perspectives are placed into communication with one another, then that which exceeds the perception of one person can be revealed in the collective. The act of conjoining faculties in communicative exchange through friendship, then, becomes the means by which to advance one's own *Bildung* practice.

Harmonious friendships are also personally beneficial because they are indispensable to the generation of new creations. In a letter to Goethe from July 21, 1797, Schiller captures how his friendship with Goethe informed his art:

> A relation thus built on reciprocal perfectibility must ever keep fresh and active, and gain the more in variety, the more harmonious it becomes…The

197

most beautiful and most fruitful way that I profit by our mutual communications, and appropriate them to myself, is always this, that I apply them immediately to the work I have in hand, and use them at once productively... And thus, I hope, shall my Wallenstein, and whatever of importance I may in future produce, contain and show in the concrete the whole system of that which in our intercourse has been able to pass into my being.[309]

The very philosophical system that these two intellectuals were constructing was used in the creation of their art through the formidable bond of friendship.

A conception of Platonic love is closely connected to the importance placed on friendship. These are not ordinary, superficial affiliations, but those of intense emotional connectivity, the truest union of souls and deepest meeting of minds. The relationship between love and friendship within this tradition is characterised by Schlegel who says:

All feelings and impulses, hence all sympathetic virtues, if they are beautiful, must be able to be referred to love. But from what can one see whether one can ascribe love to oneself or to someone else? From whether one is capable of friendship.[310]

For Schlegel, a moral education begins with the ability to love, and love is the motivation for its development.[311] Love is vitally important to this concept of social harmony because it most effectively inspires the individual to overcome their own self-interest in favour of a concern for the common good.

Those who feel a deep affinity with their beloved are more capable of acting in their interest, and this powerful dynamic represents the birth of the social bond. For Schiller, love is the "sacred fire that consumes every egotistical inclination, and the very principles of morality are scarcely a greater safeguard of the soul's chastity than love is for the nobility of the heart."[312] Love in friendship is the primordial foundation of social morality.

Beautiful souls, then, are represented as those distinguished by their resounding warmth towards others and their love of humanity. They welcome spontaneous connections and seek disparate interactions. Although they do not have to be gregarious (they can be shy or contemplative), they become sociable members of society because they value human relationships. They advance their cultivation through a compassionate understanding and interest in the lived experiences of others. Although they are open to those around them, they also maintain an intellectual autonomy. They perfect the balance between sociability and individuality, retaining their individual integrity while remaining embedded within society.

Harmonising social relationships by integrating the distinct voices of salon participants and reconciling personal conflicts and ideological divides in order to reach accord was an important dimension of the *salonnières*' role. In addition to harmonising divergent personalities, this also entailed bringing together aesthetic forms, intellectual disciplines, new ideas, and disparate ways of thinking into an integral whole. The *salonnières*' exceptional ability in this regard was thought to be due to the inner harmony that they had achieved through their own practice of the Beautiful Soul. Goethe bestowed Varnhagen with the cherished title of a beautiful soul in large part because he identified the harmony within her. In Goethe's reflections on Varnhagen, after meeting her in Carlsbad in 1795, he remarks:

> She is a girl of extraordinary intellect, who is constantly thinking and full of feeling—where can one find the like? It is a rare thing. Oh, we were constantly together, we associated in a very friendly and confidential way…She is an affectionate girl; she is strong in all her feeling and yet easy in all her utterances; the former quality gives her a high significance, the latter makes her agreeable; the former causes us to admire her great originality, and the latter makes this originality amiable, pleasing to us.[313]

Here he identifies her successful harmonisation of rationality with the passions, and originality with sociability. Then he continues:

> It cannot be denied that there are many people in the world who at least appear original; but what security have we that it is not merely appearance? That what we are inclined to take for the inspiration of a lofty mind is not merely the effect of a passing mood? – it is not so with her; she is, so far as I know her, herself at every instant, always stirred in a way peculiar to her, and yet calm.[314]

In this passage he recognises her authenticity and genuineness. With the harmony of these qualities, he bestows the sacred title: "—in short, she is what I might call a beautiful soul, the more intimately one gets to know her, the more one feels attracted and agreeably held by her."[315] Significantly, Varnhagen earned full recognition as a beautiful soul from Goethe, her idol. With his comments he affirmed her personal attainment of this philosophy as well as the triumph of the institution of the salon.

Varnhagen's salon participants greatly admired her inner harmony because it represented a well-formed spiritual constitution, a clear indicator that she was morally sound. Schleiermacher, who was known as "the connoisseur of personality," agreed with Goethe's analysis of Varnhagen, offering his own reflections on her harmoniousness:

> Just because Varnhagen at every instant is in perfect harmony, one quality balances the other; her excitability does not become hysterical, her sensitiveness sentimental, her wit ironical, her analysis vivisection, her directness does not become license nor her consciousness a mirroring of self. Thought and feeling, meditation and action, seriousness and gaiety, everything with her is of a piece; nothing contradicts or cancels, everything confirms and intensifies the rest in this harmonious nature.[316]

Harmonising the various aspects of personhood to maintain a perfect balance as Varnhagen had done was a lifelong pursuit. The even greater challenge, however, was to integrate the self into the social whole. The *salonnières* rejected the possibility of withdrawing from society. They continuously sought to unite themselves and their salon participants with others. They did this first on a smaller scale within their salons through friendship. Friendship was the symbolic representation of their social ideal. The salon quickly became a cult of friendship, a place where the pleasures of cultivating oneself were recognised by another person who shared the same values.[317]

Salons began with the immediate friends of the *salonnières* and naturally expanded to friends of friends as well as curious outsiders. Once a new guest was introduced to the group, he or she was welcomed and did not require another invitation. Salon culture depended on the *salonnière's* openness to new people, on her convivial attitude, and on her development of a strong community of friends who felt closely connected to one another by virtue of their dedication to personal interactions in this space. Salons differed from social clubs in that they did not have membership lists or fees nor a rigid structure or agenda. The *salonnière's* transformation of her home into a hospitable space for discourse allowed individuals to "gradually and gracefully become friends" developing a community around the collective appreciation of ideas, not special interests, or the parochial concerns of pre-existing social groups.[318]

In the salon, friendships allowed individuals to move beyond their own limited perspective and understand that of others. Knowledge was gained by deepening human relationships that could expand one's consciousness. In this sense, friendship was viewed as critical to intellectual success because it augmented cognitive abilities.[319] The *salonnières* not only provided the environment in which to discover a friend who could enrich one's inner world and encounter forms of association that strengthened these relationships, they also meticulously paired those people who they thought were uniquely suited to each other, making connections that would not have occurred otherwise.

The *salonnières* maintained close relationships with those who took part in their salons because they were sociable beings.[320] However, they also understood the importance of friendship in the conscious development of the Beautiful Soul. Through their auspices, many profound relationships were forged that could guide the participants' moral-aesthetic education.

The *salonnières'* closest friends were often the ones most in need of their counsel. Prince Louis Ferdinand (1772-1806), a strong supporter of Berlin's salon culture, regularly brought his personal and intellectual concerns to Varnhagen, whom he called his "moral midwife, who delivers one so softly and painlessly that a gentle feeling comes to surround even the most tormenting ideas."[321] The nobleman, Alexander von der Marwitz (1787-1814) described the profound effect that Varnhagen's friendship had on him:

> I am supposed to reassure you again and again with regard to your volumes, you write, dear Rahel. Hear then, how I receive them. I read them three or four times in a row, certain passages much more often, then I put them down with the sentiment of a miser who sees his treasure increased…and then I walk around my room for an hour and more and let the contents of your lines reverberate within me; in this mood I cannot answer…This is the effect your letters have always had on me and always will.[322]

One of the men most influenced by Varnhagen's *Bildung* guidance was the diplomat Karl Friedrich Alexander Count von Finckenstein (1772-1811) whose friendship with Varnhagen evolved into a love affair. Finckenstein insisted on his need of Varnhagen's direction:

203

> I need you. I don't know but I am so dejected although there is nothing actually wrong with me, nothing excites me, nothing engages my feelings. It is so unbearably still and dark within my soul, and so I thought a letter from you would bring me some of that consolation I usually found with you, when my soul was not well and I only had to rush to you to become content and happy again…A letter from you must make life bearable again.[323]

He often said that she had "opened his eyes" and "given him his sense of self." In a revealing statement on the effect she had in his development of a more beautiful soul he wrote, "[Y]ou have perfected my education …You have given character and form to my person by giving life and movement to all that lay dead and still within me."[324]

And yet, their relationship could not last. Varnhagen broke off their engagement because, despite all her efforts in Finckenstein's *Bildung* training, he ultimately failed to act upon her influence and achieve self-realisation. Varnhagen dismissed him (not without a measure of contempt): "I shall utilise the years during which you are away to become unacquainted with you. You can no longer persuade me. Be something, and I shall recognise you."[325]

Unfortunately, this lack of initiative to act upon the principles of the Beautiful Soul that the *salonnières* so painstakingly worked to teach was the case in other relationships too. As much time and energy as Varnhagen invested in cultivating souls and educating her salon participants, her efforts were, at times, in vain. For it was easier to acknowledge the basic tenets of the Beautiful Soul, than to consistently practice them outside the setting of the salon.

Varnhagen spent five years devoting herself to the cultivation of her friend, the writer, Rebecca Friedländer (1783-1850). She laboriously endeavoured to make Rebecca more truthful and honest and to cultivate "nobler" ideas in her.[326] But, after half a decade of these efforts, she admitted that Rebecca was incapable of achieving the moral education she had worked to give her. In a letter to Rebecca in September 1810, she remarked:

> [N]ot that you haven't gained immeasurably since our acquaintance! The entire horizon of your concepts is illuminated, a whole jumble of old opinions, judgements, and desires has been removed; entire fields have been planted anew; your mind has become more active. You have cast your eye upon a new world and let go a ridiculous, deceptive one. Yet your being has not gained in coherence. – And how is it possible that you admire emotional honesty in someone else without imme-diately becoming so yourself?[327]

She later felt guilty for her own honesty in this letter and assured her friend that she was as demanding with her as she was with Louis Ferdinand.

Perhaps the person who benefitted most from Varnhagen's counsel and was most willing to listen to her honest appraisal of his soul was her husband, Karl Varnhagen. He did not allow his vanity to interfere with her efforts to assist his *Bildung* education. He readily accepted her guidance, for he truly wanted to become cultivated in the deepest sense, and she delighted in seeing him grow. During the first year of their engagement she remarked:

> Ah how I rejoice over your development! Dear chalice, what wilt thou not contain, warmed at my breast, by my love! I am so happy and so proud and so uneasy. My spirit and my heart have a hold! This child is my beloved![328]

We can see that Varnhagen clearly took her role as *Bildung* educator seriously and those others whom she educated accepted her authority in directing their moral-aesthetic education.

Varnhagen invested endless hours in personal relationships, to understand and recognise the inherent qualities of her lovers and her friends while also attempting to identify their frailties, not out of a sense of moral superiority, but out of a sincere desire to see them improve. Her talent was to cultivate souls, and she performed it as a duty. As Karl Varnhagen said:

> As far as it was possible, possible to your nature, to understand a nature such as mine, you have understood me: through the noblest and most soulful recognition: with an insight that I do not understand, since it is not due to resemblances in our natures.[329]

Being understood with such lucid perception was a rare gift, and Rahel Varnhagen was placed on a pedestal as a muse by those whose lives she touched. Karl Varnhagen declared: "I love you so boundlessly and intensely, as neither lovers nor friends are loved: as your disciple and prophet."[330] For those such as her husband who were strong enough to accept her constructive critique, she was indispensable to their development as moral beings.

206

To self-cultivate as salon friends was a mutual relationship, one in which both parties benefited. The *salonnières* were able to develop the Beautiful Soul's theoretical framework with those who were receptive to it. An instance of this reciprocity was Varnhagen's lifelong friendship with Pauline Wiesel with whom she maintained a written correspondence for over three decades. These women were primarily concerned with discussing the Beautiful Soul, debating what its most celebrated advocates propounded, but equally developing its principles for themselves. The *salonnières* took a definite position in the evolution of the theory, and friendship was the means by which they actively contributed to this narrative.

The relationship between Varnhagen and Wiesel was also significant because it demonstrated the changing nature of friendship that the *salonnières* represented; one that attempted to solidify a common identity in *Bildung,* not by superficial social similarities but by a true understanding of souls.[331] Resemblances in personality, background, and ways of life became less important and the arbitrary differences that once dictated social dynamics were passionately challenged.

The Berlin *salonnières* were distinct from other European *salonnières* in their desire to cultivate the *Seelensfreund,* a soulmate. No longer were trivial engagements or idle pleasantries enough to sustain interactions: a more profound union was to define human relationships. Finding a friend of the soul, who comprehended the essence and intricacies of oneself, who could inspire moral development and act as a sympathetic, objective advisor along the way, was imperative for the experiential success of the Beautiful Soul. Salon participants were given the perfect environment in which to establish these life-long relationships. Loyalty to one another was enhanced by virtue of the depth and intimacy of their conversations.

Friendships of the soul superseded the limitations of individual relationships and encompassed a true concern for humanity.

Today the word "friend" is a far cry from this concept of a *Seelensfreund*. No longer is friendship associated with a profound depth of mutual understanding and sense of belonging. It is often used haphazardly and indiscriminately. We bestow the term friend upon acquaintances we barely know, so that it signifies little at all. Like the shift in its meaning, the activities we engage in with these friends barely scratch the surface of mutual comprehension or reflect our capacity to thoughtfully relate to others.

Society encourages drinking as a shortcut to social connection, eliminating some of the awkwardness and difficulty of getting to know one another. But this mode of interaction has distracted us from the fact that, without assistance from external substances, we find it difficult to relate to others. Part of the reason is that we have fewer interesting things to convey. In times when cultivating a more beautiful soul is not a priority, the imperative to enrich our mind remains unrealised. When information is readily available online, we no longer accumulate a critical body of knowledge for ourselves. Since knowledge is gained through rapid virtual transactions rather than sustained research and reflection, fewer original ideas are expressed, or imaginative anecdotes conveyed. What is not thoughtfully developed from within, cannot then act as the foundation of profound relationships.

In lieu of revealing perceptions, we resort to what we do know: the ordinary facts of our everyday lives, evanescent dramas, and gossip. But these topics will not capture our attention for long. If they do, our minds remain hardly utilised, while ideas which could compose a far more penetrating relationship are left uninterrogated. Of course, there is a time and place for idle pleasantries and simple forms of amusement, but if we do not also aspire to more than surface-level sociability, we fail to forge the bonds that are only possible through profound mutual understanding. Cultivating these friendships of the soul should not require erudite displays of complex intellectual reasoning. Communication can be much simpler and just as powerful. Meaning is generated in heterogeneous forms. It cannot, however, be created by resorting to the comfort of what is already known.

Unfortunately, the conditions do not exist for more in-depth interactions in the quotidian settings that we habitually inhabit. When we attend cocktail parties, the assumption is that we will talk about work, relationships, petty complaints and day to day issues. When we frequent professional events, we engage in small talk, discussing our vocations or repeating the same stories we have told before many times. To form stronger relationships, we must find the social contexts in which to do so and maintain a sustained commitment to the discussion of meaningful questions.

In my salon, "Does the Soul Exist?" two participants, who were friends before participating in the salon, said that it was the first time in ten years that they learned about the other's perspective on this topic. They were surprised that their assumptions were proven entirely wrong. This question opened whole new realms of interest to them, revitalising a relationship that had grown stagnant because new ideas were never raised. After they attended several salons on different topics, they further grasped the other's overarching worldview. They admitted that before this salon they believed that they possessed a strong friendship. Afterwards, they had to redefine their understanding of the word, since the soul-revealing relationship that developed was incomparable to what had previously existed. We do not realise what friendship truly means until we engage in the transcendental conversations and experiences reflected in the concept of *Seelensfreund.* Once this has occurred, it is difficult to return to the superficiality of past relationships.

To practice this philosophy today, we can think of friendship as a privilege that we make ourselves worthy of through self-cultivation. Developing intellectual faculties becomes even more significant when we may do so for the sake of others, not only for ourselves, thereby enriching their lives with the insightful reflections that we have formed. The pleasure derived from learning a fascinating fact about the universe or developing a compelling perspective on art is enhanced when it is shared, and this knowledge works to sustain the relationship. Ideas and perceptions may be understood as the gifts that we bestow to demonstrate love.

Beautiful souls find ultimate satisfaction, then, in the communication of ideas. They are aware that the great joys of friendship rest in attaining higher states of consciousness together. They know that the relationships which reach deeper terrains of understanding are the ones that are the most satisfying. They invest their finite time in nurturing these more meaningful bonds.

Like the *salonnières*, the practitioner of this philosophy will encourage their friends to overcome character weaknesses and personal shortcomings, while also demonstrating appreciation of their positive qualities and comprehension of who they are on a more fundamental level. Our friends should act as "midwives of the soul" facilitating the birth of beautiful ideas, thoughts, and creations. They will motivate us to be better people and offer something distinct that contributes to this end, while we do the same for them.

Our artful attempts to help our friends to transcend personal failings will not come from a sense of moral superiority, but rather because we genuinely desire to see them improve. The ideal relationship would be one in which we strive to bring out the best qualities in each other, favouring mutual enrichment over frivolous socialising, because we are devoted to one another's long term flourishing.

Friendships of the soul require time and devotion to reach deeper terrains of mutual understanding and form more meaningful bonds. Friendships that are merely superficially pleasurable would be considered a waste of time that could have been better spent cultivating other, deeper relationships. Perfecting the art of friendship means becoming conscious of one's interactions, determining if the dynamics are healthy, and if the person has positive qualities that enhance life.

With regards to romantic relationships, in our transactional, technological era, the landscape for love is as bleak as that of friendship. One of the great tragedies of modern society is that young people no longer believe that they can find a devoted partner in a world in which cruelty, infidelity, and a lack of commitment have become normalised. The modern individual may feel disheartened by a reality in which people regularly dehumanise each other for superficial sex, money, and quick personal gain.

However, a person only needs to depend upon themself to maintain their own romantic ideals. Although it will affirm what they know to be true if they see other people upholding good values in relationships, they do not need to rely on them to believe in the possibilities of human dignity. Understanding their power to sustain romantic ideals liberates them from the deleterious behaviour that others accept because they have lost their sense of optimism.

Cultivating the beauty of one's soul while one's partner does the same is the basis of this philosophy's conception of love. It requires never taking one's partner for granted, but rather enduringly appreciating them and devoting oneself to the relationship. People often dismiss an elevated state of love as unrealistic, but love can reach towards an ideal when individuals rise to the heights of which they are capable through the art of self-cultivation. Of course, this does not mean that loving someone is without its trials. Humans will always be flawed and act imperfectly. But love itself can transcend these shortcomings.

The Beautiful Soul's conception of love entails overcoming insincerity by cultivating quiet nobility and simple grandeur. This philosophy inspires us to love with *true* spirit and vitality, maintaining the passion and poetry of the greatest works of art and literature. The way we love reveals how we exist in the rest of our life, and whether we have maintained our ideals. Those who are apathetic and self-absorbed have allowed something inside of themselves to die. We must overcome this inner death through acts of deep, unconditional love.

CHAPTER 12

On Happiness

To live according to the philosophy of the Beautiful Soul entails engaging all that is inextricably part of the human condition, which means embracing both rationality and the senses. The theorists of the Beautiful Soul responded to the legacy of the Enlightenment and its preoccupation with reason, which they believed had triumphed at the expense of the senses, when their own philosophy placed both on equal footing. Schiller believed that the Enlightenment had failed to address humanity's dual nature of reason and the senses.[332] He observed that the human capacity for feeling was the most important need of the times.

This shift in perception came partly from the admission that people are ineluctably bound to their senses. If people are to be the bearers of human advancement, then this necessary dependence on the senses must be acknowledged. As Humboldt remarks in *On the Limits of State Action*:

> Whatever man beholds in the world around him, he perceives only through the medium of the senses; the pure essence of things is nowhere immediately revealed to him; even what inspires him with the most ardent love, and takes the strongest hold on his whole nature, is shrouded in the thickest veil.[333]

Evolving epistemological perspectives and the waning dogma of religion in popular consciousness incited this revelation. A humanist philosophy which demands that the individual internalise and develop concepts through their own lived experiences, not blindly follow abstract precepts dictated by the church or a monarch, requires that people not only accept, but actively employ their senses as a guide in navigating the material world. Plato's metaphor of reflection, in which constant, immutable ideas are represented in the world of feeling, was a vital inspiration for this new philosophical orientation, and demonstrates the possibility that objective truth can still be found through moments of sensory perception.

To overcome the dangerous comfort of reliance on institutions to guide our actions, the senses must be fully trusted. If people fear their instincts, they will only relinquish further control of their personhood and remain in servitude. As Goethe observes, "The senses do not deceive; it is the judgment that deceives."[334] Schiller argues that if the senses are brutally constrained, in what constitutes a "defective education," only bad outcomes will follow. Anything natural that is suppressed will eventually have detrimental consequences. These theorists therefore embraced the "sensuous aspects of knowledge" and saw virtue in qualities of the spirit that had previously been stifled, using them as a catalyst for new ideas.[335]

Humboldt believed that not only are the senses an inevitable part of the human condition, but they are also essential to the vitality of the soul. He claims:

> The impressions, inclinations, and passions which
> have their immediate source in the senses are those
> which first and most violently show themselves in
> human nature. Whenever, before the refining

influences of culture have given a new direction to
the soul's energies, these sensuous impressions, etc.
are not apparent, all energy is dead, and nothing
good or great can flourish. They constitute the
original source of all spontaneous activity, and all
living warmth in the soul. They bring life and
vigour to the soul; when not satisfied, they make it
active, ingenious in the invention of schemes, and
courageous in their execution; when satisfied, they
promote an easy and unhindered play of ideas.[336]

The "refining influences of culture" to which Humboldt
refers turn the senses from this raw, morally neutral energy,
into a force for good. A *Bildung* education purifies this vital
force through the guiding presence of culture and reconciles
it with reason. Goethe commented: "A man is well equipped
for all the real necessities of life if he trusts his senses, and so
cultivates them that they remain worthy of being trusted."[337]

Schiller was preoccupied with integrating sentiment and
reason and then exploring their connection to morality and
aesthetics. This is the central aim of his *Aesthetic Letters*. In
this work, Schiller identifies two drivers of human cognition
and experience: the "sensuous drive" which offers immediate
physical impressions, and the "form drive" which is constant
and eternal, establishing abstract universal laws. Schiller
believes that "our animal needs and desires provided essential
first impulses of man's spiritual perfection of both the individual and mankind as a whole."[338] He gives equal status to the
sensuous and rational faculties, a decisive break from earlier
Kantian ideas by offering a notion of freedom in which
sensuous nature is not suppressed but rather reunited with the
intellect.[339] Enlivening the senses opens the floodgates of

affect, before rationality then makes sense of new information from a more detached, reflective perspective. The harmonisation of both sense and reason can be found in the "play drive" which frees a person of the decisive command of either one. The object of the play drive is what Schiller describes as "living form" or Beauty. Experiences of beauty, then, unify these distinct, yet equally essential drives into a force that is simultaneously ephemeral (living) and eternal (form).

This symbiotic relationship which finds its union in Beauty is portrayed in the literature, particularly by Goethe, who had an astonishing gift for perceiving the smallest beauty from which he derived profound meaning. His powers of perception are apparent throughout his written work. In his novel, *The Sorrows of Young Werther*, for instance, Goethe's protagonist exclaims:

> When I first came here and looked down into that lovely valley from the hill, the way the entire scene charmed me was a marvel—That little wood! —ah if only you might walk in its shade!—That mountaintop—Ah, to view this vast landscape from there!—And the chain of hills, and the gentle valleys!—oh, to lose myself amongst them!—And I hastened there, and returned without having found what I was hoping for. Oh, distance is like the future: before our souls lies an entire and dusky vastness which overwhelms our feelings as it overwhelms our eyes, and ah! We long to surrender the whole of our being, and be filled with all the joy of one single, immense, magnificent emotion...[340]

This passionate declaration of ecstatic wonder captures the significance that was given to the senses in animating a new relationship to the world. Goethe adamantly affirmed that sensory responses play a profound role in shaping the psyche and informing the character and consciousness of the perceiver.

Perhaps the main point of convergence amongst the theorists of the Beautiful Soul was their inordinate sensitivity to sensory faculties and their acute appreciation of beauty. Goethe described it as the "poetic mood"— a state of being which impregnates experience with an aesthetic pleasure that transforms even the most banal objects into wellsprings of meaning. In a letter to Schiller on August 16, 1797, Goethe describes how such a feeling can emerge from an object which is not entirely poetic itself; referencing both the public square where he lived and his grandfather's house. These sentimental objects, which carried such symbolism for him, made an impression "when the ideal is directly united with the common."[341] This episode underscores the fact that beauty can be found in even the most mundane conditions. The sensory perceptions that make an impression upon the cultivated soul are varied and infinite. Thus, one can never blame one's external environment for a lacking play drive.

Art is the instrument Schiller identifies to induce this vital capacity for feeling; it was in art that the theorists of the Beautiful Soul found much of their inspiration. Winckelmann's moments of high elation when observing the *Apollo Belvedere*, an iconic example of the aesthetic sublimity of classical art, are significant to this tradition. Winckelmann was said to have had an ecstatic response to this sculpture, thinking of "eternal spring," ascending in "platonic rapture to the realm of incorporeal beauty."[342] Winckelmann's reaction is indicative of the inclination amongst these theorists, and their

217

fictional protagonists, to be particularly attuned to their senses, experiencing intense states of emotion derived from this acute receptivity that they had cultivated. This type of aesthetic response is connected to the Schiller-Kant debate about the respective demands of duty and inclination. Schiller believes that an "aesthetically uncultivated" moral agent will be less capable of performing moral duties.[343] The feelings that Winckelmann experienced relate to morality because they derive from the perception of pure Platonic forms.

From the impressions of a majestic landscape to the noble lines of the sculptures of Antiquity, the moral nature of this sensuous embrace of the world is distinct and can be defined in three ways. First, the emphasis on sensory experience is not associated with hedonism, vanity, or an obsession with pleasure. Nor is it an attempt to avoid higher intellectual pursuits. Quite to the contrary, the senses can stimulate both positive and negative emotional responses, and sometimes a full range of complex feelings. The entire spectrum of affect is considered intellectually significant and revealing. The aim of the senses is truth, and although happiness or pleasure might be a by-product, they are not the ends. Furthermore, the objects that excite such a sensual response are richly evocative and elicit the attention of higher faculties. Despite its visceral quality, this sensory engagement, then, evokes profound states of contemplation and reflection.

Second, and most important from an epistemological frame of reference, the emphasis on the senses is meant to establish their indispensability in generating new knowledge of the world. Although the immediate emotional response to the birds' song or the Apollo Belvedere might be dismissed as superfluous in a society that privileges rational thought above all else, which these *Bildung* thinkers believed marked the earlier phases of the Enlightenment, such experiences are considered an essential conduit to knowledge and a gateway to truth. Thus, immediate sensory experiences and their spontaneous effects upon the soul become the foundation of logical deduction and a pedagogical premise for self-cultivation. Watching a lark's parabolic trajectory in the sky, observing the fractal patterns found in nature, or contemplating the concentric circles produced by rain droplets in pools of water become sensuous opportunities to understand the universe and reach a heightened cognitive state that can never be attained from a radically rational worldview alone.

Finally, sensory impression is defined by what can be described as its transcendent nature. By this I mean that the exceptional *receptiveness* to sensory experience, not sensory experience itself, is what leads to knowledge. The senses can both obstruct hidden truths about the universe, or they can act as the vehicle for their revelation.[344] What matters, then, is the conscious spirit in which sensory material is received. That which is automatic, unimaginative, or banal, such as the mechanical consumption of a meal or the unengaged contemplation of a work of art, cannot produce greater truths or new ways of understanding life. The mind is then literally and metaphorically inured to sensory response, and, in these cases, the senses can impede, not illuminate, the path to knowledge. Reaping the benefits of the senses, therefore, requires an acute attentiveness and sensitivity to beauty that surpasses the ordinary and the quotidian; only a mindful, reflective engagement can reconcile physical, sensory input with the faculty of reason.

Transcendence is an appropriate word in this context, given that it alludes to the moral dimension of the senses. We perceive moral qualities through feeling rather than apprehend them through cognition.[345] Like the primary emotional pull of the sentiments, this feeling is the basis from which practical reason can develop. Internal excellence, therefore, becomes an obsession that originates in the passions but ultimately, through *Bildung,* is integrated with reason, producing a necessary harmonious equilibrium.

On the nature of this delicate balance, Schiller imagines three relationships. The first is when a person governs themselves according to their rationality by suppressing their senses. This, he argues, is like a monarchy in which the king represses all freedom. The second is when a person follows only his senses and is governed by instinct alone. This he compares to an ochlocracy in which the rightful sovereign is subverted by mob rule. The third is when reason and the senses come into a perfect harmony, in which neither one is sacrificed at the expense of the other, and where all parts favourably inform each other: a relationship represented by the figure of the Beautiful Soul. Unlike most people who are either a savage when their feeling dominates principles, or a barbarian when their principles destroy feeling, a beautiful soul makes nature her friend "and respects her freedom while merely curbing her caprice."[346] We can see this equilibrium in Danae, the beautiful soul of Wieland's *Bildungsroman*, *The History of Agathon*. Danae's desire for moral beauty is a passion which takes hold of her being and harmonises itself with her feelings and her faculty of reason, creating a stable and enriching pursuit.[347]

The romanticised figure of the Beautiful Soul is supposed to perfectly integrate intense emotional states and rationality with the greatest mastery, indexing the full development of their faculties, while embracing all parts of the human condition without allowing any single one to dominate. This figure is passionate and intense, receptive and awake, while also

220

remaining logical, reasonable and wise. Such is the ideal balance that the cultivated individual will seek to maintain, so that they can experience the highest sentiments that a person is capable of feeling, while also working judiciously and equitably towards rational ends.

This concern for embracing all that is human was related to a contemporary interest in people's complicated psychological states, especially the joy and the tragedy which mark worldly experiences. An ideal of "the man of feeling," and a new theory of moral sentiments emerged.[348] The theorists of the Beautiful Soul displayed joy in their "aesthetic optimism" which is pervasive throughout their writings. They decided to see this world as the most beautiful one possible and to enthusiastically partake in its beauty. Schlegel remarked: "against Candide one can counter with only an aesthetic optimism: that this world is the most beautiful."[349] These theorists' optimism was not naïve or unfounded. Rather, it was a choice, weighted by observation and experience, contingent on the belief that reality is malleable, and that therefore it is a duty to remain positive to contribute to the betterment of the world.

According to this philosophy, there is no point in adopting pessimistic stances that only further human misery. Nothing is more reprehensible than bitterness, disenchantment, and self-imposed despair. Futility born from cynicism is diametrically opposed to a concept that identifies human strength in people's capacity for improvement. A joyful disposition is an indication of a strong constitution, good character, and a product of noble feelings.[350] It is an admirable demonstration of the determination that the individual has developed to defy hardship, negativity, and resentment while overcoming life's obstacles. Happiness is considered both the precondition and the by-product of the successful attainment of the other defining features of the Beautiful Soul. According to Schiller, it is important to:

> Show by induction and by psychological means that a feeling of pleasure must flow from the combined concept of freedom and appearance, the harmony between reason and sense, which is the same as pleasure and which regularly accompanies the representation of beauty.[351]

Ill humour and indolence, on the other hand, are considered signs of self-indulgence, moral fragility, and undeveloped character.[352] These negative traits imply that the soul is sickly from neglect which is, ultimately, the failing of the individual, not the fault of an imperfect world.

Many of the fictional characters created by the theorists of the Beautiful Soul found themselves caught in this struggle to find happiness and remain optimistic despite the pain and weariness of life. Wieland's Agathon depicts a sensitive soul "for whom a single pleasant feeling is sufficient to make them forget all their woes, past and to come."[353] Goethe's novel *Werther* was revolutionary in its overt exploration of highly subjective feelings. As Werther says in one of his better moments:

> We often complain that there are so few good days and so many bad ones…but I think we are wrong to do so. If our hearts were always open, so that we could enjoy the good things God bestows on us every day, we should also have the strength to bear the misfortunes that come our way.[354]

Before Werther's descent into depression, brought on by the torturous nature of his unrequited love, he captures the vitality and joy that characterises the aesthetically awake person. In one passage Werther remarks, "It is good that my heart can feel the simple and innocent pleasure a man knows when the cabbage he eats at table is one he grew himself."[355] In another he comments, "I have never felt happier, and my feelings for nature, down to tiny pebbles and blades of grass, have never been so full and acute."[356] Much joy can be gained from becoming truly receptive to all that exists. Happiness is the product of this aesthetic sensitivity as well as the impetus for further explorations and encounters. Schiller believed that "Beauty alone makes all the world happy, and every being forgets its limitations as long as it experiences her enchantment."[357]

Beautiful souls, then, are people with joyful hearts and cheerful dispositions.[358] Their happiness can be aroused by the simplest circumstances, a consequence of their refined faculties and sensitive perception. They display a rapturous curiosity and an exuberance in partaking of what Goethe and Schiller described as the "beautiful world."[359] They are often portrayed as people who are exceptionally moved by art, nature, and human relationships, and grateful for the opportunities that are presented to them. They retain the jubilance of a mind receptive to experience, and the gratification derived from an imagination left to wander.

The theorists of the Beautiful Soul emphasised intense emotional states because, as described in relation to sensory perception, there is something distinctly moral about the elation of beautiful souls. The experience of beauty has the effect of producing a joy that is intimately connected to our pleasure in the good. Schiller argues that the happiness we find in beauty strengthens our moral sentiments. Art is moral "not only because it employs moral means in order to charm us, but also because even the pleasure which it procures us is a means of morality."[360] The quality of seeing the world in a positive light, and, consequently, reaching towards moral goodness is in line with Shaftesbury's formulation that virtue is "naturally" adorned by the qualities of beauty that arouse affect.[361] Much of the population who remain in lethargic states of emotional apathy, unmoved by the great beauty that surrounds them, are discontented because they lack essential elements of a moral nature and receptive individuality which comprises true happiness. A joyful person who feels the beauty of existence intensely, by contrast, is the product of autonomous thought, rendering them more capable of making moral choices.

The happiness in beauty also has the function of making the pursuit of a beautiful soul a joyous undertaking, one that is inherently attractive and desirable. Despite the stringent demands of this philosophy, its holistic adoption is not a burden but an exciting undertaking, one that promotes exploration, adventure, and wanderlust, all of which are an important part of becoming cultivated.

Humboldt advocated this enlightened understanding of the good life because he believed it ensured a more reflective and stable society.[362] His ideas on education afford individuals the greatest opportunities to have edifying experiences and to find fulfilment in the products of culture. The emphasis on both disciplined hard work in self-improvement, yet equally on the pleasure found in this pursuit, is liberating and satisfies the immediate experience as well as the prospects of the individual.

Delighting in sensory impressions, however, does not mean that beautiful souls are always blissful. As acutely sensitive beings, they are often depicted as enduring long periods of agony and suffering. The tragedy they experience is derived in part from their intense aesthetic sensitivity. With such vivid imaginations and multidimensional worldviews, negative emotions and unfavourable human interactions can more easily imprint a sense of melancholy upon their souls. The cultivated complexity of their minds lends itself to a sense of existential loneliness and an increased sensitivity to the harm that others cause. But, more than from this sensitive state, their greatest suffering comes from the traumas that they endure.

As we have seen, Schiller emphasises that the virtuousness of a person can only be known through trials of character and hardship. For this reason, beautiful souls are depicted in the literature as experiencing tragedies that challenge, but ultimately prove their moral worth: they are people who have triumphed, through the strength of their characters, over the unfortunate fates that befall them. Portraying these tragedies makes it harder for those who have not experienced such suffering to critique this philosophy for its disconnection from reality. The cynic can no longer justify the fact that they remain unmoved by the beauty of the world, which even those who have suffered greatly can still feel. The critique that a poetic perception receptive to beauty is somehow a privilege of those who are fortunate is thus exposed as the product of individuals who find it easier to be critical than to see.

Beautiful Souls, therefore, are not inured to negative emotions; in many ways they experience them even more acutely than others. However, they distinguish themselves in their ability to control this pain, converting it into wisdom.[363] They use negative emotions to fortify their character and to stimulate their moral development, while never allowing themselves to wallow in self-pity. The elements of tragedy that

225

the person of true cultivation endures are, then, essential to their beautiful self-realisation. Hardship expands the depth of lived experience and augments the meaning derived from beauty. According to Schiller, tragedy is a means by which to cultivate a sense of the sublime.[364] A soul who suffers but ultimately overcomes the pain and loss that they experience escapes complacency and demonstrates independent cognition.[365]

When beautiful souls endure pain, they become heroic and represent the highest form of human dignity through this demonstration of moral strength.[366] Schiller offers the example of a person who experiences severe physical pain yet overcomes it. In such a case, his "veins swell, his muscles become cramped and taut, his voice cracks, his chest is thrust out, and his lower body pressed in."[367] But his intentional movements are serene and relaxed. His stoic composure and the internal peace that he outwardly expresses during his suffering reflects his dignity. Grace and dignity unite in the beautiful soul, the ultimate expression of morality.[368] This aesthetic suffering, Schiller claims, can be witnessed in the Laocoön, the Hellenistic sculpture that Winckelmann described in *History of the Art of Antiquity* (1764). As Laocoön and his sons are slain by serpents, he maintains an internal composure rendered, in the sculpture, on the brow.[369] He valiantly battles his fear without allowing his moral nature to be degraded by physical harm. As Schiller remarks:

> An ordinary soul confines itself entirely to this suffering, and never comprehends in the sublime or the pathetic anything beyond the terrible. An independent soul, on the contrary, precisely seizes this occasion to rise to the feeling of his moral

force, in all that is most magnificent in this force,
and from every terrible object knows how to draw
out the sublime.[370]

The Laocoön, whose noble suffering is sculpted for eternity, represents this independent creature who has experienced the sublime. Schiller believes that those truly moral souls who have restrained their ego will be able to endure even the cruellest loss through the aesthetic detachment of themselves from their own experience. They gain valuable knowledge about the human condition in the aestheticized contemplation of their fate. The beautiful soul who suffers, then, can detach themself from this suffering to observe from a more objective perspective what it might teach them; therein lies their strength.

Goethe identified Susanna von Klettenberg (1723-1774), a relative of his mother, as a Laocoön-like figure who retained a sense of serenity and an aesthetically detached consideration of her position, despite her poor health and the suffering that accompanied it. In his autobiography *Poetry and Truth* (1811), Goethe tenderly describes her grace and patience, genius and liveliness, which overpowered the pain that she endured. Her steadfast morality and dedication to her principles was even more admirable given the gravity of her condition.[371] Susanna was the inspiration for the Beautiful Soul of the sixth book in *Wilhelm Meister*. This fictitious character's suffering is an important part of the moral evolution of Goethe's work. In one passage she says:

> During the nine months, which I then spent
> patiently upon a sick-bed, it appears to me the
> groundwork of my whole turn of thought was laid;
> as the first means were then afforded my mind of

developing itself in its own manner. I suffered and I loved; this was the peculiar form of my heart. In the most violent fits of coughing, in the depressing pains of fever, I lay quiet, like a snail drawn back within its house: the moment I obtained a respite, I wanted to enjoy something pleasant; and as every other pleasure was denied me, I endeavoured to amuse myself with the innocent delights of eye and ear.[372]

During this period of suffering, the Beautiful Soul defines her moral principles while still finding happiness in beauty. Once she overcomes her illness, she is more determined than ever to live according to the belief system that she has developed.

By contrast, the moment of suffering reveals the flaws in Goethe's character Werther. Although Werther's ability to think for himself, to feel deeply, and to truly grasp the meaning of aesthetic experience is admirable, he eventually succumbs to self-pity and ends his life. Ultimately, he does not live up to his own recognition that "we should all have the strength to bear the misfortunes that come our way." He demonstrates the dangers of what this philosophy sought to avoid in overindulging sentiment to the point of neurotic self-obsession. While he understands *Bildung* in theory, he is too narcissistic to grasp its humble spirit and to recognise the way that it conquers pain. In a telling passage, Werther remarks:

I have been intoxicated more than once, my passions have never been far off insanity, and I have no regrets: because I have come to realise, in my own way, that people have always felt a need to decry the extraordinary men who accomplish great things, things that seemed impossible, as intoxicated and insane.[373]

He goes on to accuse others of his own failure to maintain his poetic vision of the world. Suddenly the beauty of his perception is ruined by a sense of superiority, and the poison of bitterness that he has allowed to corrupt all that was once good in him. No longer can he continue on the path towards self-cultivation—which he alone has obstructed with his inflated ego and self-importance. His suicide is a metaphor for the dangers associated with all those who allow their vanity to corrupt the aspects of their perception that once made them beautiful, and many have interpreted *Werther* as a cautionary tale.[374] Lessing, for example, remarked that Werther is a character who is poetic but does not possess moral beauty.[375] Lessing's acknowledgement of Werther's poetic nature derives from his ability to perceive of the world in a beautiful way; but his judgement regarding the deficiency of moral beauty stems from Werther's inability to act upon this poetic perception or serve as an aspirational model for humanity.

Goethe himself chronicled his struggle with depression and thoughts of suicide during the time that he was in love with Charlotte Buff (1753-1828) who was betrothed to Johann Christian Kestner (1741-1800), fictionalized in the love triangle of *Werther*. The character of Werther may be interpreted as a depiction of the spiritual road that Goethe might have taken had he allowed soured prospects of love and the "separation of the sensual from the moral" to destroy him. We can sympathise with Goethe, the man, because he triumphed over his suffering, even in the face of a loss of innocence. He used this suffering as material for his novel, and therefore something productive came out of it. However, we cannot sympathise with Werther, his character, for the reason that Schiller touches upon in his philosophical essay "On the Tragic Art":

> I admit that the suffering of a weak soul, and the pain of a wicked character, do not procure us this enjoyment. But this is because they do not excite our pity to the same degree as the hero who suffers, or the virtuous man who struggles.[376]

Werther's appeal is diminished by his moral weakness and, perhaps most tragic of all, the beauty of his poetic vision degrades along with him.

The suffering of beautiful souls, by contrast, gives them a more compassionate disposition and a gentler nature. Through difficult experiences, they can empathise with others and create something beyond themselves. In maintaining grace and dignity and refusing to succumb to self-indulgence or cynicism, they preserve the ideal of humanity. The virtue found in the perennially optimistic beautiful soul, and the intense sense of compassion that they feel, is only heightened by the fact that they know the pain of the world.

The *salonnières,* who oscillated between the Enlightenment tradition's focus on rationality, in which they had been educated, and the emergent prominence of Romanticism's concern for the passions, readily embraced the Beautiful Soul's affirmation of the two.[377] Rationality, they understood, was necessary for their intellectual practice to arrive at knowledge with rigour. Systematic, critical thought was imperative to intellectual autonomy. The *salonnières* were highly critical of unmethodical thinking and wary of the ignorance that the unreflective subscription to ideologies can cause. However, they also believed that the passions are of equal importance. Raw emotions, while subjective, can reveal a matter in its truest form, offering visceral impressions that contain a meaning which cannot be replaced by rationality alone. Following Schiller, they believed that this undeniable dimension of the human experience will have adverse effects on personal development if it is suppressed. They welcomed the natural expression of emotions which they then strove to fuse with rational capacities.

The *salonnières* themselves were passionate individuals who lived life with an aestheticized intensity.[378] Little could be prosaic or mundane for those who wanted to know and to feel the ultimate—whose every action was a search for a Platonic divine. Herz's success as a *salonnière* was, in part, attributed to her spirited nature, a quality she had possessed since childhood.[379] She was a lively creature, animated by a vibrant and energetic psyche. She enjoyed theatrically expressing her emotions in plays as a child and later in her salon as an adult. But, more than any other *salonnière* of the time, Varnhagen was thought to have an ecstatic nature; she was considered to be a genius whose natural vivacity gave her the appellation of "the woman with the most *esprit* in the universe."[380] It was said of Varnhagen that whether she was "sorrowful or glad, ill or well, resting or active, she filled the cup of the moment to the brim with the fullness of her being."[381]

Varnhagen's brilliance was that she saw the insurmountable significance and meaning in everything.[382] She derived great meaning from seeing beauty in this deeply emotional way. She was said to have given everything, from a flower to the greatest artistic creation, an ultimate importance. She lived with the passion of the religiously devout:

> The divine was as near to her as the air, it was in
> this that her soul lived and moved and had its being.
> Indeed, it has been rightly said of her that the soul
> of the world vibrated in her soul with such strength
> that her fragile being trembled with the force of the
> God it enclosed.[383]

As Varnhagen wrote, "I confine myself to the marvel of existence in general; if this is possible, then the incomprehensible will one day be comprehended. We must become better, we must be good; that is the problem."[384] In her emotive response to the sheer miracle of existence, she found the inspiration to "become better." Her emotional states can be seen as directly connected to her social activities.

Many people recognised the exceptional power of Varnhagen's sensory perceptions which vividly coloured her emotional life. Goethe and the Romantic writer Jean Paul (1763-1825), for example, agreed that she possessed such an intensity of feeling that a flash from her soul "illuminated far wider expanses than sheets of dissertations."[385] The exhilarating quality of her passionate character drew participants to her salon and secured their steadfast allegiances. Heinrich Heine expressed his vicarious devotion to this emotionally magnanimous spirit when he wrote: "You have cheered, and fortified, and taken the rough off of me, the morose, sick man, you have supported me with word and deed, and refreshed me with macaroni and spiritual food."[386] In another passage he states:

> I run around in the world so impetuously, some-
> times people come who would like to make me
> their property, but they were always the kind that
> didn't please me much, and as long as this is the

case, I shall always have written on my collar
'*j'appartiens à* Madame Varnhagen.[387]

Despite the intense emotions that the *salonnières* exhibited and elicited in their salon participants, they did not succumb to the over sentimentalised influences of Romanticism. Emotional states were not solipsistically indulged, but rather communicated for the purpose of attaining wisdom through the influences of the rational mind. The metamorphosis of the unbridled energy of emotions into rational thought is revealed in the *salonnières'* letters that recorded the conversations in their salons.[388] Letters were thought to be "an imprint of the soul" and the "heart's blood in an envelope."[389] In passionate streams of consciousness, the *salonnières* expressed their innermost feelings, hopes, and frustrations with the world. Varnhagen recalled that in her letters it was "as if the heavy, full horizon of my soul thunders forth."[390]

Epistolary exchange was a preferred medium to represent the salon's ends, in part because it was considered a more permissible format for women. It allowed the *salonnières* to more easily contribute to the discourse on *Bildung* and to gain enduring intellectual influence.[391] The *salonnières* committed themselves to this art form because it most accurately represented self-cultivation as both an immediate and continuous pursuit. Letters explored inner realms of feeling, while also reflecting on these feelings more cogently than in a conversation when immediacy can suddenly cloud reason.

Indeed, these letters were seen as a meditative reflection on the salon's happenings, and an indication of the level of self-cultivation that a person had attained within the salons. Letters were not only a means of communication but a measure of *Bildung*.[392] The *salonnières* have rightfully been credited with transforming the epistolary into this new art form of feeling which they themselves saw as the artistic medium best suited to eternalise the ideals of self-cultivation that they practiced in their salons.[393] As Varnhagen wrote:

> I want a letter to be the portrait of the moment in which it was written: it shall be primarily a likeness, as high as any demands of art on ideal ennoblement... Happy are the lovely images in a laughing moment of nature which, far from all human imagination, could serve the most artistic as a model![394]

Thus, the integration of rationality and emotions became the methodology that the *salonnières* used to arrive at knowledge within their salons. Their prolific letters facilitated this discursive practice.

In following the philosophy of the Beautiful Soul, the *salonnières* sought to cultivate the full spectrum of emotions within their salons, reconciling the joy and the inevitable tragedy of life. The metamorphosis of mind and being that the salon demanded might appear to be a burden shorn of pleasurable qualities. But this rigorous intellectual undertaking was not an impediment to happiness, nor was it constrained by a severity that renounced pleasure. Instead, the salon was a source of great happiness, a place of ultimate fulfilment and inspiration.

Accounts of the public sphere often present communicative action in sterile terms, but if non-obligatory forms of association are not enjoyable, then people do not have the incentive to participate. Simply, but significantly, salons were attractive to participants because they made pleasurable the serious work that was at hand. Salon conversations, although intellectually demanding, were also meant to delight, to excite the imagination, to amuse, and to entertain. Salons were "the art of pleasing others through wit and refinement, which required ease of comportment and spontaneity of expression."[395] Madame de Staël (1766-1817) a French *salonnière* who had an active presence in the Berlin salon scene, summarised this vibrant spirit by calling conversation:

> A means of reciprocally and rapidly giving one another pleasure; of speaking just as quickly as one thinks; of spontaneously enjoying one's self; of being applauded without working . . . [a] sort of electricity that causes sparks to fly, and that relieves some people of the burden of their excess vivacity and awakens others from a state of painful apathy.[396]

This joyful approach to communication animated ideas and encouraged participation. The dynamic interplay between the speakers' and participants' perspectives ensured that conversation remained engaging while preventing tedious repetitions and lengthy disquisitions.[397] Conversations were relaxed and informal to foster inventiveness in thought unrestricted by rigidity or convention that would stifle conviviality. They arose from "the pure pleasure and stimulation that cultural exchange brings to an intellectually curious and cultivated group of people."[398]

The vitality of salon conversations reflected the temperaments of the *salonnières* themselves, who maintained an intense desire to live joyously. As Varnhagen said of herself, "It is still the way it used to be because my nature was not made for unhappiness. My nature was overflowing and proud wild with joy when the earth received me."[399] The joy she identified in her own spirit was the product of her *Bildung* education in which she had cultivated her ability to feel deeply. She shared this sentiment with the salon participants with whom she felt closest. In one passage she states of herself and her friend Pauline Wiesel (1778-1848):

> ...We have...a cheerful, childlike nature. And a bridge, a tree, a trip, a smell, a smile, in short the entire surface of the world engages our ten healthy senses and our precious inners. And so we'll try, a community will, must build up around such clever, cheerful, innocent creatures.[400]

Varnhagen's letters reveal the extent of her joyfulness. She uses the word *Genuss,* enjoyment, often— a fact that Veit found excessive, to which she responded:

> By the way, sir, I will use the word 'thing' [*Ding*] and 'enjoyment'[*Genuss*] as often as I want. Two charming words! What does it concern you! The enjoyment of everything at its proper time, is something that is permissible enjoyment, and therefore a full one, because an enjoyment in itself is already a pleasure, and therefore, the right one is a beautiful thing. There, with your authority! nobody can command me! I am not such a th...g! and you should not have the e...t of forbidding me words![401]

These words are emblematic of her need to continuously express happiness and to maintain optimism about the human

236

condition. She understood this to be a moral duty as much as a natural state.

In fostering an atmosphere of conviviality through their vivacity, the *salonnières* encouraged salon participants to distance themselves from personal unhappiness and pessimistic worldviews. If the *salonnières* allowed cynicism to affect their vision or diminish their ideals, they would never have been able to convince their adherents to have faith in the philosophy of the Beautiful Soul. The salon's survival was contingent upon the *salonnières'* propensity towards optimism and their abiding faith in the possibility of human improvement. Their ability to identify exactly what made conversation satisfying, and how social interactions could be pleasurable, to explore what constituted a good life and bring these elements to their salons, was an essential aspect of their social ingenuity for which they were most remembered.

Humboldt, for instance, stated that the salon of Herz gave him "some of the happiest hours of his life."[402] Varnhagen's friend, the poet and diplomat Karl Gustav Brinckmann (1764-1847), said of her:

> With what freedom and grace she knew how to animate, brighten, and warm those about her. It was impossible to withstand her gaiety...Her sallies were wonderfully unexpected...I have heard magnificent sayings of hers, true inspirations, often in a few words, which flashed through the air like lightning and reach the inmost heart.[403]

These men were aware that this happiness was not the product of chance, but rather produced in the conditions that the *salonnières* made possible.

Even though cultured pleasures were an all-pervasive force in the salon and held social interactions together, the *salonnières* did not dismiss the significance of suffering. They were, in certain respects, ineluctably drawn to tragedy, and they fluctuated between the two extremes. Tragedy, like joy, was an intense emotional state which signalled that the individual was fully awake. In her reading of Goethe's *Tasso*, Varnhagen reveals what tragedy meant to her:

> Tragic is that which we absolutely cannot comprehend, to which we must submit; tragic is that which no cleverness, no wisdom can either destroy or avoid; where our innermost nature drives, pulls, coaxes, inevitably leads and holds us; when this destroys us, and we are faced with the question: Why? Why me, why am I made for this? And all our intelligence and strength merely serve to grasp, to feel destruction or to let us be detracted from it.[404]

Varnhagen understood tragedy to be the conflict that arises between the individual, who is neither culpable nor self-destructive, and an imperfect world.[405] For the innocent person to submit to tragedy and then try to understand what it represents from an intellectual perspective is the greatest consolation. She spurned apathy, on the other hand, because it implies an intellectual deficiency that brings no greater clarity. The *salonnières* believed that it is preferable to feel something, even if it is negative, then to feel nothing at all.

With the new influences of the Romantic era, tragedy was fetishised and the *salonnières* inclination towards it only added to their allure and mystique as beautiful souls. Herz, for example, was considered "A statuesque figure swathed in melancholy... 'the tragic muse of the Romantic writers.'"[406] A perspective then emerged that this proclivity towards tragedy heightened the *salonnières'* ability to feel complex emotions and to appreciate aesthetic influences. "The Jewess, like the romantic consumptive, is a being whose affliction confers upon her a heightened sensibility."[407] The *salonnières*, however, did not romanticise their own suffering because it was acutely real to them, especially concerning the injustices they endured in their social position. They communicated their pain because this pain aroused feelings of moral responsibility which needed to be expressed in order to be overcome. In a letter to Veit in 1795, Varnhagen does not shy away from articulating the enormous unhappiness that discrimination caused her:

> I have a strange fancy: it is as if some supramundane being, just as I was thrust into this world, plunged these words with a dagger into my heart: "Yes, have sensibility, see the world as few see it, be great and noble, nor can I take from you the faculty of eternally thinking. But I add one thing more: be a Jewess!" And now my life is a slow bleeding to death. By keeping still I can delay it. Every movement is an attempt to staunch it—new death; and immobility is possible for me only in death itself... I can, if you will, derive every evil, every misfortune, every vexation from that.... this opinion is my essence.[408]

This heart-wrenching description of slowly bleeding to death graphically illustrates the psychological burdens that the *salonnières* endured, rendering the optimism they maintained in their role as *salonnière* even more admirable. Like the archetype of the Beautiful Soul, the *salonnières* did not wallow in their suffering. Rather they turned it into the impetus to further their education, to make sense of life's cruelties, and to do good. For Herz sadness from childlessness led her to turn to literature, art, and friends for happiness.[409] Varnhagen's suffering from her devalued social position and childhood experiences gave her the motivation "to be better, to feel sympathy not to be indifferent towards the poor and afflicted."[410] The weight of her pain was channelled into her efforts to ameliorate the pain of others, even those who were objectively in a better position than she. "Rahel fulfils her office of adviser with her usual art. She pours balsam on the distraught mind of the prince, and under her quiet ministration his cares vanish; he forgets his remorse and becomes again his light-hearted self."[411] Varnhagen was able to overcome her pain and do good for others through her *Bildung* education and with the guidance of Goethe's work. As she said, "The poet accompanied me unfailingly throughout my life, and what was split into unhappiness and happiness, and I could not hold together, he brought into a strong and healthy unity."[412]

In certain respects, the *salonnières* intense joy for living was the cause of their suffering and only heightened their tragedy. For those with such sensitive souls, who were so intimately aware of the beauty in the world and had a tenacious belief in the ultimate goodness in people, it was easier to be wounded by those who deceived them. The *salonnières'* belief in the virtue of others opened them to the misery of human fallibility and the scars of deception and betrayal remained.[413] The *salonnières*, however, never blamed people for the injuries they caused, nor did they acknowledge their pain from these wounds as the inevitable state of affairs. Instead, they saw their joy as the state closest to the truth; they did not permit their suffering to gain excessive psychological power over them or diminish from their conviction in the ultimate goodness of people.[414]

One poignant example of the *salonnières* resolute will in this regard is that of Varnhagen and the period of her social isolation. Around 1808 when a wave of nationalism pervaded Germany and new legislation which opposed liberalisation was implemented, the thirty-seven-year-old Varnhagen expressed her feelings of abandonment, and the suffering she endured, when many of her participants no longer attended her salon due to the changing political climate and increased antagonism towards Jews. In a letter to Brinckmann from January 1808 she writes:

> At my 'tea table' as you call it, I sit alone with my dictionaries; tea is not being served, except every eight or ten days, when Shack, who has not deserted me, asks, for it. Everything is different. Never was I so alone. Absolutely. Never so thoroughly and definitely bored. Imagine, bored! Because only cleverness, kindness, hopefulness can sustain one who has been so wronged, so devastated…I am as I was, Brinckmann; the blows have fortified the old strengths within me, and prevailed and made me truly new and more arable. I am still capable of joking, delight, and the highest suffering; only, there is nothing that can upset me completely, for I am prostrate.[415]

Despite the betrayal that she felt, having given so much only to be abandoned when circumstances changed, she continued to delight, to jest, and to sustain her salon and social activities in order to provide others with a respite from a cruel world. This, we can infer from her letters, was because her ideals were bound to a concept of a larger humanity, not to individuals. If she let her hopeful vision perish because of the injury that some had caused her, it would only prove the fragility of her beliefs.

The *salonnières* strove to become powerful, enduring, beautiful souls. They taught themselves how to make the most of the events that life brought and to productively channel the intense emotions that they experienced. They saw it as their duty to maintain their optimism while acknowledging the reality of tragedy, compassionately inspiring their salon participants to find the same strength. They overcame life's challenges and appreciated its pleasures, in the fullest expression of the human condition in all its beauty and its pain.

Despite the achievements of the *salonnières* in artfully balancing emotional states with reason and encouraging this balance in others, society today is experiencing a Dark Ages for rationality. Our ability to fairly and calmly reason appears severely stunted while feelings have been dis-equilibrated. The need to prepare cogent, balanced arguments to engage productively with others has become secondary in a society in which extremity of expression is a common feature of modern life.

The Enlightenment's achievement of enshrining reason as an indispensable human value has receded from our collective consciousness and with it, the possibilities for sustainable progress. Erroneous or false statements are no longer viewed as especially dangerous; to a terrifying degree we have accepted and even legitimised irrationality, allowing it to exist unchallenged in news articles, discursive forums, and within the communicative channels of our democracies. Out of

242

intellectual laziness and the desire to be noticed, we have unravelled the accomplishments of centuries past, threatening a descent into Medieval mentalities which breed tribalism and undermine the primacy of scientific methodologies.

Correspondingly, our emotional states remain either deficient or unhealthily developed, making it even more difficult to achieve fruitful social outcomes. Although the movement to be attuned to our emotions has proved effective in destigmatising feeling, it has also led to a measure of excess. With the legitimation of negative emotions, public displays of anger have become a regular feature of the public sphere. They shape discourse, inform policies, and win elections. Inciting bigotry, hostilities, and an ignorance bred from intolerance and discontent, the public performativity of anger has become a major social impediment.

Although we have been given free rein to pander to visceral feelings, we still have the obligation to uphold standards of decency by controlling our emotional states so that we may relate to others with a sense of balance and fairness. It is undoubtedly healthy and necessary to feel negative emotions; however, feeling emotions and expressing them are two different things. If we are not able to process and refine our feelings, then we fall prey to a brutishness unconducive to progress in a diverse, multi-cultural society.

Although we have indulged negative emotions, we appear grossly deficient in our ability to value positive emotional states. Artistic expressions and wondrous natural landscapes rarely elicit the intense sentiments that they merit in a population that seems to have forgotten what it means to feel. Marvelling at the exquisite nature of the universe, seeing life as a divine force that awakens intense expressions of passion is a way of being that has been lost. When we visit museums, we do not bask in the glory of the *Apollo Belvedere* as Winckelmann did. We stand in front of the most famous work of art for just long enough to check it off a list, ignoring those works that are perhaps even greater but have not been reproduced for sale in museum stores or turned into a meme. A crowd of oblivious people mechanically makes their pilgrimage to the Mona Lisa, never having stopped to observe the masterpieces around it.

Our engagement with nature is often similarly mundane. When we climb a mountain, rarely will we absorb the majesty of the sweeping view beyond the few minutes that it takes to catch our breath. We may exclaim how awesome it is and pose for a picture with our friends, but this is the extent of the impression that the landscape makes upon us. We may go to great expense to visit national parks, but if an experience of nature has not been defined as such through the demarcation of fences that indicate it is something that we should care about, then we remain largely unmoved. To witness a person walk down the street and spontaneously stop to observe an ancient tree or marvel at the exquisite system of veins in a leaf would be an anomaly. Any genuine, unmediated experience of awe in the natural world is rare to find and may very well be belittled in our painfully cynical society.

When our culture tells us that expressions of feelings should be mistrusted, disguised or even heavily medicated, it is no wonder that large portions of the population have become automatons, going through the motions of engaging their senses but feeling nothing in return. Uncultivated sensory faculties and a deadened relationship to the world can be observed in the glazed eyes of consumerism and the tranquilised demeanour that we embody as we cart ourselves through shopping mall and Disneyland realities. Unfortunately, the monotonous environments we live within have been shorn of beauty to reflect a sterilised vision of progress that prioritises easy profits over human needs and feeling. We must, therefore, forge communities that restore our ability to experience a profoundness of being.

In a salon on "Anger," we discussed the state of emotions and the spaces that influence them. Participants were torn between the importance of expressing anger and the problems this may pose for progress and social comity. In the debate, anger was often conflated with "emotional intelligence" and passion for a cause and indulged in based on this pretext. A salon is valuable in this sense because it vividly reflects popular ideas that may be influencing society's direction. The general attitude toward negative emotions, however, was incongruous with the way participants perceived these emotional states and behaviours when they occurred within the salon itself. One participant, for example, was overly truculent in conversation. He blurted out his opinions with a hostility that appeared divisive. Though his behaviour was not extreme, salon participants bristled, demonstrating that hostility is, in fact, not valued in public forums.

Within my salons, I have witnessed time and again that people do not reward the expression of negative emotional states and they instinctually disconnect. By contrast, when someone communicates an idea with passion, or is visibly moved by the impressions gained from the questions that are explored, the community favourably perceives them and is particularly receptive to their opinions. Thus, much can be learned about the effect of emotions on social life in a discursive space such as a salon; often closely observing actual behaviours is more revealing than what is verbally communicated.

To practice the Beautiful Soul means to educate ourselves on the nature of our emotional states and the effects that they may have, inducing positive feelings while comprehending the sources of negative emotions and controlling them so that they may be used to our advantage. The many passions we feel that could be categorised as negative, such as rage, loathing, disgust, annoyance, jealousy, and envy, all serve a valuable function. Practicing this philosophy does not mean suppressing them, but rather, finding ways to control them while enhancing the possibility of experiencing positive emotional states such as ecstasy, amazement, serenity, love, optimism, and gratitude within constructive environments that elicit these responses within us.

Beautiful souls are portrayed by Goethe and Schiller as supremely harmonious. Their faculties are harmonised, and this inner harmony is externally apparent in a self-possessed nature. They feel passionately but they do not descend into histrionics. They have the fortitude to extrapolate beyond their singular experiences, bridling negative emotions to view situations from a fair and more objective perspective. The control that they exhibit in taming visceral emotions through the development of rational faculties allows their positive feelings to flourish freely.

Of course, there are also many instances in which negative emotions serve an essential function and should not be avoided. Therefore, one must distinguish between negative emotional states that are poisonous and unproductive and those that are invaluable warning signs. If my best friend succeeds in her career, I should be overjoyed for her. There is no conceivable benefit to anyone involved in my feeling envious of her good fortune. She is in a better position, and I do not lose anything from her happiness. Envy reveals a flaw in my character. However, if my partner is flirtatious with other women and I am jealous, perhaps my jealousy stems from a serious problem. Jealousy, in this case, may prevent me from investing further in an unhealthy relationship. Ultimately, the individual must determine if their negative emotions are constructive or if they do not serve them well and should be conquered.

To practice the Beautiful Soul today means to have the strength to overcome the malaise that has defined twenty-first century society, daring to feel by cultivating the ability to perceive beauty and experience wonder. Beautiful souls are cognitively alert, wholly consumed by sensorial impressions. Their positive passions are not genetic endowments but cultivated states formed through practice. They view situations and ideas from a logical perspective, while retaining an intensity for living which animates their relationships in the world.

With regards to the contentment discovered in the balance of emotions with reason, it is difficult to discuss happiness today in relationship to the past because our understanding of this word has been corrupted. The change in its meaning reveals the vast re-conception of the ends we choose to prioritise and the social values to which we subscribe. No longer are popular definitions of happiness inextricably associated with virtue, excellence, and the attainment of practical wisdom. Nor are they grounded in the Greek notion of *Eudaimonia* which, as we have seen, is translated as human flourishing and is etymologically composed of the words *eu* (good) and *daimon* (spirit). The modern definition of happiness emphasises accumulating great wealth, far beyond what is necessary for a healthy subsistence, exerting power over others, and receiving public accolades by achieving celebrity status.

The aphorism that "money can't buy happiness" was once a widely shared sentiment. But today happiness is conceived in popular culture as a finite commodity for which we must compete relentlessly. Yet those who strive for material emblems of success often find themselves in a prolonged state of pain in the pursuit of that which they do not yet possess, or wholly disconsolate if they win this zero-sum game yet realise its ultimate futility. The modern individual remains in a vicious cycle with no apparent release from their suffering, all because they did not deeply consider the ends that are intrinsically valuable.

This analysis of our current condition might seem overly pessimistic. Surely people comprehend that there is more to happiness than quantifiable material pursuits. However popular culture has so strongly reinforced a consumerist interpretation that many go against what they know to be right. One needs only to observe the values advanced in advertisements, the lyrics of the latest Top Fifty Billboard songs, and social media content to realise just how pervasive and insidious this message has become.

Instead of exposing the lewd debasement of happiness propagated by the entertainment industry, news sources now try to find the sense of "empowerment" and "artistic merit" that these songs and social media displays possess. These sources, too, have become part of the money-worshipping entertainment industry that desires not to inform or enlighten but to share in the profits. Ignominious ends are so reinforced in cultural definitions of happiness that they have become normalised.

Of course, the most popular songs and social media samplings are not an entirely accurate metric of people's perceptions. They are, however, representative of our times and remain the ubiquitous definitions which young people, in need of a direction, will pursue. This is not an innocuous facet of modern cultural life that can be ignored because it is just a lyric, a passing comment on the news, or a YouTube feed. This is the degraded value system by which history will remember us.

In a salon on "The Good Life," participants were asked their definition of happiness. Their ideas reflect the problems of a wider social trend. Most expressed a conception commensurate with the Beautiful Soul, finding purpose and satisfaction in good deeds, committed love, virtuous personality traits, and meaningful work. Many admitted, however, that they deprioritised these ends to pursue wealth, short term sexual gratification, and career success. They knew that this did not fulfil them, but they still felt inclined to remain on the same course, deflecting happiness to a time in the distant future when they could find meaning once again.

Within this salon, the tensions between the past and present were made apparent as participants discussed their pursuit of modern conceptions of happiness while intellectually and emotionally affirming classical notions. Evidently, the privileging of ends that did not ultimately make them happy was a formula for disaster; they were aware of the joylessness with which they approached life and the regrets they would inevitably have on their death bed. However, social pressure is a powerful force. They could not ultimately rid themselves of what they believed others would perceive constituted happiness. Public perception and social standing were prioritised over their own satisfaction, revealing a pervasive threat to true self-realisation today.

The idea brought to light within this salon is that the pursuit of happiness requires the character strength to overcome socially imposed expectations. It begins by clarifying one's own conception of happiness and then forming the resolve to live by it. Evidently not everyone can reach the same level of happiness since so many factors, from clinical depression, poverty, and difficult environmental circumstances remain outside of our control. However, to a large degree it is within our power to be happy, and where it is possible, we can view it as our moral responsibility to make the most of our good fortune. We must differentiate between when we are unhappy out of truly unfavourable circumstances, and when we are unhappy because we are morally frail.

There are many people who, no matter how lucky they are or how desirable their situation may be, are miserable for no apparent reason. Although they may blame their circumstances, ultimately their unhappiness is caused by their own character weakness. Instead of spending a fortune on therapy or taking medication and never resolving their discontentment, they could find the inner strength to deliberately change their perspective. According to the Beautiful Soul, the inclination to waste the possibility of happiness out of self-indulgence must be overcome. If we have been given the opportunity to lead a good life, then it is our responsibility to actualise this possibility when others are not so fortunate.

The *salonnières* might act as our inspiration in this regard. These formidable women chose to be happy because they saw it as a moral necessity. Since they thought deeply about the nature of happiness, balanced their emotional states with reason, and valued profound ends, they were able to achieve contentment even during the most painful periods of their lives.

The modern practitioner of the Beautiful Soul will overcome the major psychological inhibiters of happiness today: emotional ennui, superficiality, and apathy. Instead of favouring hedonistic indulgences, sedated comforts, and transient pleasures, their happiness will be defined by the burgeoning of the virtues and ideals in which they believe. They will prioritise joy found in the attainment of knowledge, the appreciation of beauty, and human relationships. Although this will not inure them to pain, it will make them better able to overcome it since their life holds value beyond ephemeral pursuits.

In practicing this philosophy, we strive to become the magical person who is illuminated from within by a spark of life. This beautiful disposition is exceedingly rare, but it can be cultivated through gratitude and a developed consciousness. In enacting the Beautiful Soul, we overcome a state of "soul death" by consciously harmonising our emotions, employing our rationality, cultivating our sensory faculties, and harnessing suffering to expand our empathy.

CHAPTER 13

On the Journey Towards the Ideal

THE features of a Beautiful Soul are rendered tangible through the literal and metaphorical undertaking of a journey.[416] The journey, in its literal sense, is a joyful period, usually taken in one's youth from the late teens to early twenties when the individual then ventures out. By undertaking an arduous adventure to develop their true self, they are freed from the stultifying comfort of their upbringing and the narrow perspectives of their close-knit social circle. This deeply revealing journey serves as the transition from childhood to an enlightened adulthood during which the individual over-comes intellectual infantilism by enriching their aesthetic and emotional faculties. It is a time for youthful discovery to encounter the mysterious and the unknown, placing oneself in new situations and absorbing the impressions that they offer.[417] Schiller writes:

> Thus his culture will consist of two things: first, providing the receptive faculty with the most multifarious contacts with the world, and as regards feeling, pushing passivity to its fullest extent; secondly, securing for the determining faculty the fullest independence from the receptive, and as regards reason, pushing activity to its fullest extent. Where both qualities are united, Man will combine

> the greatest fullness of existence with the utmost
> self-dependence and freedom, and instead of
> abandoning himself to the world he will rather draw
> it into himself with the whole infinity of its phe-
> nomena, and subject it to the unity of his reason.[418]

On a journey of self-discovery, the questing youth can make richly varied contacts in the world and test the limits of their understanding through "cultural cross fertilisations" in which they embrace lived experiences disparate from their own.[419] In doing so they induce epiphanies and awaken dormant aspects of their personhood. They also strengthen their character through the hardships that they endure along the way and the challenges that are posed to their assumptions.

What it means to cross-fertilise is to adopt a cosmopolitan attitude, to embrace different cultures and come to understand their systems of knowledge. This epistemological process rejects myopic, insular thinking and the notion that ideas should be limited to the circles of one's ancestry. Education should extend to the traditions and wisdom of other peoples. Goethe captured this cosmopolitan spirit when he argued that the epoch of World literature had arrived.[420] These theorists did not focus education within a specific discipline or intellectual tradition, but rather encouraged the acquisition of knowledge through a complete immersion in the wider world. They considered a cosmopolitan perspective to be the best way to expand the material from which to form a self-determined identity. As Schleiermacher comments:

> Hence I cannot develop myself in isolation, as the
> artist does. In isolation all the juices of my mind
> dry up, and the course of my thought is arrested. I

must get out and join a community with other spirits, to see the many forms of humanity and what is alien to me, to know what can become of myself, and to determine more securely through give and take my own nature.[421]

The experience of the alien is not feared or automatically judged but considered rationally and assimilated into the rest of one's value system if it is determined to be true. Goethe readily acknowledged that he found his influences in different cultural traditions arguing that we can thank "a thousand influences of the great world, from which we appropriate what we can and what is suitable to us. What is important is to have a soul which loves truth and receives it wherever it can find it."[422] The discovery of truth is supremely important to the *Bildung* journey, and truth can be found in many places, but never in parochial isolation.

In drawing on various traditions from an early age, the individual discovers and rediscovers themself, overcoming their own weaknesses through experimentation while solidifying the values they will come to hold later in life. The moving encounters of their youth, in which the Platonic forms are revealed through experience, inspire a life dedicated to their pursuit. Beauty is the compass in this revelatory journey, helping the traveller navigate through new social milieus and sustaining their natural inclination towards moral goodness. Beauty also serves "to maximise contacts with the world" which can consequently lead to a fuller truth.[423]

Goethe describes the Platonic structure of the poetic person who discovers themself through their *Bildung* journey. They search for a common humanity found not within the arbitrary boundaries of territorial divisions, but in a universal quest for Beauty, Truth and Goodness:

The poet may, as a man and citizen, love his native land; but the native land of his poetic energies and poetic action is the Good, Noble, and Beautiful, which is confined to no province nor country, which he is to seize upon and body forth wherever he finds it. Therein is he like the eagle, which hovers, with free gaze, over all countries, and to which it is of no consequence whether the hare, on which he pounces down is running through Prussia or through Saxony.[424]

That patriotism could expand to something that is universal, based upon shared values, and not upon inherited territorial boundaries, is one of the ways in which this philosophy is extraordinarily progressive, striving for a unifying consciousness of all of humanity. Nationalism becomes a shared Platonic ideal that anyone can hold, and identity is found in values that supersede geographical, ethnic, and historical frames of reference.

Although it is the individual who undertakes this journey, they do so in a spirit of camaraderie with others working towards this common end. *Bildung* represents the willingness to explore concepts through a web of interconnected relationships marked by the desire to forge affinities through encounters of the mind. Sustained interaction and dialogue play a vital role in this process of self-discovery.

The journey was not only a metaphor portrayed in the *Bildungsroman*. The theorists of the Beautiful Soul often had revelatory experiences of travel and discovery in their youth. The Grand Tour, the *Bildungsreise* in the German context, was an educational journey that took the young bourgeoisie across Europe to witness the artistic and cultural marvels of classical antiquity and the Renaissance, while improving their language skills and discovering themselves through encounters with other peoples and cultures. Goethe, like his character Wilhelm, was profoundly influenced by his travels—in his case in Italy from 1786-1788, which he chronicled in *Italian Journey* (1816).[425] His experiences viewing objects from antiquity and immersing himself in Italian traditions inspired his ideas on aesthetic education. Some of the finest hours of his life, when he enjoyed the most elevated feelings, were had during this time.[426]

Perhaps from their personal experiences, the theorists of the Beautiful Soul recognised the power of youthful explorations to solidify personal moral frameworks and systems of understanding. They believed that if the optimism, excitement, and energy of one's early youth is fully actualised, then it will inform the moral and intellectual trajectory of a person's subsequent life. From this perspective youthful ideals are not meant to be sustained in the abstract, but rather firmly embedded within the world. Even though the process of aspiring to live a life of noble ideals can begin at any age, it is most advantageous to start early when the mind is still malleable and open to the possibilities of change.

Once the initial journey of self-discovery has taken place in one's youth, either in the literal or figurative sense, the metaphor of the *Bildungsreise* continues with the corresponding duty to systematically integrate oneself into the fabric of society in deeper relationships with others. To be self-cultivated means to remain endlessly open to new knowledge. None of the features of the concept are a given; all require continual effort, re-interpretation, revision, and a commitment to elaborate upon the values discovered in young adulthood.

In the end, the journey is a metaphor for the life of a beautiful soul. This life is not without its missteps and misfortunes, but it is lived with dynamic purpose and there is an evolution that can be traced from beginning to end. As Goethe declared "He is the happiest man who can set the end of his life in connection with the beginning."[427]

Bildung itself is implemented through this journey and the life cycle of the people who enact it. In the future, if the larger social reality reflects the structures of the Beautiful Soul, it will be far easier for new generations to adapt its basic tenets, hold its values, and educate themselves accordingly. It is always harder to be a pioneer in unchartered terrains of thought than to follow a well-trodden path. To ensure social progress while this transformation is taking place is, according to Schiller, like the work of a mechanic who fixes a watch as its wheels turn. Measures must be taken to support a society that is trying to emancipate itself without having to resort to devastating deconstruction through revolution. Encouraging citizens to start their *Bildung* journey by breaking from the structures of their predetermined environment is the best way to mend an imperfect society as it continues to spin.

The characteristics that comprise the beautiful soul's journey can be understood as the pursuit of Platonic perfection. This concept is a forward-looking meditation on what the human condition can become if individuals aspire to improve their present state, and in doing so, optimise their capacities through concerted action. In affirming an ideal in which Beauty, Truth, and Goodness are the objective values, the theorists of the Beautiful Soul challenge people to rise above the imperfections that impede their capacity to fully utilise their faculties. As Schiller writes: "the soul swells with noblest emotions when a divine ideal is placed before it."[428] Like the instinctual desire to find one's ultimate *telos*, a vital life force stimulates the soul into the pursuit of perfection.

Through the voice of Wilhelm in *Wilhelm Meister*, Goethe claims that most people live impoverished, fragmented existences but that within them, an energy can be harnessed to achieve the ideal.[429] This force is as tenacious as the will to live; it is a primordial urge that acts as the catalyst for the ascent out of personal imperfections and bleak social realities. Even the most ordinary individuals can achieve the extraordinary when this energy is recognised and set in motion. *Entfremdung,* or alienation, a term that Hegel concretised in his *Phenomenology of Spirit* (1807), but was earlier explored by Fichte and Schiller, can be employed here to describe the impoverished state to which Goethe refers.[430] The alienated human soul waits to be animated by this inner spark, facilitated by the right environmental conditions. It seeks to triumph over the gravitational pull towards mediocrity, coming closer to the ideals towards which every life is ultimately directed. Fichte addresses human limitations by uniting the phenomenal and the spiritual world:

> Insofar as man is spirit, therefore, he is not merely a part of this world but rather the ground of its existence. And by virtue of his consciousness and reason, it is within his power to reassert his primacy over it, by coming to recognise where the true dependence lies.[431]

Within this framework, he develops a concept in which people can rise above their current state and attain the ultimate ideal. In a similar vein, Schiller demonstrates the discrepancy between people's present condition and their essential nature. But he believed it is their purpose and destiny to harmonise the two in order to approach the realm of perfection.[432] Schiller concludes that a spark is struck, and a person is on their way to the ideal, if they risk the reality of their material conditions for the "embellishment of [their] existence," preferring form over substance.[433] Goethe argues that this expressed inclination towards perfection, which transcends the base demands of earthly comforts, is the true measure of a person. As one of his maxims notes: "Perfection is the measure of heaven, and the wish to be perfect the measure of man."[434]

Despite the seeming utopian nature of this perspective, the philosophy of the Beautiful Soul acknowledges human embeddedness in an imperfect reality and the inevitability of incompleteness, or even failure, in one's attempt towards self-cultivation. Its theorists were aware of the impracticality of principles that advance utopic visions without considering the frailty and moral flaws to which humans are naturally inclined. They avoid the hypocrisy of demanding unattainable ends in the development of a humanist philosophy that is meant to empower, not to oppress people.

They also concede that the ideals of one's youth might be more difficult to maintain when the realities of everyday life dismantle the dreams of the past. In a passage of Schiller's poem, "The Ideals", he captures the sad truth implicit in this sentiment:

> The glorious suns my youth enchanting
> Have set in never-ending night;
> Those blest ideals now are wanting
> That swelled my heart with mad delight.
> The offspring of my dream hath perished,
> My faith in being passed away;
> The godlike hopes that once I cherish
> Are now reality's sad prey.[435]

However, acknowledging the experiences that might with time compromise one's youthful ideals does not mean accepting defeat. To preserve one's idealism is not a function of living under perfect circumstances, but rather a choice that requires effort and provides a source of resolve, meaning, and direction. To dismiss ideals as nothing more than the charming follies of one's youth, not a real state of affairs, is understandable when the poetic spirit of what one once felt has been lost. But ultimately, such a perspective diminishes the prospects of the adult who has allowed themself to forget the great beauty of what they have experienced in the past. Although comprehensible given the strains of daily life, this is perhaps the most tragic mistake of all.

Even if a pure ideal can never be fully achieved by people who are inevitably bound to human shortcomings, the will to strive towards ideals is what is most important. As the beautiful soul of *Wilhelm Meister* says, what matters is "That I am still advancing, never retrograding; that my conduct is approximating more and more to the image I have formed of perfection."[436] As Goethe reflects in his autobiography, "All men of a good disposition feel, with increasing cultivation, that they have a double part to play in the world—a real one and an ideal one, and in this feeling is the ground of everything noble to be sought."[437] In his *Aesthetic Letters*, Schiller similarly respects both the inevitable constraints of the real and the prospects of the ideal. He maintains that the ideal can be preserved if reality does not injure form, or form injure reality. His poem, "The Ideal and the Real Life", elegantly captures this sentiment:

> The weavers of the web—the fates—but sway
> The matter and the things of clay;

Safe from change that time to matter gives,
Nature's blest playmate, free at will to stray
With gods a god, amidst the fields of day,
The form, the archetype, serenely lives.
Wouldn't thou soar heavenward on its joyous wing?
Cast from thee, earth, the bitter and the real,
High from this cramped and dungeon being, spring
Into the realm of the ideal![438]

The final phrase, "spring into the realm of the ideal," powerfully expresses the forward looking, aspirational tenor of this philosophy. In the spirit of this phrase, Schiller and Goethe analysed their own limitations and weaknesses, while tracing their development. In constantly striving for perfection, they shed their faults and slowly reached closer to the ideal.[439] This is the ethos with which they hoped people would embrace life to sustain the rigorous standards upon which this philosophy is founded.

Beyond their personal conviction in the ideals they espoused, their acute understanding of the human condition reveals the psychological need for such ideals. In *On the Limits of State Action*, Humboldt explicitly expresses this sentiment based on his observations that an ideal is highly motivating and offers an irreplaceable sense of purpose:

> The idea of perfection will still hover in front of a man, even if he is not accustomed to think in terms of the sum of all moral excellence in one absolute ideal, and to conceive of himself as in a relation with an ideal being: it will be to him the incentive to activity, and the stuff of all his happiness.[440]

An unalloyed ideal is considered essential to inspire humanity, for, just as most people would not

imagine God as vengeful and merciless, no one would want to pursue a humanist concept that is profoundly pessimistic about the possibilities of improving the human condition.

But, unlike Christianity, which, according to Goethe and Schiller, espouses a sterile, joyless ideal, this philosophy is life giving and fully embraces humanity. Both poets admired the Greeks, for, as Schiller declaims in his poem "The Gods of Greece," their Gods were more human, and their humans were more divine.[441] To become godlike, or to theoretically have the capacity to possess qualities of the divine, is integrated into this concept. As Schlegel writes, "every good person becomes more and more God. To become God, to be human, to cultivate oneself, are expressions that all mean the same thing."[442] The aim of this idea of perfection is to inspire humans to believe in something greater than themselves without succumbing to the fear or subservience that other ideologies require. Humboldt argues:

> This very idea of perfection, the goal of all his actions, is really not a mere cold abstraction of the reason but a warm impulse of the heart, which draws his own being towards that of others. For in them too there exists a similar capacity for greater perfection, and this he may be able to elicit or improve upon.[443]

The theorists of the Beautiful Soul, however, identified a significant problem: most individuals with influence in character development, such as teachers, speak not of the ideal, but of the imperfect real, and, in doing so, inhibit the attainment of higher ends.[444] To propagate ideals becomes the responsibility of those who hold positions of creative power. Artists and intellectuals are responsible because, through their use of the imagination, they can most compellingly portray the ideal and make people believe in what otherwise might appear futile. They have the unique ability to lift their work above reality while retaining the indispensable influences of the sensual world.[445] Fiction, especially, can grapple with everyday concerns while descriptively portraying ideals that reality might not allow. Goethe argues that the tendency to see oneself in the noblest characters of novels and "place oneself on equality with something higher" is healthy and necessary to fight the boredom of everyday life and to preserve the vision of something greater.[446]

Since this concept is intended not only for abstract contemplation, but also as a foundational belief system and a practical philosophy, its theorists deployed fiction to convey its core elements to a wider public. Literary accounts serve to advance a perfect, God-like ideal to inspire awe and admiration that is motivating and life-affirming. At the same time, they depict the tribulations of persons who exhibit characteristics of goodness, yet, nevertheless, possess significant human shortcomings. This integration of an affirmative, enlightening ideal with compassion for such limitations offers a compelling framework for an optimistic, yet realistic assessment of the human condition.

The artful amalgamation of the real and the ideal in both philosophy and literature is a gift particular to the theorists of the Beautiful Soul. Wieland's originality, for example, is that his writing maintains an ideal while also exploring concrete human realities.[447] Goethe and Schiller portray characters who popularise the concept with great efficacy because they are vulnerable to the same imperfections and excesses as any ordinary person. None of their characters can be said to have achieved the perfect state of the Beautiful Soul: their short-comings are made apparent, and it is their struggles in this journey, not the end itself, that are most insightful.

Literary creations, such as Wilhelm Meister, are undoubtedly on a *Bildung* odyssey, but they never fully attain the status of *die schöne Seele*. Schiller, for example, was not certain that Wilhelm had truly become self-cultivated because Goethe's protagonist never demonstrates the ability to perform "a proper aesthetic judgment."[448] Such literary characters' frustrations with the world, missteps, misfortunes, and feelings of existential uncertainty, loss, and loneliness are all part of what makes their story compelling. If these authors had depicted supremely beautiful souls who were perfect from the beginning, there would be no lessons learned or questions for practical consideration. Wilhelm Meister's story is not only about the development of his personal capacities but, from another perspective, it is about his practical attempts to live in the world.[449] It is within this realistic orientation that elements of the ideal can be found. As Schiller remarks *à propos Wilhelm Meister* in a letter to Goethe on July 2, 1796:

> If I had to express in so many words the goal which Wilhelm has finally reached after so many aberrations, I should say he enters from an empty and undefined Ideal into a defined actual life, but without thereby forfeiting the idealising power.[450]

Commensurate with this interpretation, the ideal is discovered, therefore, not in the end state of the characters but rather in accordance with their will to seek ideals in the definition of their lives. This focus resonates with the definition of moral beauty which, as we have seen, is found not in an inherent condition but rather in the process of an individual overcoming personal failures, having their character tested under trying circumstances, and ultimately improving their internal constitution despite hardship and pain.

The fundamentally human depiction of the pursuit of inner perfection in the literature reveals important aspects of this philosophy and addresses two of the main areas of concern or potential weakness in its reception. The first concern responds to one of the strongest critiques of the concept. The premise of this critique is that as soon a beautiful soul enters the imperfect world, they necessarily become corrupted and cannot achieve their idealised ends. Hegel tried to dismiss the ideal of the Beautiful Soul on the assumption that, by virtue of operating in an unbeautiful world, they will inevitably become corrupted and, in effect, self-liquidating.[451]

Yet, as the literary accounts demonstrate, this concept is aspirational and does not require perfect realisation. The individual can cultivate themselves and, in the process, come closer to this ideal. They do not have to arrive at the ideal to validate its existence or to justify its pursuit. Therefore, this critique does not detract from the validity of the value system that was being promoted. Hegel was commenting on the responsibility of the individual and the nature of the human condition. Nevertheless, his scepticism about the concept makes clear the high expectations placed on the Beautiful Soul to remain true to itself but also have demonstrable effects in the world. The literature on the Beautiful Soul reveals the intent of its proponents to respond to this critique by employing poetry, novels, and plays to humanise the concept and to demonstrate that it can be compatible with lived experience but still retain philosophical purity.

The second critique is one of a more contemporary nature. The words "perfectibility" and "ideal" in reference to humanity often have negative connotations, especially in the German context. The perfection of the human soul, a beautiful ideal to some, might signal an ideology ripe for fascist manipulation in which hierarchies of "superior" souls are created. However, it would be a mistake to impose a twentieth century understanding of these words on their eighteenth and nineteenth century formulation. The term "perfection" in this philosophy has nothing to do with conditions of birth, and therefore cannot be associated with racial theories. It is in fact precisely the opposite: perfection is framed in reference to cultivated states of immaterial being. The Beautiful Soul offers the antithesis of hierarchical structures, class stratification, or ethnic chauvinism— a point which becomes only further apparent when considered in relation to the concept's centrality of subjective expression, egalitarianism, and a concern for the social good.

An exception to this foundational perspective is Johann Caspar Lavater (1741-1801), a Swiss pastor and philosopher of the controversial field of physiognomy. In a distorted appropriation of the concept, with pseudo-scientific observations, he suggested that beautiful souls are necessarily housed in beautiful bodies, thereby introducing a physical criterion to a distinctly non-corporeal concept. Lavater's conflation of corporeal essence with cognitive and spiritual capacities presents an ideological threat to the legitimacy of the Beautiful Soul. His bastardisation of the philosophy's original intent has been well-recognised by scholars and is considered an apocryphal anomaly.[452] The unfortunate rise of the cult of physiognomy around 1775, when Lavater published *Essays on*

Physiognomy, demonstrates how a concept can be grotesquely misappropriated and subsequently haunted by an illegitimate legacy that represents its opposite. However detrimental Lavater's ideas were, they had the positive effect of eliciting a clear rejection of such arguments, which then reinforced the true spirit of this philosophy.

The rhetoric of the Beautiful Soul on the concept of perfection was demonstrated to be the antithesis of dogmatic substantiations of human inferiority or fascist ideologies. It accomplished a dual feat of resurrecting the perfected ends of antiquity while rescuing notions of the ideal from their perversion. If this philosophy had held greater prevalence in popular culture in the twentieth century, as it did in the late eighteenth and early nineteenth centuries, then perhaps the course of history would have been different and the tragic developments in Germany could have been contested with an ideology that was diametrically opposed to physiological determinism.

Since the concept of the ideal in this philosophy is reinterpreted within a humanist framework with the intention of worldly realisation, individuals must never lower their aspirations to anything less than the perfection of their soul. If values of kindness and benevolence, as represented by the ideal form of the Good, are diminished to mere displays of power and wealth in a society where material gain triumphs over moral standing, then political figures will serve only themselves, and citizens will seek nothing more than their immediate needs. This will keep humanity subjected to animalistic impulses that possess no moral beauty. However, if duties associated with human decency are affirmed as reflecting the ideal, then people will find greater incentive to work towards its realisation.

Schiller argues that a vulgar mind will disgrace the noblest things by treating them as mundane. A great mind, by contrast, will ennoble even the smallest, most common things.[453] In his opinion, the Dutch and Flemish painters were examples of the former, and the Greeks and Italians were examples of the latter: elevating every creation to the ideal and, consequently, elevating humanity. The aims of the cultivated individual can never be lowered in order to attain them with greater ease.[454] Like a painting crudely rendered, the superficial person will not excite virtue in others. But, like the elegant form of a Greek statue which remains eternally inspiring, those who maintain a nobility of soul will animate the moral beauty in others.

On September 20, 1780 Goethe wrote that "this desire to raise up as high as possible the pyramid of my existence—whose basis and foundation were given to me—outweighs everything else and can hardly be forgotten even for a moment. I dare not tarry. I am already at an advanced age, and perhaps fate will break me in the middle of life and the Tower of Babel will remain an incomplete stump. At least they should be able to say it was a daring attempt."[455] Goethe's attempt to reach the pinnacle of his existence produced a body of work that inspired others in their own pursuit of self-cultivation.

Like Goethe, the *salonnières* inspired their contemporaries to pursue ideals through self-cultivation. They were able to witness their efforts to heal society without violent or destructively reactionary means by tracing the *Bildung* journey of their salon participants in their salons. As Schleiermacher notes in reference to the salons of Varnhagen and Herz, to engage in such social relations:

> Provided the individual with opportunities to go beyond his own limits to become acquainted with other and foreign worlds, so that by and by no

human manifestation would remain unknown to him and even the strangest characters and circumstances would become familiar ('friendly and, as it were, neighbourly') to him. This task was accomplished by means of freely associating rational people engaged in mutual education or *Bildung*.[456]

Schleiermacher understood that the salons initiated a *Bildung* journey, introducing individuals to new worlds and ways of being. The *salonnières* concurred that their salons represented a developmental transition from childhood to enlightened adulthood, and they had strong views on what such a journey should entail. Schlegel agreed with her husband that a man's journey involves three stages: of boyhood, cultivated young adulthood, and maturity in love. But she believed that women should go through the same three stages, though they were frequently excluded from the second.[457] In her *Bildungsroman*, Schlegel's character Florentin depicts this "inner pilgrimage" by traveling widely and discovering important lessons along the way.[458]

Participants often embarked upon this journey in the salon at a critical moment in their lives when they were young, impressionable and open to change. People entered salons at a time in their young adulthood when their love affairs, friendships, interests, and professions were being experimented with and solidified.[459] The salon afforded them practical forays into culture, philosophy, and the arts that the fictitious journey of the *Bildungsroman* could only represent. In this space, individuals shaped their identity, matured their faculties, and developed a concrete belief system in communication with others.

The metaphor of the journey within the salon underscored

the fact that the Beautiful Soul is a pursuit which requires no material resources. Humboldt's revelatory *Bildung* journey, for example, occurred, not through physical travel but within the intellectual landscape of Herz and Varnhagen's homes. He attributed much of his professional success and the social relationships which most influenced him at a formative time of his life to their salons.[460]

The journey was, therefore, not necessarily one of physical movement—although it was sometimes portrayed as such in the literature for clarity—but rather an intellectual movement across the psycho-social terrains of the urban salons. If new ideas were explored, assumptions questioned, and other cultural traditions discovered, it could occur within these local spaces as it had for Humboldt. Indeed, the individual who was able to enliven their surroundings with their intellect would gain from the revelations that were to come in their subsequent physical travels; they would have the internal resources to find greater fulfilment in their relationship to the wider world.

In creating the environment for the *Bildung* journey to take place, the *salonnières* maintained Platonic ideals and reflected them in their salons. The beautiful environments that they created were a physical representation of the abstract form of Beauty in whose grace they found inspiration. Since Beauty and Truth, according to this philosophy, are inextricably intertwined, then creating a beautiful atmosphere was conducive to the pursuit of Truth. Conversations were undertaken upon the basic assumption that through shared intellectual practice, absolute knowledge could be found. With the manifestation of Truth came Goodness by making oneself receptive to other people and ideas. Thus, these ideals were both embedded in and formed by the very structure of the salons. Structure and process aligned in the pursuit of Platonic perfection.

The *salonnières* understood that they must have the courage to pursue the ideal for if they allowed pessimism to impede moral growth, then their lack of conviction would demonstrate short-sightedness and frailty. As Varnhagen commented: "My whole belief is in the conviction of progress, of the perfectibility and development of the universe to even better understanding and welfare in the highest sense."[461] This was as much a statement of what she believed to be true as a declaration of the way she had decided to live, which, in its affirmative style, demonstrated her attainment of the Beautiful Soul.

To pursue the ideal, however, did not mean that the *salonnières* held others accountable to a specific definition of the concept. Rather, they developed each individual's specific relationship to the Platonic Triad while also interrogating the possibilities of objective knowledge. The *salonnières* encouraged experimentation in the evolution of the self and appreciated the inevitability of human failings along the way. To participate in a salon meant to implicitly acknowledge one's own limitations, and the inevitable uncertainties and fallacies of the reality in which one exists, while at the same time moving beyond these imperfections towards a shared, mutually articulated end.

In the case of Varnhagen, her view of society "included both the idealism which creates the future, and the realism which forms the present."[462] She often vocalised her desire to overcome the imperfections that she identified in the world. "Rahel escaped from a present in which she believed there was not yet any place for her, and her refuge was not the past but a better future. That was why she pleaded: 'When I am dead, rescue the image of my soul.'"[463] Varnhagen's concern for the future represented a shared characteristic, a rare attribute that the most prominent *salonnières* exhibited, which was a precondition for the establishment of their salons. Varnhagen never assumed or unquestioningly accepted a single, static reality, contending that many distinct realities can be cultivated within the soul. She acknowledged that all social realities are constructs shaped by human thought and activity and that the individual can transform them through the power of their will. She had the audacious vision to see beyond what was and imagine what could be; the idealism to believe in the development of a new, more perfect world; and the audacity to deploy her innate agency to bring the latent ideal into existence.

The *salonnières* adopted the ideals specific to the Beautiful Soul because they represented an alternative to their present, imperfect reality and proposed an elegant theory of what could exist. Grounded in a German philosophical tradition that granted them the freedom to contribute to its development, the Beautiful Soul affirmed an ideal that was far removed from their existing reality.[464] And yet it still seemed feasible to implement within the cultural context of Germany at the time. The way they systematically implemented their ideals suggests that the *salonnières* considered them to be as pragmatic and achievable as they were aspirational. Instead of containing them within an abstract realm of philosophical discourse, they demonstrated the viability of their idealism through practice.

But, despite the objective attractiveness and feasibility of the ideals that they espoused, to change social reality proved difficult. Opposition against emancipation remained intense. For the aristocrats and elite, the prevailing societal structures benefited their social and economic status and so it was easy to assume them "natural" and necessary. Likewise, the lack of economic resources, social standing, and political imagination of a large percentage of the population inhibited their capacity to envisage alternative realities. These conditions, in effect, validated and naturalised the status quo.

However, even when it seemed futile to maintain such a utopic ideal, and progress was thwarted by apathy and concerted resistance, the *salonnières* preserved their faith in "the world's eternal perfectibility."[465] During the time of riots against Jews around 1819, for example, Varnhagen and her brother, Ludwig Robert, concurred that despite these momentary relapses, the world still moved forward, and progress was possible if they maintained constancy.[466] "It's moving, the world," Varnhagen observed.[467] Even though she knew that within her own lifetime she almost certainly would not see the developments that she hoped to witness, the possibility that they would occur for future generations was enough to keep her optimism alive. "This old earth must be made brighter and future men must be better and happier."[468] Varnhagen was convinced that knowledge of what *should* be would triumph, even if it required waiting "a thousand years for the sunshine that is to make the plant grow!"[469] Such a long-term, selfless perspective was precisely what made her vision feasible, for she was not blinded by the prospect of immediate success.

Despite the tragic ends to her love affairs, financial troubles, the instabilities of war, and the humiliation she endured from never being fully accepted in society, Varnhagen remained hopeful throughout her life, echoing statements in her youth as an older woman: "I believe completely in the progression, the perfectibility, the continued improvement of the universe, toward ever greater understanding and wealth in the highest sense; happiness and the giving of happiness."[470] With regards to the challenges of her time, such as the French occupation and the Wars of Liberation, she was one of the few members of her social circle who continued to have faith that the fundamental principles of the French Revolution could still be achieved. She maintained her youthful ideals throughout her life and did not allow cynicism to corrupt what she believed was morally and politically possible.[471]

Although the *salonnières* possessed constant hope that sustained their activities, the beautiful world that they envisioned required more than their personal conviction. Like any democratic undertaking, the challenge of inclusivity depended on the cooperation and consensus of others from all sides of the social spectrum. The only way to transform a flawed social order was if another, more perfect reality was manifested, not simply in philosophical essays, but in its real-world enactment. A discursive space was necessary to facilitate this shift in perception. The *salonnières* understood that they would first have to make their vision tangible before it would be widely accepted.

Their salons became the physical representation of the ideals of the Beautiful Soul, a controlled environment in which they oversaw the rules and the structures that governed the small worlds that they created.[472] By enacting the ideal through the systematic implementation of the principles of the Beautiful Soul, by empirically demonstrating that new forms of social order were indeed possible, desirable, and ultimately necessary, the *salonnières* made alternative realities psychologically tenable. In blurring the apparently intractable divide between the real and ideal, by showing that elements of the ideal could emerge within the present, imperfect circumstances, the dominant critique of the Beautiful Soul as a misbegotten and unrealistic goal was shown to be nothing more than a deficient understanding of what was possible.

The salon as an intimate, semi-private institution that flourished in the domestic setting of the home, detached from the decision-making powers of a monarchy or state, was uniquely suited to serve the *salonnières'* utopic ends. It allowed them to freely examine the merits and problems associated with their ideology and to control those social structures required to achieve the ideals they promulgated. They no longer had to accept imperfect social conditions but could, instead, invent principles that regulated ideas and actions. By bringing the Beautiful Soul's philosophy to life in their salons, by making the ideal the very structure upon which social interactions were based, they demonstrated that the Platonic Triad was not a nebulous concept detached from human activity, but a viable principle for governing society as the ancient Greeks had professed.

Today, it may be more difficult to embark upon the *Bildungsreise* because the ideals that are inextricably connected to that journey have been systematically undermined. Modernity became a cynical project that destroyed the ancient vision of Beauty, Goodness, and Truth. It is, of course, understandable why society took this turn. After the tragedies of the two World Wars, maintaining idealism might seem impossible given the horrifying extent of the devastation and innumerable lives lost. However, ideals have never been maintained in times of flourishing. Indeed, it is often during catastrophic periods of social conflict, warfare, and cultural decline when they are turned to and needed most.

The belief in ideals is not about representing the world as it is, but rather maintaining faith that a more perfect reality can exist and will eventually be attainable by taking responsibility for our own actions. If every person aspired to be kinder, wiser, more benevolent, rational, and forgiving, then naturally we would have fewer problems in the world. Social progress begins by acknowledging our duty and capacity to shape reality for the better by improving our own inner life. It requires a fearless commitment to counter the decline in values and the threats to human decency.

Within my salons I noticed that participants often distance themselves from expressing idealistic beliefs. Ironically the decline of ideals is responsible for many of the social and environmental catastrophes that we are experiencing. Yet people seem afraid to imagine alternative structures that could restore a broken society because they might be labelled as naïve. I found it surprising that many people who take part in salons, even the most seemingly optimistic among them, maintain such cynical views.

Whether it has been in a salon on politics, love, or religion, many participants reject the notion that life has a greater meaning beyond immediate experiences or that we should have faith in the prospects for human progress. Participants seem to have absorbed the pervasive idea that the idealist is somehow "out of touch with reality." Cynicism and a detached posture of self-conscious irony is actively encouraged, not critiqued, because this stance is believed to be the norm of social behaviour. Only after numerous events during which a measure of intimacy was reached did some of the salon participants reveal that they are truly idealists.

It is perverse that the idealistic viewpoint that takes the greatest moral strength to maintain, and promises more positive outcomes, is so severely undermined that people are embarrassed to express it—while believing in nothing so as never to be held accountable is considered admirable. Tragically, pessimism, selfishness, and indifference are the idols of these cynical times, dismantling the great ideals of the past.

The pursuit of self-cultivation, however, demands idealism. We must have the strength of character to uphold ideals and live by them. Cynicism stands in diametrical opposition to a philosophy that places ultimate faith in the human capacity to improve. No matter what personal trials we may have endured or social challenges we face, we can decide to remain optimistic. We can choose how we view reality and what we wish to believe. Nihilism is a way of perceiving the world that often justifies character weakness. It is not a more accurate representation of reality. Having the inner strength to challenge a nihilistic mentality, and the will to strive towards greater values, is a demonstration of a nobility of character and a preliminary act towards the cultivation of a more beautiful soul.

CHAPTER 14

On Creating a Beautiful Life

B EAUTY is the defining feature of the Beautiful Soul, the quality that unifies all aspects of this philosophy. In its simplest formulation, this concept maintains the Greek notion that the beautiful possesses the characteristics of the good and that the good features in all manifestations of the beautiful. The relationship is elegantly summarised by Goethe who remarks "The beautiful is not different from the good: The beautiful is the good which shows itself to us pleasingly veiled."[473]

According to Goethe, only people with uncultivated moral faculties will fail to comprehend and internalise the full significance of this union, for those whose morality has been developed are ineluctably drawn to beauty.[474] Schlegel affirms that beauty is the pleasurable manifestation of the good and he postulates that reaching towards a metaphysical beauty can only occur through *Bildung*.[475] In cultivating one's aesthetic faculties, one therefore comes closer to the good:

> If we have properly trained our "taste" and have
> thus adequately exercised the appropriate faculties
> of our mind, we will always and unerringly desire
> what is good because it is at the same time beauti-
> ful, that is, in conformity, or harmonious, with our
> "natural" constitution.[476]

The relationship between the two is considered a natural union, the most basic law of the universe. Goethe claims, "The beautiful is a manifestation of secret laws of nature, which, without its presence, would never have been revealed."[477]

Schiller conceptually links beauty and goodness to truth when he argues in his *Aesthetic Letters* that beauty requires a pure concept of human nature and that this concept, rather than being born from experience, follows a "transcendental way" to truth.[478] He clarifies his definition of beauty by distinguishing two types. The first is an "energising beauty" that excites us and elicits an immediate response. This beauty is required for the "sensuous man" whose emotions are too intense and must be rebalanced with form and thought. The second is a "melting beauty" which is calming. This beauty is required for the "spiritual man" whose concern for form and abstract thought must be conjoined with the senses and his ability to feel. Energising beauty alone can become an excessive force, and melting beauty can become too constrained, but brought together they represent perfection.

For Schiller, aesthetic experience, therefore, is a dynamic equilibrium between the senses and form. In what he refers to as "the aesthetic state," the ideal condition towards which we should aspire, our consciousness will be dictated neither by the passions nor by reason alone. Thus, Schiller makes the transcendental deduction that beauty is the balancing point between reason and the senses. Aesthetic experience liberates us from uncultivated impressions and volatile emotions through the serene, freeing effect of beauty on the human soul. Simultaneously, it arouses excitement about *a priori* knowledge and abstract ends. This aesthetic intermediary state is discussed by Schiller as the "play drive," a concept alluded to previously, which took inspiration from both Winckelmann's notion that art is the product of gaiety, as well as from Goethe's earlier writings.[479] The play drive has "as its object to suppress time in time, to reconcile the state of transition or becoming with absolute being, change with identity."[480] Schiller's interpretation of beauty, then, allows for the reconciliation of the passions with rationality and facilitates the harmonious integration of opposing human faculties.

For both Schiller and Goethe, listening to a beautiful musical composition, for example, places the subject in a state of sublime serenity which momentarily releases him from the volatile pull of his passions. This harmonious state is active and awake, fully present in the immediate sensory experience, while also remaining intellectually detached, immersed in the conceptual realm. Goethe believes that music "should set free the joy of living, moral confidence, whole-hearted energy, and above all, the impulse of reason; it should encourage the spirit of clearness of thought, the sense of the eternal contempt for pettiness, and nothingness."[481] Schiller makes a similar argument when talking about beauty more generally: "beauty is, to be sure, the work of free contemplation, and we step with her into the world of ideas—but, it must be observed, without thereby leaving the world of sense, as is the case with cognition of truth."[482] Beauty can combine the positive, world-disclosing dimensions of emotion with the enlightening meditations of the rational mind:

> Beauty is therefore certainly an object for us, since reflection is the condition under which we have a sensation of it; but it is at the same time a state of our personality, since feeling is the condition under which we have a conception of it. It is then certainly form, because we contemplate it; but it is at the

same time life, because we feel it. In a word, it is at once our state and our act.[483]

Beauty possesses the unique ability to restore a divided nature and balance the soul. This, we will see, has the function of making humans more capable of productively contributing to and existing within a social whole.

Although the beauty found in art and nature is material, in the sense that it physically exists in the world, it contains an eternal, disembodied essence: the immutable form of the beautiful. Thus, a divine dimension is discovered within every worldly experience of beauty, and thereby sensory impression enters the conceptual realm.

Furthermore, beauty, according to Schiller, has the distinct ability to excite both the imagination and the intellect.[484] Its wide scope gives it an all-pervasive force in positively shaping those who choose to embrace its powers, and by extension, the social structures to which these people are bound. In its imaginativeness, beauty offers the individual release from a conventional reality of blunted emotions and unlived possibilities. Beauty inspires an acute receptivity to the world.

Goethe's poetic imagination, for example, was excited when he went on "image hunts," solitary walks where he found symbolic meaning when he was struck by what he often referred to as an "*aperçu*"—the transformative suddenness of an impression brought about by natural beauty.[485] The unexpected immediacy of the experience overcame the anticipated routines of daily life and thus his artistic creativity formed within the vital exercise of his imagination.

In relationship to the intellect, beauty provides a means to access greater truths, to perceive the elegance of the universe, and to illuminate from within the ultimate purpose of existence. As Schiller writes in his poem "The Artists," "Only through beauty's morning gate didst thou the land of knowledge find."[486] Beauty brings a simplicity to thought and a clarity in our understanding of the nature of being and the value of worldly associations. To Schiller, the beauty of symmetry and reoccurring forms in nature follows rules that uncover fundamental dimensions of knowledge.[487] Goethe affirms that a mathematical equation or scientific theory that is beautiful clearly communicates the theoretical truth that it seeks to reveal, solidifying understanding through an aesthetic elegance that mirrors natural systems.[488] Thus, the spectrum of human achievement, from the imaginativeness of the arts and humanities to the primal truths found in mathematics and the sciences, are immeasurably enhanced by, if not indivisibly tied to, beauty.

The ineluctable indeterminateness of aesthetic experience is precisely what makes it valuable in expanding one's consciousness. Beauty offers profound "satisfaction without any interest" that is a phenomenon complete in and of itself.[489] Ironically, since it seeks no accomplishment or specific end, the most important aims can be achieved because they come about organically without strain or force.[490] The ennobled mind that perceives of beauty wants for nothing. It finds pleasure in the contemplation of the phenomenon and does not desire to appropriate the objects that it observes. It is free of the dependence on resources beyond its basic subsistence and does not fear dispossessing that which it never wishes to possess. These insights are based on Kant and Shaftesbury's earlier notions on the disinterested and representational nature of beauty. In his *Critique of Judgement* (1790), Kant argues that if something depends on beauty or if one's interests are interlaced with one's judgement, then the judgement cannot be considered one of pure taste.[491] Similarly, in his dialogue "The Moralists" (1709) Shaftesbury claims that observing a lovely landscape is a gratifying experience in itself. The rolling hills, resplendent colours, and trees that dot the horizon will arouse feelings of intense sensory and intellectual pleasure, bringing elation with a calming clarity. If the encounter with beauty has been true, it will not cross a person's mind to desire to acquire the landscape; the thought would be absurd, for its appreciation is complete.[492]

Beauty is therefore demonstrated to be the most absolute phenomenon, the only time when the individual is entirely present in the perceptual realm, momentarily released from the shackles of their will and liberated from the tyranny of necessity. The disinterested, immaterial nature of beauty reinforces the fact that the Beautiful Soul is a theory that is available to all. Everyone can delight in the gentle sway of a willow's branches, or a mountain landscape suffused in golden light. Schiller remarks that "the sublime, like the beautiful, is spread profusely throughout nature, and the faculty to feel both one and the other has been given to all men."[493] This common feeling unveils the universality that underpins existence, giving aesthetics the form and structure of ethics and its universal laws.

In its universality, beauty provides a basis upon which positive social relationships can be developed, acting as a point of commonality for collective exchange. Since there is a natural human inclination to want to share beautiful experiences, these can afford an opportunity to bond individuals in a moment of ultimate meaning, conveying ineffable feelings that cut to the core of existence. Unlike material objects, which are thought to evoke acquisitiveness, beauty in its infiniteness is meant to be shared. The meaning found in observing a landscape or listening to music is only intensified and enhanced with others. During the experience of beauty, therefore, either in nature or in art, the individual is made receptive to those around them, and becomes attuned to their position, which amplifies their aptitude for making sound moral judgements. The beauty of literature allows the reader to empathise with the character by putting themself in their place as if it were their own. We comprehend the plight of Oliver Twist through the beauty of Dicken's words, despite not having experienced his suffering ourselves.

In satiating our souls and suppressing selfish desires, beauty brings a source of happiness in meaning which allows us to look beyond ourselves and makes us more capable of giving and receiving love. In this sense, beauty is actively conducive to reciprocity and positive relationships, the very foundation of justice and the social bond. Aesthetic sensitivity increases a beautiful soul's capacity to act as a moral citizen, loving partner, and benevolent friend.

Schiller draws on Kant when he argues that the good is attained by cultivating the subjective experience of beauty which, by opening one's horizons and developing the senses, strengthens faculties of empathy that lead to compassion for others and concern for the well-being of nature and humanity. The act of looking at a beautiful painting, for example, elevates a person beyond ego and self-absorption into a realm of universal concern and contemplation. "As the instrument or expression of human reason, art is thus the activity responsible for creating the perfection necessary to happiness and morality, and its manifestations, as Leibniz wrote, is a soul that is correspondingly "beautiful."[494] The sublime knowledge derived from the experience of the beautiful inspires the desire for the good and awakens the sense of possibility necessary to live in its image.

The story of *Saint Cecilia, or The Power of Music* (1810) by Heinrich von Kleist (1777-1811) perhaps most powerfully expresses this sentiment.[495] As the sixteenth century legend goes, four brothers decide to attack a convent during the time of a village celebration. However, as they are about to begin their attack, they hear orchestral music being played within its walls. They are so overcome by its beauty and moved by the unexpected effect that it has upon their souls, that they withdraw, and the convent is saved. Evidently, the story is exaggerated for dramatic effect, but the message remains compelling: in the face of great beauty, moral feelings are spontaneously aroused.

Beauty can both engender moral sentiments and suppress immoral propensities. In his essay on "The Moral Utility of Aesthetic Manners" (1796), Schiller argues that, like a lunatic who fears an impending fit of madness and removes the knives in his vicinity to avoid bloodshed, man should seek the salutary bonds which aesthetics offers so that his internal imbalances are put to rest and he causes no harm.[496] The formation of taste, which seeks this higher beauty, therefore, is an exercise in the good, one that holds a moral urgency. Schlegel asserts, "Correct taste, one could say, is the developed feeling of an ethically noble mind. It is impossible, moreover, that the taste of an immoral man could be correct and in harmony with itself."[497] Schiller argues that taste stimulates our inclination to take part in moral duty and more easily allows us to practice virtue. Furthermore, taste gives a virtuous direction to the soul and differentiates between negative influences and those that are morally desirable.[498] The concept of taste implicitly introduces a hierarchy in which some things are considered tasteless and others tasteful, a hierarchy believed to correspond with moral weakness and moral strength. Just as morality needs laws to function, rules must be established to maintain aesthetic standards. The cultivation of taste necessitates an objective conception of beauty and a set of values towards which to aspire.

Schiller, however, makes clear that taste is not enough to make a particular action moral. He concedes that "morality could never have any other foundation than her own."[499] After liberating the individual from their instincts, taste can present a new set of constraints because of its association with pleasure which cannot determine morality. However, even if taste is insufficient, it greatly assists in moral development by freeing the individual from brutal appetites and replacing them with "nobler and gentler inclinations."[500] These inclinations may not be virtues in themselves, but they share something in common with virtue, and, combined with a rational inclination towards moral law, they can more easily produce moral outcomes.

Cultivating taste and creating beautiful environments in the physical world or in the intellect is far more than a preference for certain aesthetic impressions. It is the vehicle through which transcendental truths are revealed—the means by which one accesses abstract moral laws and deontological ends, bringing them from the domain of concept to the earthly realm. Those without taste express more than just poor aesthetic judgement: they allow misguided pleasures to blind them to ultimate moral principles, the knowledge of which could have been reached through the cultivation of their aesthetic faculties.

Eckermann reflects on Goethe's meticulous efforts to refine his tastes and act as a moral educator in this regard when he comments in a conversation on February 26, 1823:

> We then looked at the drawings and engravings. Goethe takes great interest in forming my taste he

shows me only what is complete, and endeavours to make me apprehend the intention of the artist; he would have me think and feel only with the thoughts and feelings of the noblest beings. 'This' said he, 'is the way to cultivate what we call taste. Taste should be educated by contemplation, not of the tolerably good, but of the truly excellent.'[501]

For the theorists of the Beautiful Soul, the cultivation of taste by contemplating the truly excellent as a moral exercise extends to the production of their own artistic creations. To produce works that are worthy of representing an objective beauty is their highest aspiration. Their contemporaries believed that they had succeeded in this regard, and they were successful in arousing the moral effects that they had hoped to elicit in their readers. As Schlegel remarks of Goethe:

This great artist opens up a prospect to an entirely new level of *Bildung*. His works are an irrefutable attestation that the objective is possible and that the hope for the beautiful is not an empty delusion of reason. The objective is attained here already.[502]

Schiller shared Schlegel's sentiments, particularly regarding Goethe's *Wilhelm Meister*. He praised Goethe for producing a work that arouses the feeling of the beautiful and the moral sentiments that accompany it:

I cannot describe to you how deeply the truth, the beautiful vitality, the simple fullness of this work, has affected me. The excitement into which it has thrown my mind will subside when I shall have perfectly mastered it, and that will be an important crisis in my being. This excitement is the effect of

287

the Beautiful, and only the Beautiful proceeds thence, that my intellect is not yet entirely in accordance with my feelings. I understand now perfectly what you mean when you say that it is strictly the Beautiful, the True, that can move you even to tears. Tranquil and deep, clear, and yet like nature unintelligible is this work; and all, even the most trivial collateral incident, shows the clearness, the equanimity of the mind whence it flowed.[503]

The beauty in *Wilhelm Meister* inspired a corresponding beauty in its reader and we can clearly see here how works of art can have a moralising effect.

Although the creation of art which represents the beautiful is moral, to make art with the intention of morality is to assume a function that would destroy its capacity to elicit this faculty. As Goethe writes:

In this sphere moral effects are required above all things; and here at once arises a dissension between the class that produces and that which uses; for a good work of art can, and will indeed, have moral consequences; but to require moral ends of the artist, is to destroy his profession.[504]

Furthermore, although beauty and goodness are metaphysically intertwined, beautiful art can still be produced by morally imperfect people. Those who deny this proposition would be required to eliminate most of the artistic works from world history. However, the moral beauty of art can transcend the imperfections of its creators, and therefore still have the capacity to inspire a sense of the good in people. Just like a terrible human being can create and raise a child who is good, so, too, can beauty arise and exist independently from its origins.

As Schiller remarks in observing a Greek sculpture: "Man brought something here into being, that is more than he himself is, that hints at something greater than his own species—does this perhaps prove, that man is now less than he will be?"[505] Having granted this concession, the aim of the Beautiful Soul is to make both beautiful souls out of artists, and art from beautiful souls. Only when the wholly moral person produces works of beauty will these works reach perfection and most favourably serve humanity's advancement. A moral-aesthetic education fosters an improvement of the human condition as a whole, ennobling souls and their creations through beauty.[506]

Although immoral people might superficially appear to appreciate beauty, this philosophy would argue that they do not really understand the *spirit* of beauty, since they do not have a strong notion of the good, and so their perception of it is warped or one dimensional. A cruel person might appear to appreciate Beethoven's concertos, and even genuinely believe in the sincerity of their own experience, but they will not have grasped its essence because the beauty of the work of art is only fully revealed and understood by the person who is good.

The practitioner of the Beautiful Soul integrates the experience of the beautiful into their daily reality by reading, observing nature, listening to music, and engaging in poetic conversations to make themself more receptive to others and the world around them. They follow Goethe's prescription that "a man should hear a little music, read a little poetry, and see a fine picture every day of his life in order that worldly cares may not obliterate the sense of the beautiful which God has implanted in the human soul."[507] With this vision of beauty incorporated into their lived experience, they create aesthetically moving works in their given metier that reflect the moral nature that they have developed through the refinement of their taste. Beauty acts as the channel through which they both awaken and sustain the will to exist and to create in a spirit of kinship and solidarity with others.

The aim of a moral-aesthetic education is to turn life itself into a work of art. The classic ideal of the Beautiful Soul foregrounds the proposition that humans can indeed become works of art.[508] According to Schiller, the spontaneous goodness that beautiful souls exude and the relationship between the naturalness of their composure, and the ease with which they perform moral duties, is the product of their aesthetic development. The harmonisation of their virtuous characteristics follows both aesthetic and moral laws and thus their life becomes art.[509]

Although contemplating art is considered important to the cultivation of the Beautiful Soul, it is not what defines the aestheticization of life. Rather, it is the goodness that comes from the "aesthetic pleasure inherent in human excellence" that distinguishes it.[510] A virtuous person is aesthetically gratifying to observe, and the pursuit of inner perfection brings a pleasure to its subject that is similar to that found in contemplating artistic creations. When beautiful souls perform moral actions, they feel the same type of ecstasy that they derive from their immediate experience of art.

This important clarification saves Schiller from the critique of naïveté: although it is theoretically possible that people can be so moved by contemplating beauty that they will become ennobled, as in Heinrich von Kleist's story of Saint Cecilia, the theory does not hinge on practically realising this outcome. The theory instead makes acute observations on the nature of the beautiful and the sensations that it elicits, which inspire its construction of the ideal person. It is more of a reflection on the human condition informed by a study of aesthetics than a reflection on art and its consequences, although the two are intimately interconnected.

In analysing the feelings aroused by profound aesthetic moments, we can learn lessons about the nature of the human experience as an artistic creation and contemplate art in a way that is world revealing. Aesthetics defines a mode of perceiving that glorifies life. Beauty becomes "the means by which humanity can be elevated to its highest and most proper station. Art, that is, ought to be designed to transfigure us all into beautiful souls."[511]

The theorists of the Beautiful Soul took inspiration from the Greeks, especially Plotinus's idea that life is an "odyssey," during which an individual must "sculpt away impurities" until the soul transforms into a "work of art," becoming virtuous by attaining self-knowledge (*gnothi seauton*.)"[512] As Plotinus says:

> Withdraw within yourself and examine yourself. If you do not yet therein discover beauty, do as the artist, who cuts off, polishes, purifies until he has adorned his statue with all the marks of beauty. Remove from your soul, therefore, all that is superfluous, straighten out all that is crooked, purify and illuminate what is obscure, and do not cease perfecting your statue until the divine resplendence of virtue shines forth upon your sight, until you see temperance in its holy purity seated in your breast.[513]

This artistic process heightens human sensitivity to all aspects of living. If every action sculpts the ultimate form of a person's life, then each part is critical to the value of the final composition. Whether it is in personal relationships, vocational pursuits, or intellectual queries, all elements of one's daily existence can hold an aesthetic significance. Goethe, especially, affirms this view, arguing that life is the greatest work of art, more important than his traditionally artistic literary and theatrical pursuits. In a letter to Reinhard on January 22, 1811, he writes, "I recall a complimentary reproach once made by a friend of my youth. He said, what you live is better than what you write, and it would please me if that were still true."[514]

The definition of an artist, therefore, expanded and, from this enlightened perspective, anyone who lived with beauty could be considered one. Schlegel writes, "An artist is everyone who makes the goal and centre of his existence the development of his mind."[515] Schleiermacher argues that once we become aware of our being as an entirely original creation, life becomes art and the individual an artist who is poeticising his unique existence.[516] Schlegel posits that "Just as the Greeks termed those who rhythmically organised the ethical bountifulness of their inner minds, and ordered it into harmony, musicians; thus I term those who love beauty artists."[517] Since art is, according to Goethe, "essentially noble," those who become artists of existence ennoble their life while boldly exercising their sovereign rights.[518]

Implicit to this new conception of the artist is a performativity bound to the creativity of the Beautiful Soul. Those who accept the principles of this philosophy passionately enact them; a life undertaken with aesthetic refinement is likened to a dramatic art form. The performativity of being transforms the basic material of existence into a poetic force that elevates existence into the infinite realm.[519] Like any performative art form, a performance is contained within the limited space-time dimension of the stage, and yet its ephemeral nature is transcended when the work exemplifies the greatest of human achievements. In the same way, existence for humans is limited by the impending approach of death, but when life becomes beautiful, elements of it are always sustained in a dimension of the universe, where space and time collapse and the transient is eternalised.

Goethe and Schiller were preoccupied with theatre as a moralising artistic form because it exemplifies the aestheticized life of beautiful souls. Besides literature, theatre and opera offer the closest representations of life. Sculpture and painting are immobile, and music is too abstract, but theatre is an intense encapsulation of existence. We can understand how a life might become aesthetic through these poets' discussion of the stage.

Schiller offers the clearest illustration in his essay "The Stage as a Moral Institution" (1784). Here he argues that theatre comes to the aid of justice because it magnifies the thousands of vices that are left unnoticed in our world. It also serves as the handmaid of philosophy, revealing its high principles in a lovely form. Of course, as Schiller concedes, the stage cannot remove egoism and many vices remain while many virtues make no impression on the "cold-hearted spectators."[520] But even with this admission, he argues that the stage is undeniably a particularly powerful guide for civic life and makes a great impression on its audience by vitally expressing noble ideals while exposing ignoble actions. This is also the line of argumentation that Goethe takes in *Poetry and Truth* when he defends the theatre against his father, who considers it useless, and explains that vice in prosperity and virtue in misfortune are set right by "poetical justice."[521]

According to Goethe and Schiller, a feeling of compassion for our fellow human is brought about through the stage when suffering is expressed in aesthetic form, and this spectacle gives us courage to persevere in the face of inequity and to struggle for the good. The suffering of others becomes personal here, and we feel with the greatest intensity a perspective other than our own. The stage teaches us to be considerate of the unfortunate and to judge in fairness and with empathy for "we can only pronounce on a man when we know his whole being and circumstances."[522] It allows us to observe, from a multifaceted perspective, the condition of others by virtue of the objective position that the spectator holds. We maintain an intellectual omnipresence and our attention is focused on the situation at hand. Schiller succinctly summarises the breadth of the moralising powers that the stage represents when he comments:

> The stage is an institution combining amusement with instruction, rest with exertion, where no faculty of the mind is overstrained, no pleasure enjoyed at the cost of the whole. When melancholy gnaws the heart, when trouble poisons our solitude, when we are disgusted with the world, and a thousand worries oppress us, or when our energies are destroyed by over-exercise, the stage revives us, we dream of another sphere, we recover ourselves, our torpid nature is roused by noble passions, our blood circulates more healthily. The unhappy man forgets his tears in weeping for another. The happy man is calmed, the secure made provident…the

individual shares in the general ecstasy and his breast has now only space for an emotion: he is a man.[523]

This description mirrors the life and attributes of a beautiful soul, who combines passion with rationality, who pursues an ideal, who embodies compassion and overcomes their own suffering to bear the imprint of humanity upon their soul. We observe, then, that in constructing this concept, Schiller practices what he professes, making deductions from the truths uncovered in the theatre to form a perfected concept of humanity by studying the favourable psychological effects intrinsic to the experience of art. The life of a beautiful soul most closely resembles opera and the theatre because it poetically captures this infinite conception of humankind within every act. From listening to the euphonious bells of a church toll, to studying the Delphic visage of a figure deep in thought or tracing the subtle spectrum of colours as day dissolves into night, every experience can hold the aesthetic intensity and significance that one usually only becomes receptive to when it is staged. If, like a playwright or a poet, we concentrate on small details of life and give them the momentousness that they deserve, then every facet of being can become illuminated, and life will hold a sacrality worthy of being preserved.

Like the theatre, the aesthetic lives of beautiful souls are explicitly expressed in the communicative exchanges that they maintain, which artfully concretise their poetic sentiments. Communication is central to this concept of lived beauty because it is inherently performative. Like the sociability and friendship that emerges from an inner harmony, the ability to communicate comes from the beauty that they perceive.

According to widespread eighteenth-century definitions, such as Kant's in his *Critique of Judgement*, art is "a kind of representation that is purposive in itself and though without an end, nevertheless promotes the cultivation of the mental powers for sociable communication."[524] Following Kant, Schiller believes that "our pleasure in beauty is inseparably linked to its communicability" so that by living beautifully we will necessarily become more communicative.[525] He argues that all forms of communications that do not have beauty as their fundamental principle will divide society, while "the communication of the Beautiful unites society, because it relates to what is common to them all."[526] Meanwhile Goethe emphasises the fact that beauty assists in the art of the mutual communication of ideas. Schlegel's neologism, *symphilosophy,* meaning to philosophise together, represents this understanding of aesthetic communication which was readily adopted in the space of the salon.[527]

Schiller, whose aesthetic-communicative views are inspired by Socrates, argues that the Socratic method of discourse best represents, first, the Good because it progresses from the known to the unknown, and second, the Beautiful because it advances from both the head and the heart.[528] Socrates in some interpretations is thought to exemplify the Beautiful Soul of antiquity because he engaged in beautiful discourse.[529] Schiller elaborates upon what he means with respect to the performativity of aesthetic communication when he argues that speaking, in its widest sense, includes every physical phenomenon which can represent a state of the soul.[530] Thus, gesture and music, for example, could be included in this definition. This generality of terms is necessary for communication to become *the* activity that determines the artful living of the Beautiful Soul.

According to Schleiermacher, a language developed in this expansive sense becomes "the clearest mirror of the times, a work of art in which its spirit comes to self-knowledge."[531] By forming their own aesthetic language, people can both create and communicate the content of their soul. However, if this language has not been developed or if the power of speech is dissolved, then, according to Schleiermacher, the inner world is lacking:

> Someone knows nothing of their inner development and has never felt the depths of humanity in themselves, if the foundation stones of their language have crumbled into dust, if the power of their speech has dissolved into empty phrases and superficial polish, and if their loftiest rhetoric degenerates into an idle play of sounds. No one can live harmoniously according to a simple beautiful moral than he who strives after his inner development, and so belongs to a future world. No one can become a true artist in the use of language than he who has looked into himself with a free view and taken possession of the inner essence of humanity.[532]

Schlegel argues that the publicness of *Bildung* through language is the only way to elevate the mind and that sociability is the solution to the sulking pride and strange caprices which result from excessive solitude.[533] Thus, the soul performatively secures its beauty through language while seeking to unify every discursive act into a greater transcendent whole.

This interpretation of the aesthetic lives of beautiful souls, realised in communication with others, is represented by the concept of a beautiful humanity. Goethe was occupied with portraying life as a work of art which comes about through a labyrinth of poetic experiences constructed in a social environment that fosters beautiful perception. He passionately explored ideas for forming a more beautiful humanity and for understanding the world as a poetic whole.[534] Schiller believed that together the naïve and the sentimental poet can create this ideal—"for the idea of a beautiful humanity is not exhausted by either, but can only be presented in the union of both."[535] He describes the people who would comprise a beautiful humanity, arguing that they are active but not to an unhealthy extreme; that they believe in an ideal without remaining cognitively detached; and that they accept the reality of human affairs without being enslaved by them. In this case, the poles of extravagance, on the one hand, and excessive passivity, on the other hand, are transcended to produce human flourishing. Every person who has beautified their soul and lives in communicative accord with those who have done the same can take part in forming this beautiful humanity: a new community of people distinguished not by their class, gender, race, religion, or region, but by their intellect, compassion, and reason. Elaborating upon ancient Greek notions of an "Aesthetic State," the theorists of the Beautiful Soul envisioned a new poetic world order in which this beautiful humanity could exist, the aesthetic assumptions of which would have important political consequences.

This revival of the Hellenistic notion of an Aesthetic State can be traced to Italian influences from the early Renaissance, particularly in the writings of the Florentine humanist Leonardo Bruni (1370-1444). Bruni developed ideas on an ideal city, "an aesthetic vision of a material city of suitable splendour to house political virtues."[536] Within this aesthetically structured state, in which the artists are political visionaries, intellectual life and community would thrive and a golden age for music, architecture, poetry, literature, and rhetoric would flourish.[537] The Italian resurrection of "the life of beauty in community" was expanded upon by Shaftesbury, who formulated ideas on the ideal political order, comprised of artful dialogue and aesthetic principles, where musicians are the founders of the state. His aesthetic interpretation of political life according to the Athenian model greatly influenced the Germans.[538]

Following Shaftesbury, Winckelmann's revival of classicism in German intellectual culture included notions on an Aesthetic State which centre around art as gaiety, political freedom, and beauty as the universal goal of Man. Goethe and Schiller drew from these ideas in their own writings, especially in *Wilhelm Meister* and in the *Aesthetic Letters* respectively, which can be seen as their most definitive attempts to delineate the nature of this Aesthetic State. In *Wilhelm Meister*, for example, The Society of the Tower represents a community of cultivated peoples striving to live according to aesthetic principles. In the *Aesthetic Letters,* Schiller argues that only the Aesthetic State can fairly reconcile the position of the individual with the communal will, a unity which is achieved through aesthetic education.

Goethe, Schiller, Weiland, and Herder endeavoured to put these ideas into practice, transforming Weimar into a centre for self-cultivation and the site for this Aesthetic State to emerge.[539] Weimar was compared by contemporaries to ancient Athens, a place where the Greek emphasis on community and beautiful dialogue could be developed. It became a city where artists and intellectuals congregated as aesthetic humanists in a common quest to make social and political life more beautiful. *Salonnières,* such as Madame de Stäel, found inspiration for their salons in the creative happenings and bohemian gatherings of this flourishing city of aesthetically minded people, which Goethe cheerfully remarked "has ten thousand poets and some inhabitants."[540]

Wieland was a particularly influential figure in Weimar's literary scene. His ideas on virtuous citizens brought into being through the fine arts, especially the art of conversation, was foundational to the lived, communicative beauty that the Beautiful Soul espoused.[541] *The History of Agathon* is a model of this Aesthetic State, following the hero Agathon from tyranny to "the land of beautiful souls, of utopian republics."[542] But the theorists of this philosophy were aware that to systematically bring this utopian republic into being outside of the poetic circles of Weimar, from which these ideas naturally sprung, was a formidable challenge, one which required a political theory which either worked within the current imperfect structures or else rewrote them.

Humboldt's *The Limits of State Action* is an aesthetically grounded political work that attempts to pragmatically assess how political institutions can advance this concept of man as a work of art and to evaluate their efficacy in reaching this end. These theorists generally agreed, however, that a flawed political state is insufficient to support the development of beautiful souls. Beauty is identified as the essential instrument to create the social conditions necessary for a more beautiful humanity to emerge. As Schiller remarks:

> All improvement in the political sphere must proceed from the ennobling of the character. But, subject to the influence of a social constitution still barbarous, how can character become ennobled?

It would then be necessary to seek for this end an instrument that the state does not furnish, and to open sources that would have preserved themselves pure in the midst of political corruption. I have now reached the point to which all the considerations tended that have engaged me up to the present time. This instrument is the art of the beautiful; these sources are open to us in its immortal models.[543]

Aesthetics, for Schiller, offers a political alternative to the status quo and a theory of justice which does not depend on existing models that are fundamentally flawed.[544] If, according to Schiller, people do exercise their political power to form this more beautiful humanity, then the state will not have to intervene and need only assist in the enhancement of the finer instincts that have already been developed. But if people are in conflict internally and with one another, then the state will be required to "assume the full severity of the law."[545] These theorists arrived at aesthetics to define their political ideals because they believed it was the only solution to the political crises that they observed. Aesthetics offers the distinct promise of inducing greater freedom of the internal world which, in their diagnosis, was severely lacking and the major cause of turmoil. Their project was to transform the passive and uninformed citizen into an enlightened member of a new republic through moral-aesthetic education.

The individual works of art (the cultivated souls) as a community (a beautiful humanity) comprise this total work of art (the Aesthetic State.) If this Aesthetic State comes into fruition, its ruler will be "the artist of artists" which, according to the theorists' theatrical analogies, is the director in a play comprised of actors.[546] But this Aesthetic State will only come about through an aesthetic revolution, one whose basis is self-cultivation. Despite the obvious obstacles for the implementation of this pacifist revolution over one of brute force, they were hopeful that it would still arise. Schlegel, for example, acknowledges that like plants' or animals' natural development which eventually perishes, human *Bildung* can easily regress— as indeed he believed was the case in Europe around 1795 when he published *On the Study of Greek Poetry*. However, again using analogies of the theatre, he argues that even when we assume that "aesthetic vitality" has died, one may observe that in fact "this drama is far from over":

> It is truly wonderful how in our age the demand for the objective is everywhere astir, how the belief in the beautiful is being awakened, and unequivocal symptoms announce a more refined taste. The moment indeed seems ripe for an aesthetic revolution, by means of which the objective could become dominant in the aesthetic development [*Bildung*] of the moderns.[547]

Schlegel's optimism is instructive in that it shows us that even in times of great political distress, there is always a distinct possibility that the noble ideals which appear all but lost are only in temporary abeyance, waiting for the moment when humanity believes in them once more.

Beautiful souls are revolutionary figures because they can lead the struggle for the restitution of these ideals. They are the vanguard of progress, radically reformulating what it means to be human and how to harmoniously exist in a social whole. They become the archetypal members of a beautiful humanity and the model citizens of this Aesthetic State.

However, as we have seen from Schiller's observation, beautiful souls can only exist in theory within the current political reality and the morally destitute social environments which accompany it. So, the question then becomes, how do they come into being in the physical world? Now we may witness the union of concept and institution: for beautiful souls who lead this aesthetic revolution are cultivated within salons:

> This aesthetic whole would be a *Bildungsanstalt*, a society in which people would educate one another through the free exchange of their personalities and ideas. The Romantic salons, in Berlin and Jena, were fledgling attempts to put this ideal into practice. If life were only one grand salon, one long learning experience in which everyone participated, the Romantics believed, then society would indeed become a work of art, and this life "the most beautiful of all possible worlds."[548]

The Beautiful Soul thus left the pages of literature and philosophy and was born in the real world through salon culture.

Since beauty is the cornerstone of the Beautiful Soul, the feature that coalesces the disparate parts of cultivated person-hood, the *salonnières* sought to exemplify the beautiful. Beauty governed their lives, shaped their character, and informed their actions in the world; a world which Varnhagen often referred to, like Goethe and Schiller, as "The Beautiful World."[549]

The *salonnières* understood beauty to be the guiding force of their salons. They believed that life without beauty has no purpose, no direction forward, no pathway to knowledge. In its absence there is little impetus to cultivate oneself or to aspire towards a more perfect reality. The *salonnières* were aware of the humanising qualities of beauty, which can teach morality, turn selfishness into a concern for the collective will, tame brutish impulses, and ennoble existence. "How to beautify the earth" was the enduring theme towards which Varnhagen's life was directed.[550]

The beauty that the *salonnières* nurtured in their salons began with the poetic atmosphere that they created. This was as important to discourse as the active moderation of conversations, for it influenced the psychological state of those present to one conducive to intellectual suppleness and social receptivity. If the space was shorn of beauty, if it did not excite the imagination or evoke a sense of poetry, then it would fail to induce an animated engagement with the ideas presented. And so, the salon was a place one came to in order to be transported to another, more beautiful world where social interactions were precipitated by the *salonnières'* heightened aesthetic sensibility.

In order to understand the importance of beauty to the institution of the salon, we must imagine what it was like to partake in salon culture. On a typical day in the first salon of Varnhagen, which lasted from 1790 to 1806, guests would climb the stairs to the attic room in her family home on Jägerstraße where her salon took place. The atmosphere was not grand like her later salon (1821-1832), in the elegant and spacious blue rooms of the house on Mauerstraße where she lived with her husband. Nor, at this time, could she provide the lavish dinners that she did subsequently. However, the atmosphere was cosy and inviting, the perfect place for intimate and unpretentious conversations.

Upon entering the space, the guests might find Varnhagen deep in conversation with Friedrich Schlegel, the poet Johann Ludwig Tieck (1773-1853), or his brother the sculptor, Christian Friedrich Tieck (1776-1851). With her characteristic gaiety she would greet them, offering a poetic aphorism or idea communicated with the wit and imaginativeness for which she was so admired by her friends. The newcomers might contemplate the ideas she had portrayed with the aesthetic sensitivity one gives to a painting, for she had turned the spoken word into a work of art and the mind was awakened to new possibilities by this verbal aestheticism.

Within the space of the salon, Varnhagen's inner psychological state would be revealed through her aesthetic choices. The room was elegantly furnished with a piano and flowers as the focal points. Select books were displayed to reflect the ideas discussed in the salon. Gotthold Ephraim Lessing's bust was prominently featured to represent the ideals of the Enlightenment; next to this icon, the bust of Schleiermacher symbolised the rules of sociability that governed the salon; and the bust of Prince Louis Ferdinand indexed an individual whose soul Varnhagen had sculpted.[551] This triptych of the salon's influences, values, and aspirations, respectively, was emblematic of the *salonnières'* desire to embody ideas in the physical world. As those present subconsciously processed the illustrious intellectual figures of the salon rendered in stone, tea and sweets might be served as the Romantic poets discussed the literary works of Jean Paul or Friedrich de la Motte Fouqué (1777-1843), placed on the table by the authors themselves for salon guests to read and discuss.

Once the guests had absorbed the inspired aesthetic of their surroundings and the initial conversations had ended, those present would be seated. The salon almost always began with the contemplation of an aesthetic form; a reading from a passage of a play by Goethe, letters by Schiller, or a book by Schlegel. After listening to the literary work, a vibrant conversation would ensue. The author would often be present to convey the essential aspects of their art and to hear the perspectives that emerged. Both giving and receiving constructive criticism was itself a work of art within the salon, for the discussion was exquisitely communicated by these poets of conversation, who captured all the beauty of the spoken word. Varnhagen understood conversations to be highly aesthetic, a living art form, and this appreciation was apparent in the way that she facilitated the salon.[552]

After hours of artful conversation, the salon would transition to yet another aesthetic form: music. The conversation had been pushed to new intellectual terrains and when the limits of current knowledge were reached, music provided a sense of unity and completion. In the intimate setting of the home, with the immediacy of sensory impressions, the power of music was more intensely felt.[553] Bach, Schubert, Mozart, and Beethoven, were some of the composers who were most loved in the salons of this time.

Prince Louis could be found at the piano playing a mélange of classical pieces as he sought Varnhagen's counsel on the questions raised in the salon. The conclusions drawn in conversation might be examined further by a diplomat and a rising poet as they drank wine on a chaise lounge and listened to Prince Louis play. The salon would slowly fade only after hours of conversation and a full engagement with the spectrum of aesthetic forms upon which salon sociability was structured.

The decision to have the salon take place in the home, where objects and artifacts were displayed, rendered material the inner workings of the *salonnières'* mind and represented the ideals she hoped to reach through conversation. This proffered intimacy of exposing her own intellectual state through aesthetic arrangement opened guests to the possibility of representing themselves with equal depth, which, in turn, contributed to the clarity and meaning of the conversations that took place. The familiarity of this environment was one more conducive to free-flowing conversation than some sterile public setting which lacked intimacy.

The aesthetic of the physical space emphasised the welcoming, non-utilitarian spirit of the salon, one that encouraged the expression of spontaneous thought unhindered by the fear of public scrutiny. A strong ethos of reciprocity was reinforced by the *salonnière's* preliminary act of generosity in opening her home to others. Guests felt comfortable speaking openly in this welcoming, personal environment that she had tastefully created, and they were moved by the desire to contribute to the beauty of this space. The domestic setting of the salon symbolised the public-private dimensions of self-cultivation. *Bildung* was a highly personal activity, and therefore it took place in the private setting of the home. However, now the home was opened to an educated public.[554]

The *salonnières* contributed to the symbolically rich environment by offering their participants material for the creative imagination to flourish. The visual arts, music, poetry and literature all formed essential elements of this space: fruit bowls on tables carefully composed as a mimetic representation of a still life; chamber music resonating in a room perfumed by elaborate floral arrangements; paintings hung strategically on the walls to evoke contemplation; and verses of poetry elegantly spoken were just a few of the evocative embellishments that composed this world.

Within the context of these aesthetic influences, a new

reality emerged. The composition of this reality varied among salons in the emphasis given to certain art forms or intellectual traditions. In some salons drafts of novels were read, poetry recited, or new compositions performed.[555] Almost all the Berlin salons had a musical component. Music was considered the most important of the salon's arts because it most closely related to *Bildung*.

Struck by both the depth of the conversations and the pleasure found in this unique form of aestheticized communion, participants were often left feeling deeply inspired. As one exclaimed: "How greatly that circle inspired and spurred me on cannot be put into words."[556] The atmosphere of the salon imparted a special spirit, one that was widely felt, yet remained elusive. Varnhagen attempted to describe the nature of this spirit in a fragment from her letters when she said that it was "a capable good will…not visible."[557] Here, the connection between beauty and goodness becomes apparent, for goodness seemed to flow naturally from the beauty that was created in the salon. The distinct inspirational spirit that emerged within the salon proved critical to its success.

The *salonnières* emphasised beauty found in artistic forms because its appreciation does not require extensive knowledge in a specific intellectual tradition. Beauty provides a shared lexicon that catalyses conversation amongst a diverse public. It undergirded the salon insofar as it inspired the cultivation of common faculties. Intellectual exploration was enhanced by aesthetic sensibility; social interactions were stimulated by the equalising encounter with the beautiful.

After listening to a piece of music together, mutual understanding could be achieved through a shared emotional response. The immediacy and inclusiveness of the experience was positively disarming and encouraged intense discussion.

Varnhagen expanded the musical offerings in her second salon because she perceived the bond that her participants experienced in the presence of music.[558] Beauty, then, was the basis of language and sociability: the foundation of a common system of knowledge and affect. By refining the ability to differentiate colour or composition in a painting, a person exercised the acute perception necessary to interpret facial expressions or to consider the significance of word choice. Sensory receptiveness meant a more cultivated ability to comprehend social interactions and the psychological intricacies of personhood.

Reading aloud, a widespread practice of the Enlightenment era, contributed to the aesthetic communication of ideas and was an important element of the salon.[559] Herz, for example, described her salon as comprised of a heterogeneous group of individuals who shared the desire and ability to read well.[560] Reading was an incarnation of Enlightenment principles, a way of both effectively communicating ideas while evoking the poetry of the written word.[561] Aphorisms, anecdotes, novellas, travel writing, poems and memoirs, all provided lyrical content for salon conversation.[562] As Varnhagen said, "a drama, a novel…must be a complete expression of the world; everything that appears there will be beautiful."[563]

Reading played an important role in the salon because the *salonnières* believed that understanding the subtleties of another person's worldview was the basis for social cohesion. Hearing passages from a book that presented the compelling story of a protagonist induced empathy for the character and the author in a way that a non-aesthetic form could not. Suddenly, the position of a person from a very different social background or circumstance was not so easily categorised as otherness—nor did it elicit feelings of distrust and misunderstanding. By placing the reader into the psyche of the Other as if it were their own, works of literature inspired a sense of togetherness that might otherwise be inconceivable. Aesthetic activity eschewed hierarchy, for everyone shared equally in its educating powers. Cultivation of taste and sensibilities meant cultivation of social perception and of processes of communication which led to the prospect of mutual understanding.

The *salonnières* employed beauty to induce states of empathy which acted as the basis for constructive social exchanges. Artistic forms were intended to heighten the cognitive capacity and emotional depth of salon participants to enable them to truly listen to others and to grasp their different circumstances in the world. By creating opportunities for the appreciation of beauty through the art displayed or performed in the space of the salon, and by their emphasis on aesthetics in lectures, the *salonnières* governed their spaces with the sensitivity found in the act of aesthetic contemplation.[564] The decision to share a beautiful experience created a foundational atmosphere of conviviality and collaboration.

Discourse itself proved to be the most influential art form of the Beautiful Soul and the one that most defined the spirit of the salon. The ability of conversation to elevate the human spirit through the aesthetic pleasure derived from the effective spoken word merged with the functional aspects of conversations to convey knowledge. This felicitous marriage turned the laborious process of self-improvement into a gratifying undertaking, one in which the joys of communication were pronounced.[565] Like contemplation of a beautiful landscape, whose aesthetic value stimulates a vibrant affirmation of being that excites a desire to share, reflection on ideas rendered beautiful in salon discourse awakened a search for meaning in communion with others.

The philosophical perspective of the time, in which the moral function of aesthetics lies in its communicability, was especially pronounced in the reciprocal art of conversation. When communication becomes art, it fulfils beauty's natural ends of mutuality more obviously than other art forms, ones where the shared dimension is present, but not as immediately apparent. Music can excite a desire to be shared that might lead to empathy and understanding. Inter-subjectivity, however, is the very foundation of conversation and, as such, when beautified, its moral effects are even more perceptible. Those who spoke beautifully were recognised for their ability to raise conversation to a work of art. With their artistry, no longer did communication serve merely to transfer knowledge, but rather to poetically derive and creatively express knowledge.

Beauty could be found everywhere within the communicative acts that took place in the salon. There was beauty in hand gestures and pauses, in silences and proclamations, in the repositioning of two words. It was detected in the increased decibels of a voice which gave away the passion of their speaker or in the gentlest pause taken to gracefully allow another person to enter the conversation. Beauty was found in the moment when two perspectives merged in harmonious accord while retaining their individual integrity, or the triumphant times when the argument deemed closest to the Good was won without self-righteousness or flattery.

Goethe and Schiller's ideas on the sociable nature of beauty seemed destined to be proven in the setting of the salon. No longer was beauty imprisoned within the perimeters of a frame or a stage, now it informed the nuances of social existence in a communicative form in which the benefits of aestheticized human interactions were palpable. Within every discursive act, there existed the possibility of a reawakening to oneself and to other people in the world.

Life in the salon became the ultimate work of art, and the salon participants, artists in living. Like an artist whose visceral impulse to create converges with the rigorous logic of aesthetic principles, the *salonnières* established their salons with a similar sensibility, combining the originality of their guests' personalities with the aestheticized structures of sociability, giving form to content. In doing so, they mediated the aestheticization of their own lives and the lives of others, composing the life forces present into a total work of art in which all the other art forms were vibrantly represented. Their poetic endeavours were founded upon Goethe's idea that humanity might become morally and intellectually beautiful. They were perhaps the only people who concretely attempted to actualise this vision by systematically working to beautify the souls of those in their circles and beyond.

A beautiful life could not be taken up casually; it necessitated entering a sustained aesthetic state. As Varnhagen remarked "One cannot become an artist at six o'clock in the evening."[566] She was certain that the true artists, both of a particular form and of living, were those who perennially lived as such. With its continuity and immediacy, the salon made entrance into this aesthetic state viable. Varnhagen believed that:

> The positive of life consists in living out what is immediately before us...To feel the present moment, to be able to deal with it, that is the art of living; the more we have of this in us, the more positive we shall be, and the more positive will be our experiences.[567]

Like any performative art form, the salon's creativity came from its temporal constraints of having to actualise ideas and aspirations in the present. Gentz, who affectionately described Varnhagen's methods of communication as "fresh aromatic strawberries, to which however, mould and roots are still hanging" captured the sweetness in the raw immediacy of her lived, communicative style.[568]

The salon represented the art of living beautifully insofar as the immediate and un-replicable relationships of the mind were of an indispensably creative nature. As Varnhagen remarked:

> In all of life as in art, its practice and contemplation, ever more relations must be set forth (this alone means living), not because we live more this way: no repetition could achieve that. But with each particular relationship something new is created; and for this reason alone its increase is desirable, invigorating, joyful, noble, real.[569]

Living beautifully found expression in the salon through the multitudinous relationships that the *salonnières* provided among people, art, and ideas. Varnhagen believed that life should be a work of art and that her salon was a representation of this art of living.[570] She wanted to transform the entirety of existence into an art form, not just an existence juxtaposed with forms of art.[571] She spoke to an inclination shared by many of the other *salonnières* when she said that "Man is a work of art…given to himself as a task. Material, artist, and workshop (are contained) within ourselves."[572] With this statement she not only affirmed the aesthetic nature of being, but she also alluded to the innate potential of *Bildung*,

313

suggesting that life can become art, but only if the materials invested in people are actively used. Just like any other creative act, a beautiful life is not given, it is consciously formed.

The *salonnières'* vision, however, required legitimation, for, despite their belief that conversation (and the art of beautiful living that it epitomised) is of equal or greater value than the art forms of painting, literature, or music, unsurprisingly the dominant social and ideological perspective did not concur.[573] This was, perhaps, not simply because the idea was radical but rather that sociability was not typically implemented in such a philosophical way. The domain of conversation, consumed normally by idleness and pleasantries, had been transformed into something entirely different. Thus, what the *salonnières* sought to legitimise was, in fact, an entirely new art form. The *salonnières'* understanding of their art, and the barriers to its realisation, is reflected in a reoccurring dream recounted by Varnhagen:

> I saw men of every…age, from about 17 years on…facial expressions (and colour) from all nations which art the power of imagination, and reality had ever shown me; whole worlds of the imagination streamed from my brain which I never thought were contained therein. All the national dress which I ever saw in such books where they are collected, in the theatres, or in the world, were there in actuality. Men with helmets, without helmets, with curly hair; with caps, and turbans of every kind; with coats, with jackets, with tight, with very flowing clothes…The most beautiful little boots, sandals, and strange shoes they wore…they often also went barefoot…The sculptors, however,

had bare arms, as the women now have; that's how you recognised them. Many of the men carried their tools in their hands. The noise was almost supernatural, because they all spoke and judged their works. The crowd prevented them and me from coming close to the works of art, and most remained quite far. For me, however, the artists were the works of art, and I was busy observing them with infinite care, and my dream lasted a very long time.[574]

In this moving description, she explains that no matter how absorbing the art on display may have been to the crowd, the art form that interested her most was observing the artists themselves. In juxtaposing the lives of others with the visual arts, she makes their aestheticized existence as significant as more established art forms, a powerful testament to the importance that she perceives in the institution of the salon. She imagines a utopia in which a heterogeneous group of people join to live harmoniously according to aesthetic principles. But her dream also suggests that she felt alone in her perception.

There is great significance in the fact that this vision came to her in a dream. The *salonnières* feared that their ideals would remain in the dream world and were constantly cognisant of the need to apply the material of the imagination to physical reality. Despite the frustrations that Varnhagen faced from her pioneering efforts, many salon participants did recognise that life in the salon became a work of art and saw Varnhagen as an artist of living beautifully. Jean Paul, for example, said of Varnhagen, "She is an artist, she begins an entirely new sphere, she is an exceptional being, in conflict

315

with ordinary life and raised high above it."[575] Bettina von Arnim described Varnhagen as a person whose most beautiful feature was her "penetration of the individual" which she described as a divine work of art.[576] Karl Varnhagen believed that Rahel Varnhagen had a "talent for life" which made everything she did beautiful.[577]

Schlegel was also considered an artist by her contemporaries. In his novel *Lucinde (*1799), Friedrich Schlegel said of his wife that she "was an artist, and passionately worshiped beauty."[578] His understanding of an artist was one "who possessed a certain approach to life characterised by poetry, a certain kind of feeling or intuition manifest in creative imagination."[579] Salon participants agreed that an artist was a person who could "transform situations and people into the beautiful."[580]

The patrons of the salons viewed the *salonnières* as artists because they did not separate life from art and saw beauty everywhere.[581] From salon sociability and human interactions, to nature, music and literature, the world was an endless source of aesthetic inspiration. Primary accounts reveal the breadth and extent to which Varnhagen perceived of the world in this way. Jean Paul extolled her for treating all of life poetically: "Winged one!— in every sense you treat life poetically and consequently life treats you in the same way. You bring the lofty freedom of poetry into the sphere of reality, and expect to find again the same beauties here as there."[582] One anonymous visitor recalled how moved Varnhagen was by the music played in her salon:

> The conversation first touched upon a question of religious orthodoxy and then passed to music, one of the foreign visitors taking up the cudgels on

behalf of Rossini; a celebrated singer went to the
piano and gave songs by Schubert and Beethoven,
to which Rahel listened with tears in her eyes and
a happy smile.[583]

When traveling, Varnhagen went to great lengths to
discover new aesthetic experiences. In one instance, she visited
every convent and monastery in a region, not for their religious
significance but for their sensory qualities. In particular, she
was delighted by a Mozart mass organised in her honour.[584]
Her appreciation of beauty encompassed nature as well. So
moved was she by the landscapes that she discovered in
Silesia, that she could not put her experience of them into
words.[585] Flowers, she believed, were her medicine and when
human art forms disappointed her, she found solace in the
purity of natural scenery.[586] Even in her old age she proclaimed
that she found beauty in the same wide variety of things that
she had always loved, among them "air, flowers, fields, music,
the theatre, discussion, that is, sociality, order, cleanliness,
elegance, wit, consistency of thought."[587] With her sensitive
perception she mastered the art of living beautifully.

Varnhagen believed that the artist of living must be sincere
if they were to become "one of the elect of mankind" who
could take part in forming a more beautiful humanity.[588] Her
perspective reflects the tenet of this philosophy that a creation
of the highest value is one that originates from a person who
is morally cultivated. For if a person's intentions are not
beautiful, then the creation itself, as perfect as it may seem,
will be wrought with contradictions and tensions. Art, and
artful living that is created by a person with a beautiful soul,
however, possess a purity that is both aesthetically pleasing
and morally sound.

By aestheticizing the everyday in conversation and making life within the salon beautiful, the *salonnières* provided a degree of detachment from reality that served to bring humanity closer to ideals. The relationship between the real and ideal was ultimately reconciled through an aesthetic state that lifted reality closer to perfection. In this intermediate state, the lines between reality and imagination were blurred.

Like an actor whose experimentation with different characters reveals the wider scope of lived experience, salon participants contemplated their innumerable, more perfect selves within this imaginative space. The *salonnières* facilitated the process of aesthetic development by assembling the sets in which to play out different ideas and ways of being. The space of the salon was constantly evolving to reflect this practice. The art that was displayed, the books that were read, the musical compositions that were performed, and the objects presented for study became the material props that were used to develop the art of living beautifully. The ideas that were discussed were perpetually in flux so that, like the actor or musician who changes repertoire, the subject matter of this aesthetic practice developed with time and new experiences.

The performativity of speaking in the salon enabled those in pursuit of the Beautiful Soul to express themselves in a manner that allowed for public critique. Self-cultivation transformed from an inward, contemplative process to a collaborative performative art form. Since there was no quantifiable metric for assessing the soul, interpretations of one's own development through the expression of ideas in the salon became the means to encourage this process. The performativity of self-cultivation harnessed the collective wisdom of a receptive community dedicated to mutual enlightenment. The soul was afforded a place to be sculpted before its final reveal.

In this respect, we can understand the salon as a rehearsal for reality, a space in which participants had the performative freedom to test the possibilities of what they could become through an aesthetic performance of the ideal. The salon became the theatre of the Beautiful Soul whose curtains could eventually open on to a new, more beautiful world. Indeed, the salon is often analogised to the theatre in the literature: "the meeting places of those who had learned how to represent themselves through conversation."[589] Goethe's Wilhelm Meister, who becomes an actor in the theatre, is often compared to a cultivated participant in salon conversation.[590]

The *salonnières* would most likely have welcomed this analogy since they saw the theatre as having a similar function and significance to their salons. As Varnhagen remarked, "A city without a theatre...is like a person with his eyes shut: a place without a breadth of fresh air...In our time and our cities (the theatre) is the one general (institution), where the circle of joy, of intellect, of participation and the gathering...of all classes is drawn together."[591] Varnhagen shared Schiller's conception of the theatre as a critical space to witness moral development and social change.[592] Her views on theatre inevitably informed the performative dimensions of her salon.

The purpose of this theatre of the Beautiful Soul was threefold. First, its liminal status between imagination and reality made more believable the possibilities of change. The very act of exercising different realities, such as new norms of social status and distinct value systems, rendered them tangible even when they had not yet permeated society. Since the salon was still a part of the world, not the imagination, these ideas came closer to being realised. Thus, change could be accelerated because the great barrier between what was and what could be had been transgressed. The second purpose was to examine the content of this rehearsed material: questioning developments within the self and the community in order to avoid irrational action through considered reflection before salon life was then translated to the world at large. Finally, debate over social problems, political ideas, and alternative realities were made appealing and less divisive through their aesthetic enactment.

The aspirational end of this new performative art form was to achieve the transcendent state of the Beautiful Soul. If each person worked towards this end, a more beautiful humanity would eventually emerge. The *salonnières* were the "explorer of souls" and the "leader of souls."[593] Their role was to bring this more beautiful humanity into being.

Since the intellectually and aesthetically scintillating time of the *salonnières*, our relationship to beauty has fundamentally changed. Today we might intuitively understand what beauty means when we exclaim, "what a beautiful sunset" or, "look at this beautiful work of art." Yet the word now often connotes little more than surface level appearances. Instead of representing a universal quest for meaning, beauty has been appropriated by entertainment and cosmetic industries to sell merchandise which categorises us according to the possession of an arbitrary set of physical traits. Beauty is warped to reflect the distorted cultural values and shallow ends that we are told we should pursue.

The extent to which societal understandings of beauty have degraded was first made apparent to me in a nascent attempt to start a salon when I pursued my undergraduate degree at Yale University. I founded an organisation called *The Movement for Beauty and Justice*. The purpose of the organisation was to foster positive social relationships through the experience of the beautiful in art, nature, and conversation. The idea was grounded in my reading of Goethe and Schiller's moral aesthetic philosophy. The organisation was founded upon the simple premise that if people come together to engage in beautiful activities, these soul enriching experiences will encourage the empathy necessary to the practice of morality. The movement brought many different types of people together whose discussions were catalysed by the collective appreciation of beauty in the world.

However, despite the success of the events, the organisation experienced its fair share of criticism. The idea that beauty could lead to improved forms of human sociability was ridiculed. The problem lay in the fact that those people who were unfamiliar with the purpose or activities of the organisation automatically dismissed it when they heard the word "beauty." They misconstrued the activities based on a simple misinterpretation of a word, superficially conflating beauty with fashion and physical appearances.

Some years later at a philosophy festival, I gave a talk on beauty and being where it became apparent that the meaning of the word beauty had become even further disfigured. At one point, in a self-indulgent provocation, a scholar equated beauty with the derrière of a reality television star. Such smug intellectualism masked as populism perverts the significance of concepts and words. Subsequently, an audience member offered the apocryphal suggestion that since people of the lower socio-economic classes cannot appreciate more sophisticated forms of beauty, the very discussion of the term beauty is "elitist." This comment brought back memories of a common critique lodged against beauty in my university days.

The critique of elitism is perplexing given that art, culture, and ideas are increasingly accessible. Almost all cultural institutions have made their productions affordable and widely available to a public. Moreover, most experiences of beauty do not require material resources. We can all appreciate the changing formation of clouds or the composition of a majestic landscape, so it does not make sense that something so universal would be considered anti-democratic.

We live in times when intellectuals who bring knowledge to others are considered "out of touch with the people." The attempt to make the world a more beautiful place through the proliferation of the arts is labelled an elitist excess. Appreciating a masterful work of literature or listening to a transcendentally beautiful piece of music is excoriated as an indulgence of the rich. Yet, our society finds it acceptable when people *actively* flaunt social and economic inequalities displaying their luxury clothing, expensive holidays, fancy cars, and the exclusive events that they attend, in popular culture and on social media. When further interrogated, this critique of elitism is not grounded in a solicitous concern about accessibility, but rather in the apocryphal belief that people of disadvantaged socio-economic classes cannot truly appreciate beauty. A gross prejudice against the working class fuels this belief, for it assumes that they are somehow unable to appreciate beauty. The critique of that which is labelled elitist is, in other words, inherently elitist.

Some may worry that introducing any aesthetic judgement or hierarchy of values is anti-democratic. But how can building with the cheapest materials to make the most profit with the least consideration of their detrimental effects on the human psyche possibly be good for humanity? Why should vulgar television shows and sexualised music videos be given the same legitimacy as art and literature that strives to understand the human condition with nuance and sensitivity? How could a crude, unthoughtful tweet be allowed to replace serious discourse in the public sphere?

If we legitimise the opinions of the most superficial people because we assume that the population is too ignorant to understand anything else, or if we embrace the ugliness of cities that have become desolate wastelands so as not to offend those subjugated to these eye sores, we fail humanity. The more we lower standards from our own prejudices, transforming the world into a bleak and uninspired place because we are not courageous enough to uphold a rigorous system of values, the more we lose the capacity for aspiration. It is easy to sit back and let society crumble. Claiming that the appreciation of beauty is elitist is the weak way out. However, the loss of this essential value is not democratic. To make this claim demonstrates a lack of faith in human capacities.

The goal should not be to reduce life to the lowest common denominator so that architecture becomes desolate, politics brutal, art vulgar, culture diminished, and ideas vacuous. It should be to elevate humanity by promoting the building of beautiful cities, the advancement of ideals, the greater accessibility of culture, and the encouragement of intellectual ambition. Expecting more, because we believe that every person deserves and is capable of more, is the most deeply progressive view. In returning to aesthetics to inform our value system, we should have faith that *all* people are able to appreciate beauty and create it in their own unique ways by virtue of the faculties with which every person has been endowed. Just like the ability to love, the capacity to derive a sense of purpose from beauty represents a fundamental part of what it means to be human.

The theorists of the Beautiful Soul and the *salonnières*

shared an acute aesthetic sensitivity that illuminated their perception of the world and provided them with an eternal wellspring of inspiration. The same verdant landscape that might make little more than a pleasing impression on one individual, brought irradiating hues of meaning to these thinkers. This sensibility they shared was as enigmatic and mysterious as genius, and it distinguished them from their contemporaries. But, despite their unique capacities, they were the first to acknowledge that the appreciation of beauty can be cultivated and matured. Schiller wrote extensively on aesthetic education because the desire to educate people on the importance of beauty for enriching the human spirit, and his belief that *all* people are capable of its appreciation, was the central claim of his revelatory philosophical treatise.

If we wish to share the inspired vision for humanity that the theorists of the Beautiful Soul maintained, we must undertake an aesthetic education. Only by becoming receptive to deeper forms of aesthetic perception will we recapture the true meaning of beauty. When fully utilising our faculties, we discover that beauty is everywhere, from the light which refracts through glass to the resplendent colours of fruit ripened by a glowing sun. A constant stream of sensory impressions surrounds us from which we can derive immense meaning. The redeeming fact of human existence is that in the face of true beauty, we all have the capacity to be moved deeply.

But in a society in which experiences of profound feeling are often categorised as psychological maladies, even the most obvious and overpowering forms of beauty can fail to make an impression on us. The tedious and isolating monotony of modern existence has the effect of deadening our senses and we easily forget the great beauty of the world. Practicing this philosophy means becoming alive once more through the refinement of aesthetic faculties. We aspire to render ourselves conscious of the everyday forms of beauty that surround us, which are immediately apparent yet go unappreciated. We can imagine that we are removing a clouded lens that obstructed our vision to see reality with the brilliant clarity it possesses. Aesthetic sensitivity permeates all aspects of our lived reality to develop the expansive perception that this philosophy demands. By constantly searching for beauty in everyday existence, contemplating its significance, creating beautiful atmospheres in our mind, and communicating this beauty, we reach an elation and feeling of unity with the world that we did not know was possible. In inspiring states of cognition that transcend material reality with all its injuries, disappointments, and suffering, beauty preserves ideals within us and makes apparent what is important in life.

The problem, however, is that the harmonious psychological effect inspired by the immediate experience of beauty and the elevated feelings that arise from this experience are ultimately transient. The poetic force we may feel while watching a powerful film dissipates upon the return to quotidian reality. The wonder and elation brought about by observing a constellation in a clear sky subsides when time fades night's majesty. In listening to music, a person might feel a sense of ultimate fulfilment and existential tranquillity, an expansive connectedness to others and a desire for the good. But this feeling will eventually subside, diluted by the disenchanting return to reality and the tedious demands of the will. To lose the force of the initial aesthetic experience is to diminish its power.

But what if we were able to capture the noble feelings that arise during and immediately after an experience of beauty in a sustained aesthetic state, as if to identify and bottle a precious substance? What if life itself could become a work of art, a poem of being in the act of becoming? What if every aspect of reality was impregnated with the loveliness that we feel when observing a masterful painting and this transcendent feeling was the basis from which we developed ourselves and improved the world?

It is the task of this philosophy, then, to capture these transient moments of beauty and sustain a continuous aesthetic state of being. This aesthetic state is "a particular way of looking at things" that mirrors the immediate response to art and nature, but for a sustained period.[594] It is the primary condition for life to become art and to immortalise one's being in the act of becoming. Beauty, then, is not only an object of philosophical interest but also a mode of living, a way of looking at the world and existing within it. By developing our ability to see beauty in this enduring sense, life itself becomes a work of art.

Today, the idea of living beautifully is particularly compelling, and in many respects revolutionary. It offers a radical break from the overwhelming sense of despondency and the unpoetic nature of these times. Imagining life as a work of art gives individuals the agency to transform existence into something which is ultimately significant under even the most imperfect social conditions. Poeticising the everyday by reshaping perception offers an intense meaning that previously only our experiences in literature or at the theatre allowed. By explicitly bringing aesthetics into the realm of daily life we may find the enduring strength particular to the artist whose ideas, liberated from the bonds of reality, can reach toward the infinite. Suddenly we become the protagonist of a novel, the lead character of a film, directing ourselves within a world that we have chosen to create.

Knowledge that our life is but an infinitesimal story in the history of the universe might make us believe that it is insignificant, and therefore unworthy of investing in with such care and intensity. But this philosophy shows us that our individual existence has an importance far greater than a symphony, or any other artistic creation. It encourages us to mould ourselves into something more momentous than what we assumed could be, by believing so fully in our innate capacities. The conviction in the extraordinariness of a life that an ordinary person can lead challenges us to make something ultimately beautiful in the finite time we have on earth.

If there is one thing that my salons have taught me it is that, despite our shortcomings, humans can continuously conceive new ways to render existence supremely beautiful. By adopting the eye of a visitor in a museum to observe people, as Varnhagen did within her own salons, time and again, I have seen this living art form become imaginatively manifest.

Those who wish to practice this philosophy today might take up the art of living systematically by approaching every aspect of experience with an aesthetic sensitivity, harmoniously composing enlightened thoughts and virtuous actions, familial relationships, professional pursuits, and social responsibilities, into a beautiful, unified whole.

CHAPTER 15

The Future of the Beautiful Soul

A T this point, a sceptical reader might ask "were beautiful souls actually cultivated within the eighteenth and nineteenth century salons?" Such a question is essential to determine if this might become a viable philosophy in today's world. Accounts of the time give a clear sense that people *believed* that their soul had, indeed, improved. Whether or not this was actually the case is inevitably a point of contention. We can never come to a definitive conclusion since there is no objective metric to the cultivation of beautiful souls; moreover, the philosophy itself contends that no human is ultimately capable of attaining a perfected form of this desired state.

Evidently the anti-Semitism that was perpetuated by some of the salon participants suggests that beautiful souls had, in fact, not been cultivated. However, multiple primary accounts of tolerance and empathy expressed in social relationships within the salons could point in the opposite direction. It is, in the end, futile to engage in such a debate; the very idea of a competition to achieve and display this exalted state negates the very principles upon which the concept was grounded. We should judge this philosophy on the quality of the ideas and principles that defined the Beautiful Soul and the way *salon-nières* chose to enact them. We can, however, argue more definitively that the salon is remembered as one of the most beloved institutions in European history. Even people who were not necessarily strong enough to fulfil its high moral demands respected its ideals and admired its activities.

What happened to the Beautiful Soul after the late eighteenth and early nineteenth centuries? The concept retained some salience throughout the nineteenth century but attempts at contributing to this tradition were less original and rigorous than in the Age of Goethe. Some ventures could not truly claim to be a part of this tradition and others appropriated the phrase "Beautiful Soul" in diametric opposition to its principles.[595] In certain circles of the *Bildungsbürgertum,* the concept was adopted as a passing fashion, a badge that could be worn, a term that could be employed cavalierly without underlying knowledge of its philosophical aims. In many instances *Bildung* became little more than a sign of approval for a bourgeois career in the civil service. It was associated primarily with training in the ancient languages and pursuit of a university degree. The deeper ideals of self-cultivation envisioned by Goethe and Schiller were all but lost.[596]

Bildung became disconnected from its ultimate end of cultivating a beautiful soul, and the nature of its meaning consequently changed. I do not explore the evolution of *Bildung* after the period that this book covers; to do so would be to inaccurately conflate topics. Just as it would be fruitless to equate *Bildung* in its original sixteenth century religious sense with *Bildung* in its eighteenth-century humanistic definition, any appropriations of the terms following this period constitute a fundamentally separate tradition. Indeed, the reduction of the concept's former meaning was met with contempt by later philosophers such as Friedrich Nietzsche (1844-1900) who, in a mocking passage referring to the latter-day advocates of the Beautiful Soul, remarked that:

> They despised the body, they left it out of account; even more, they treated it like an enemy. They were insane enough to believe that one could carry around a 'beautiful soul' in some cadaverous miscarriage...And to make it comprehensible to others, they had to employ the concept of 'beautiful soul' differently, to revalue its natural value, until finally a pale, sickly, idiotically enthusiastic creature was perceived as 'perfection,' as 'angelic,' as transfigured, as a higher form of human being.[597]

The figure of the Beautiful Soul was debased by rationalisation and "Christianisation" in Nietzsche's eyes.

Part of the reason for the conceptual degradation of the Beautiful Soul was that any attempt to implement an idea intended to radically redesign the philosophical and structural constitution of society requires visionaries who can translate complex principles into pragmatic action and intervene when concepts are misrepresented. Before people liberated themselves through self-cultivation, they needed guidance from mentors cognisant of and expert in these principles and practices. Varnhagen was this kind of visionary. People willingly followed her because of her exceptional personality and ability to imagine the world in a different way. With her demise, a poetic philosophy in pursuit of higher ideals was reduced to an institutionalised educational model.

However, a strong philosophy should, in theory, survive beyond the death of its creators and greatest proponents. Therefore, this explanation of decline is only partial. The principal reason for the superficial appropriation and diminishment of the Beautiful Soul was the accelerating influences of industrialisation and the market economy. In a capitalist society progressively more preoccupied with individual status and wealth, collective concerns of the soul became secondary, if not irrelevant. The dramatic changes that occurred in the economic sphere seeped into the philosophical sphere whose underlying value system decayed. Perceptions of human worth and success hinged on material acquisition, not on a rigorous process of moral and intellectual cultivation. Monetary gain took precedence over human dignity; it became easier to buy one's social value in the marketplace than to consider the state of one's soul and work towards its improvement.

As for the salons, some positive social outcomes were achieved. The 1812 edict of Jewish emancipation, for instance, gave Jews the right to become citizens of Berlin and ended the heavy taxes placed upon them. This policy came into being in large part because the *salonnières* demonstrated that the Jews were an essential part of German culture and society.[598] However, a rise in antisemitism which began during the Pamphlet War of 1803 and continued throughout the early nineteenth century, eroded many salon friendships.[599] This antisemitism not only had negative implications for the Jewish *salonnières*, but it also undermined the tolerance and egalitarianism that salon culture encouraged. With the rise of these exclusionary sentiments, a fundamentally progressive institution lost its salience and social influence.

In addition to the death of the most brilliant *salonnières* and the dawn of a new era of religious intolerance, industrialisation contributed to the demise of salon culture. As Marie von Bunsen (1860-1941), a chronicler of salon culture, commented, "aside from the catastrophes of war and inflation" the salon's disappearance was due to "the acceleration, the Americanisation of our existence, the restless need for travel and variety, the increase in hotel hospitality, the clubs, the passion for sports."[600] In a society that increasingly prioritised economic growth above all else, the desire to engage the intellect and cultivate moral faculties became less urgent. With a shift in values from collective pursuits of the mind to self-interested material pleasures came a shift in the ways one chose to associate with others and spend one's time. Individual salons continued, but a thriving salon culture comprised of *salonnières* who collaborated with one another did not survive. Those individual salons that did exist mirrored the changing times, taking on more of a club atmosphere by prioritising special interests and political affiliations which contradicted their former non-utilitarian spirit. Economic changes in the value system, therefore, meant a loss of public interest in *Bildung* and *die schöne Seele*. The critical ideological foundations of salon culture began to dissolve.

The theorists of the Beautiful Soul anticipated that an ethic of unbridled capitalism would imperil this ideal and undermine the community structures from which it was born. In a final letter to Humboldt, just prior to his death, on March 17, 1832, having observed a time of transition following the July Revolution in 1830, Goethe speculates that his ideas would not find favour in the modern age. Like Schiller, he saw technological change, industrial activity, mechanical developments and an ideology of economic growth to be in contradiction with the ideals of the past.[601] However, he also believed that the Beautiful Soul's story was far from over. Like the centuries between ancient Greece and Weimar Classicism, fallow periods might exist, but the legacy would continue. Paired with the dynamism of modern times, the Beautiful Soul would eventually flourish once more.

However, as capitalism intensified into a hegemonic system in the twentieth century, there were no substantive attempts to revive this philosophy or salon culture. Any such efforts were isolated, underdeveloped, misrepresented or did not reach the original spirit. Adam Smith (1723-1790) replaced Wilhelm von Humboldt as one of the most influential scholars of the eighteenth century. Changes in the activities that people pursued and the priorities that they chose may be understood as a reflection of the new and divergent understandings of liberalism and social values that these theorists professed.[602] Furthermore, on a larger political scale, Germany embarked upon an antithetical course with the rise of fascism and its corresponding racial theories that were in direct conflict with the principles of the Beautiful Soul and the ideological foundation of the Jewish salons. As society suffered the tragedies of the modern age, this utopic model for community life, and most especially, this idealistic philosophy, were all but forgotten amidst the chaos and destruction of industrial change and the aftermath of war.

In the twenty-first century, the original concept and institution of the salon have all but receded from our memory and collective consciousness. The Beautiful Soul has been lost in the popular vernacular; it also became an obscure domain of scholarship. Meanwhile, salons have come to be associated with initiatives that are in stark contradiction to their original values. Lectures and speaker events are often considered a "salon" in the contemporary context. However, this is a misrepresentation of the term, at least in its traditional sense. Implicit to the definition of a salon is the *collective* exchange of ideas through the art of conversation and a lack of distinction between those who present and those who participate. There is, by contrast, no participation in a speaker event except, perhaps, through a few questions posed by a passive audience which only reinforces a hierarchy of knowledge that was eschewed in the salons. The sterile, hotel conference room-like setting of such events, devoid of beauty, is in patent contradiction to the intimate, aesthetically curated atmosphere of the salon that was so crucial to its success. Social interactions are rendered superficial by the uninspired arena setting in which ideas cannot be collectively interrogated and critiqued. These types of talks are often seen as "networking opportunities," the instrumental jargon of the modern age. To network is to implicitly expect something out of someone else, to see them as a tool of one's own material advancement. How contrary this is to the non-utilitarian, idealistic spirit of the salon!

Similarly, internet forums are, at times, referred to colloquially as the public sphere and online salons.[603] Yet this, too, fundamentally misses the original intent of the salon. The internet can in theory foster the kind of egalitarian, communicative exchanges that the salon sought to create by bringing people who might not otherwise meet in contact with one another. However, the *type* of interactions that emerge often undermines egalitarianism itself. Unlike the highly personal space of the salon, with its culture of politeness and civility, the anonymity of the internet, lacking structures or rules of etiquette, can induce cruelty, bigotry, and deep misunderstandings that fester without accountability. Habitués of online forums may never witness or fully appreciate the negative implications of their online words and actions. Furthermore, internet exchanges can theoretically be insightful, continuous, and knowledge producing, but they very often are just the opposite. The sustained contact of the salon, so critical to the formation of soul-changing relationships, has been replaced by quickly changing newsfeeds and superficial interactions with thousands of strangers. Consequently, online exchanges often suffer from a lack of intellectual rigour and sustained interrogation of critical concepts.

Although there have been no major attempts to revitalise the Beautiful Soul or the institution of the salon, and communicative exchanges have, in many respects, taken a turn for the worse, this does not mean that this tradition cannot be revived. Indeed, it is precisely these negative developments that heighten the need for a restoration of this value system. The Beautiful Soul may appear naïve and outdated in the context of an increasingly cynical modernity. However, extreme pragmatism and the universal embrace of instrumental principles has exhausted itself and, arguably, proven profoundly ineffective in advancing human happiness and dignity.

Over the course of this book, we have seen that among the modern ills we face that could be addressed by this philosophy and salon culture is the deterioration of standards of human decency and the change in our relationship to beauty. I have argued that cross-cultural values of kindness, humility, and compassion have been replaced by ego-driven aims of material gain, vanity, and self-aggrandisement. Ideals that would maintain human dignity have been undermined by a cynicism that evades moral responsibility. It is easier to assume that the world is cruel and contribute to its cruelty than to maintain the will towards idealism and positively shape society's course. It is easier to inure one's emotions to experience, to exist as a half-dead being, and to be selfish, than it is to see beauty, to feel deeply, and to retain a belief in something greater than oneself. Moral cowardice and sensory apathy are symptoms of our current age as we suffer through a global crisis of values which leaves us feeling purposeless, degraded, and alone.

The word beauty, once connected to a transcendental ideal and an immaterial state of the soul, has been reduced to surface appearances. The *salonnières* who perceived the world in a beautiful way have been replaced by pop icons who unashamedly extol wealth, power, and personal display at the expense of deeper inquiry into the values that make life worth living. All too often politicians and institutional leaders appear to lack the principles and integrity that would command respect. Disillusioned by the moral turpitude and the sorry displays of unbeautiful character traits that we see all around us, we succumb to these commonplace vices: they have become the norm. The values that gain traction are those bound to the desires of specific interest groups that divide the social world into increasingly unequal factions. No longer is our concern for humanity but rather for the limited circles of people with whom we associate. Cosmopolitan ideals have been replaced by a surge of tribalist sentiments and sectarian populism. Nationalism and rising inequalities threaten peace, security, and social cohesion.

This crisis of values is accompanied by a distinct loss of purpose. Schiller and Goethe's discussion of the fragmentation of modern society was a prescient harbinger of the contemporary state of the world. The individual has arguably become more fragmented than ever before, disconnected from his labour and enslaved to structures beyond his control or comprehension. Often professions are pursued entirely for profit while promising a happiness that never materialises. In such cases it is easy to forget what reason there is in continuing to exist when most of one's waking hours are spent on activities divorced from a greater meaning.

Having lost a sense of communal life, society is threatened by an epidemic of loneliness. Where there were once "Friends of the Soul" and "Societies of Virtue," there are now people extracting practical benefit from each other. Meanwhile, mass hysteria, gratuitous cruelty, and witch hunts without trial fuelled by online exchanges can be likened to the mob mentalities that Goethe and Schiller warned against. History repeats itself in the mania caused by the irrational actions of an uninformed crowd. As people become more resentful and divided, as views become more provocative and extreme, as valuable ends and just means are thwarted by ignorance and irrationality, it appears that somewhere along the path towards progress, humanity lost its way.

In keeping with the cynicism that defines our times, Robert Norton, who wrote the only other book published about the Beautiful Soul in the English language in 1995, suggests that we should bid this ideal "a final and clear-eyed farewell."[604] His conclusion relegates its historical legacy to the realm of irrelevance, as a beautiful but evanescent concept that has outlived its day. By contrast, I have argued that it was in fundamental respects reached during the intensely productive, albeit brief, period when philosophy and institution came together as one, and that there is no compelling reason why this cannot be achieved once more. Indeed, a renaissance of the philosophy of the Beautiful Soul represents a beacon of hope for restoring a deeply fractured society.

The theorists of the Beautiful Soul and the *salonnières* taught us important lessons: to expand our mind, refine our faculties, increase our empathy, and hone our ability to perceive the beauty in this world. They remind us to maintain faith in the Good, to act with a nobility of spirit, to find humane forms of shared existence, and to improve the lives of others. If we still believe in these beautiful ideals, then it is not only possible, but also in our best interest to revive them once more. For, as the theorists of the Beautiful Soul maintained, we still have the capacity to form a more virtuous humanity. To create the most beautiful of worlds is the duty we owe to ourselves and to posterity. No matter what circumstances we have been born into or what trials we may face, we have the choice to maintain a nobility of soul. It is this which defines us, this which unites us, this which determines the worth of the existence that was led. In the end, to poetically reconstruct the world by living a beautiful life is the most radical political act.

ENDNOTES

[1] Robert Edward Norton, *The Beautiful Soul: Aesthetic Morality in the Eighteenth Century* (Ithaca: Cornell University Press, 1995), p. 251.

[2] Ibid., p. IX.

[3] Suzanne L. Marchand, *Down from Olympus: Archaeology and Philhellenism in Germany, 1750-1970* (Princeton: Princeton University Press, 2003), p. 3.

[4] Friedrich Schiller, *On the Aesthetic Education of Man, trans. by Reginald Snell* (New York: Dover Publications, 2004), pp. 37-38.

[5] Frederick Beiser, 'Schiller and Pessimism', in *Aesthetic Reason and Imaginative Freedom: Friedrich Schiller and Philosophy,* ed. by María del Rosario Acosta López, Jeffrey L. Powell (Albany: State University of New York, 2018), pp. 83-101(p.94).

[6] Johann Peter Eckermann, *Conversations of Goethe with Eckermann and Soret*, trans. by John Oxenford (London: Smith, Elder & Co., 1850), p. 204.

[7] Johann Wolfgang von Goethe, *Collected Works of Johann Wolfgang von Goethe* (Hastings, East Sussex: Delphi Classics, 2013), p. 3535.

[8] Eckermann, *Conversations of Goethe*, p. 265.

[9] Humphry Trevelyan, *Goethe and the Greeks* (Cambridge: Cambridge University Press, 2008), p. xxxviii.

[10] Ibid., p. xvii.

[11] James Conant, 'Nietzsche's Perfectionism: A Reading of Schopenhauer as Educator', in *Nietzsche's Postmoralism: Essays on Nietzsche's Prelude to Philosophy's Future,* ed. by Richard Schacht (Cambridge: Cambridge University Press, 2000), pp. 181-258 (p. 252).

[12] Bas van Bommel, 'Between "Bildung" and "Wissenschaft": The 19th century German Ideal of Scientific Education', *European History Online*, (2015), 12-14 (p. 3).

[13] Johann Gottfried von Herder, *Outlines of a Philosophy of the History of Man,* trans. by T. Churchill (London: Bergman Publishers, 1800), p. 107.

[14] Friedrich Schlegel, *On the Study of Greek Poetry*, ed. and trans. by Stuart Barnett (New York: Suny Press, 2001)

[15] Joachim Whaley, 'The Transformation of the Aufklärung: From the Idea of Power to the Power of Ideas', in *Cultures of Power in Europe during the Long Eighteenth Century,* ed. by Hamish Scott and Brendan Simms

(Cambridge: Cambridge University Press, 2007), pp.158-179 (p. 158).

[16] Frederick C. Beiser, *Enlightenment, Revolution, and Romanticism: The Genesis of Modern German Political Thought, 1790-1800* (Cambridge/Mass.: Harvard University Press, 1992), p. 56.

[17] Frank A. Kafker, James Michael Laux, and Darline Gay Levy (eds.), *The French Revolution: Conflicting Interpretations* (Florida: Krieger Publishing Company, 2002), p. 222.

[18] Beiser, *Enlightenment, Revolution, and Romanticism*, p.10.

[19] Norton, *The Beautiful Soul,* p. 138.

[20] James van Horn Melton, *The Rise of the Public in Enlightenment Europe: New Approaches to European History* (Cambridge: Cambridge University Press, 2001), pp. 215-216.

[21] Bernhard Giesen, 'Cosmopolitans, Patriots, Jacobins, and Romantics', *Daedalus,* vol. 127, no.3 (1998), 221-250 (p.230).

[22] Ibid., p. 231.

[23] Van Horn Melton, *The Rise of the Public in Enlightenment Europe*, p. 216.

[24] Ibid., p. 220.

[25] Deborah Hertz, *Jewish High Society in Old Regime Berlin* (Syracuse: Syracuse University Press, 2005), p. 81.

[26] Ibid., p. 44.

[27] Ibid., p. 96.

[28] Dan Cohn Sherbok, *Judaism: History, Belief and Practice* (New York: Routledge, 2017), p. 243.

[29] Heidi Thomann Tewarson, *Rahel Levin Varnhagen: The Life and Work of a German Jewish Intellectual* (Nebraska: University of Nebraska Press, 1998), p. 25.

[30] Roswitha Burwick, 'From Aesthetic Teas to the World of Noble Reformers: The Berlin Salonière (1780 to 1848)', *Pacific Coast Philology*, vol. 29, no.2 (1994), 129-142 (p.129).

[31] Van Horn Melton, *The Rise of the Public in Enlightenment Europe*, p. 207.

[32] Hertz, *Jewish High Society in Old Regime Berlin*, p.19.

[33] Leo W. Riegert, 'The Practical Side of Bildung: From Moses Mendelssohn's "Was heißt aufklären?" to Karl Emil Franzos's Moschko von Parma', in *Yearbook for European Jewish Literature Studies,* ed. by Alfred Bodenheimer and Liska Vivian, vol.1, no.1 (2014), 255-279 (p.255).

[34] Yael Sela Teichler, 'Music, Acculturation, and Haskalah between Berlin and Königsberg in the 1780's', *The Jewish Quarterly Review,* vol. 103, no. 3 (2013), 352-384 (p.354).

[35] Liliane Weissberg, 'Stepping Out', *New German Critique*, no. 53 (1991), 149-162 (p.150).

[36] Sela Teichler, 'Music, Acculturation, and Haskalah', p. 375.

[37] Alexander Altmann, 'Das Menschenbild und die Bildung des Menschen nach Moses Mendelssohn', *Mendelssohn-Studien,* vol 1. (1972), 11-28.

[38] Sela Teichler, 'Music, Acculturation, and Haskalah', p. 373.

[39] Thomann Tewarson, *Rahel Levin Varnhagen,* p. 27.

[40] Ibid., p. 132.

[41] Arendt, *Rahel Varnhagen*, p. 56.

[42] Valerian Tornius, *Salons: Pictures of Society through Five Centuries*, trans. by Agnes Platt and Lilian Wonderley (New York: Cosmopolitan Book Corporation, 1929, p. 253.

[43] Ibid., p. 257.

[44] Burwick, 'From Aesthetic Teas to the World of Noble Reformers', p.132.

[45] Hertz, *Jewish High Society in Old Regime Berlin*, p. 108.

[46] Donovan Anderson, 'Franco-German Conversations: Rahel Levin and Sophie von Grotthuß in Dialogue with Germaine de Staël', *German Studies Review*, vol. 29, no. 3 (2006), 559-577 (p.566).

[47] Hertz, *Jewish High Society in Old Regime Berlin*, p. 179.s

[48] Petra Wilhelmy Dollinger, 'Berlin Salons: Late Eighteenth to Early Twentieth Century', *Jewish Women: A Comprehensive Historical Encyclopedia: Jewish Women's Archive,* (2009), 1-1 (p.1).

[49] Tornius, *Salons*, p. 260.

[50] Anderson, 'Franco-German Conversations', p. 559.

[51] Wilhelmy Dollinger, *Berlin Salons*, p. 1.

[52] Arendt, *Rahel Varnhagen*, pp. 34-35.

[53] Ibid., pp.188-189.

[54] Ibid., p. 114.

[55] Tornius, *Salons*, p. 300.

[56] Arendt, *Rahel Varnhagen*, p. 112.

[57] Novalis, 'Pollen', in *The Early Political Writings of the German Romantics*, ed. and trans. by Frederick C. Beiser, (Cambridge: Cambridge University Press, 1996), pp. 9-31 (p.11).

[58] J. W. Burrow, 'Introduction' in *The Limits of State Action,* by Wilhelm von Humboldt, trans. by J. W. Burrow (London: Cambridge University Press, 1969), p. liv.

[59] Friedrich Schiller, *Essays Aesthetic and Philosophical*, trans. by John Weiss (London: George Bell & Sons, 1884), p. 293.

[60] Schiller, *On the Aesthetic Education of Man,* p. 31.

[61] Ibid., p. 73.

[62] Nicholas Boyle, *Goethe: The Poet and the Age: Volume II: Revolution and Renunciation, 1790-1803* (Oxford: Oxford University Press, 2003), p. 30.

[63] Johann Wolfgang von Goethe, *The Maxims and Reflections of Goethe,*

trans. by Bailey Saunders (New York: The Macmillan Company, 1906), p.8.

64 Schiller, *On the Aesthetic Education of Man*, p. 38.

65 Wilhelm von Humboldt, *Gesammelte Schriften: Ausgabe der Preussischen Akademie der Wissenschaften,* vols. I-XVII, (1903-36), vol. 2, p. 117.

66 Schiller, *Essays Aesthetic and Philosophical*, p. 134.

67 See the "Confessions of a Beautiful Soul" = Book VI in Johann Wolfgang von Goethe, *Wilhelm Meister's Apprenticeship and Travels*, trans. by Thomas Carlyle (London: Chapman and Hall, 1874), pp. 321-372.

68 Schleiermacher 'Monologues II and III', p. 182.

69 Schiller, *Essays Aesthetic and Philosophical*, p. 350.

70 Goethe, *The Maxims and Reflections,* p. 61.

71 Humboldt, *The Limits of State Action,* p. 13.

72 David Kettler and Gerhard Lauer, 'The "Other Germany" and the Question of Bildung: Weimar to Bonn', in *Exile, Science, and Bildung: The Contested Legacies of German Intellectual Figures*, ed. by David Ketller and Gerhard Lauer (New York: Palgrave Macmillan, 2005), pp.1-18 (p. 13).

73 Schlegel, *On the Study of Greek Poetry*, p. 37.

74 Goethe, *Wilhelm Meister*, pp. 359-360.

75 Ibid., p. 368.

76 Ibid., p. 211.

77 Thomann Tewarson, *Rahel Levin Varnhagen,* p. 32.

78 Ibid., p. 32.

79 Weissberg, 'Stepping Out', p. 153.

80 Ibid., p. 144.

81 Arendt, *Rahel Varnhagen*, p. 155.

82 Ibid., p.129.

83 Ellen Karolina Sofia Key, *Rahel Varnhagen: A Portrait* (Bremen: Erscheinungsort, 2013), p. 40.

84 See Hans Adler, 'Herder's Concept of Humanität', in *A Companion to the Works of Johann Gottfried Herder,* ed. by Hans Adler and Wulf Koepke (Rochester: Camden House, 2009), pp. 93-116.

85 Van Horn Melton, *The Rise of the Public in Enlightenment Europe*, p. 201.

86 Key, *Rahel Varnhagen*, p. 41.

87 Norton, *The Beautiful Soul,* p. 131.

88 Rebekka Horlacher, *The Educated Subject and the German Concept of Bildung: A Comparative Cultural History* (London: Routledge, 2015), p. 42.

89 Ibid., p. 42.

90 See Aristotle, *The Nicomachean Ethics,* trans. by J.A.K. Thomson (London: Penguin Classics, 2004)

91 Schiller, *Essays Aesthetic and Philosophical*, p. 134.

92 See F.C. White, 'Beauty of Soul and Speech in Plato's Symposium', *The*

Classical Quarterly, vol. 58, no. 1 (2008), 69-81 and Plato, *Plato Complete Works,* ed. by John M. Cooper (London: Hackett Publishing Company, 1997), pp. 483-494.

[93] Goethe, *The Maxims and Reflections,* p. 148.

[94] Friedrich Schiller, 'Kallias or Concerning Beauty: Letters to Gottfried Körner', in *Classic and Romantic German Aesthetics,* ed. and trans. by J. M. Bernstein (Cambridge: Cambridge University Press, 2010), pp. 145-185 (p. 174).

[95] Schiller, *Essays Aesthetic and Philosophical,* p. 169.

[96] Ibid., p. 203.

[97] Ibid., p. 203.

[98] Ibid., p. 203.

[99] Norton, *The Beautiful Soul,* p. 163.

[100] Schiller, *Essays Aesthetic and Philosophical,* p. 275.

[101] Louis K. Dupre, *The Enlightenment and the Intellectual Foundations of Modern Culture* (New Haven: Yale University Press, 2004), p. 126.

[102] Ibid., p. 202.

[103] Ibid., p. 134.

[104] Ibid., p. 135.

[105] Ibid., p. 135.

[106] Anne Margaret Baxley, 'The Beautiful Soul and the Autocratic Agent: Schiller's and Kant's "Children of the House"', *Journal of the History of Philosophy*, vol. 41, no. 4 (2003), 493-514 (p.496).

[107] Schiller, *On the Aesthetic Education of Man,* p. 83.

[108] Key, *Rahel Varnhagen,* p. 53.

[109] Ibid., p. 42.

[110] Ibid., p. 41.

[111] Ibid., p. 41.

[112] Ibid., p. 53.

[113] Ibid., p. 67.

[114] Hertz, *Jewish High Society in Old Regime Berlin,* p. 118.

[115] Marjanne E. Goozé, 'Posing for Posterity: The Representations and Portrayals of Henriette Herz as 'Beautiful Jewess', in *Body Dialectics in the Age of Goethe*, ed. by Marianne Henn and Holger A. Pausch (Amsterdam: Rodopi, 2003), pp. 67-97 (p.76).

[116] Henriette Herz, 'Ein Tugendbund-Wilhelm von Humboldt' in *Ihr Leben und ihre Erinnerungen*, trans. by Herausgegeben von J. Fürst (Berlin: Berliner Ausgabe, 2015), pp. 91-96.

[117] Ibid., p. 76.

[118] Liliane Weissberg and Rahel Varnhagen, 'Writing on the Wall: Letters of Rahel Varnhagen', *New German Critique*, no. 36 (1985), 157-173 (p.158).

[119] Wilhelmy Dollinger, Die Berliner Salons, p. 65.

[120] Herz, *Ihr Leben und ihre Erinnerungen*, p. 93.

[121] Jeffrey A. Grossman, *The Discourse on Yiddish in Germany from the Enlightenment to the Second Empire* (Rochester: Camden House, 2000), p. 70.

[122] Carol Diethe, *Towards Emancipation: German Women Writers of the Nineteenth Century* (New York: Berghahn Books, 1998), p. 22.

[123] Gerlinde Roder-Bolton, George Eliot in Germany, 1854-55: "Cherished Memories"(London: Routledge, 2017), p. 124.

[124] Thomann Tewarson, *Rahel Levin Varnhagen,* p. 22.

[125] Ibid., p. 22.

[126] Key, *Rahel Varnhagen*, p. 53.

[127] Ibid., p.172.

[128] Ibid., p. 49.

[129] Bilski and Braun, *Jewish Women and their Salons*, p. 28.

[130] Steven D. Kale, 'Women, Salons and Sociability as Constitutional Problems in the Political Writings of Madame de Staël', *Historical Reflections*, vol. 32, no. 2 (2006), 209-338 (p.319).

[131] Key, *Rahel Varnhagen*, p. 224.

[132] Thomann Tewarson, *Rahel Levin Varnhagen,* p. 183.

[133] Arendt, *Rahel Varnhagen*, p. 19.

[134] Thomann Tewarson, *Rahel Levin Varnhagen,* p. 1.

[135] Ibid., p. 72.

[136] Key, *Rahel Varnhagen*, p. 221.

[137] Van Horn Melton, *The Rise of the Public in Enlightenment Europe*, p. 202.

[138] Kale, 'Women, Salons and Sociability', p. 320.

[139] Arendt, *Rahel Varnhagen*, p. 154.

[140] Ibid., p. 154.

[141] Kale, 'Women, Salons and Sociability', p. 318.

[142] Van Horn Melton, *The Rise of the Public in Enlightenment Europe*, p. 207.

[143] Weissberg and Varnhagen, 'Writing on the Wall', p. 159.

[144] Key, *Rahel Varnhagen*, p. 226.

[145] Bilski and Braun, *Jewish Women and their Salons*, pp. 28-29.

[146] For an examination of the French salons see Dena Goodman, *The Republic of Letters* (Ithaca: Cornell University Press, 1994)

[147] Goethe, *Poetry and Truth*, p. 144.

[148] T. J. Reed, *Light in Germany: Scenes from an Unknown Enlightenment* (Chicago: University of Chicago Press, 2015), pp. 148-149.

[149] Novalis, 'Pollen', pp. 24-25.

[150] See Schiller, *On the Aesthetic Education of Man*, pp. 25-27.

[151] Schiller, *Essays Aesthetic and Philosophical*, p. 240.

[152] Humboldt, *The Limits of State Action*, p. 22.

[153] Schleiermacher 'Monologues II and III', p. 178.

[154] Schiller, *On the Aesthetic Education of Man*, pp. 35-36.

[155] Reed, *Light in Germany,* p. 126.

[156] Friedrich Schiller and Johann Wolfgang von Goethe, *Correspondence Between Schiller and Goethe,* trans. by George H. Calvert (London: Wiley and Putnam, 1845), p. 237.

[157] Humboldt, 'Theory of Bildung', p. 235.

[158] Helmut Thielicke, *Modern Faith and Thought* (Michigan: William B. Eerdmans, 1990), p. 174.

[159] Schiller, *On the Aesthetic Education of Man*, p. 40.

[160] Ibid., p. 26.

[161] Schiller, 'Kallias', p. 170.

[162] Hertz, *Jewish High Society in Old Regime Berlin,* p. 12.

[163] Kay Goodman, 'Poesis and Praxis in Rahel Varnhagen's Letters', *New German Critique*, no. 27 (1982), p. 130.

[164] Thomann Tewarson, *Rahel Levin Varnhagen*, p. 32.

[165] William Rasch, 'Ideal Sociability: Friedrich Schleiermacher and the Ambivalence of Extrasocial Spaces', in *Gender in Transition: Discourse and Practice in German Speaking Europe, 1750-1830*, ed. by Ulrike Gleixner and Marion W. Gray (Ann Arbor: The University of Michigan Press, 2006), pp. 319-341 (pp. 3
28-329).

[166] Ibid., p. 330.

[167] Ibid., p. 330.

[168] Van Horn Melton, *The Rise of the Public in Enlightenment Europe*, p. 222.

[169] Rasch, 'Ideal Sociability', p. 330.

[170] Key, *Rahel Varnhagen*, p. 226.

[171] Friedrich Schiller, *Essays, Aesthetic and Philosophical (London: George Bell and Sons, 1875), p. 61.*

[172] Schiller, *On the Aesthetic Education of Man*, p. 91.

[173] Beiser, *The Romantic Imperative*, p. 100.

[174] Ibid., p. 100.

[175] Boyle, *Goethe*, pp. 30-31.

[176] See, e.g., Quentin Skinner, *Liberty before Liberalism* (Cambridge: Cambridge University Press, 1998).

[177] Schlegel, 'Ideas', p. 139.

[178] Goethe, *The Maxims and Reflections,* p. 75.

[179] Immanuel Kant, *An Answer to the Question: 'What Is Enlightenment?'*, trans. by H.B. Nisbet (London: Penguin Books, 2009), p. 5.

[180] Ibid., p.5.

[181] Humboldt, *The Limits of State Action,* p. 36.

[182] Schiller, *On the Aesthetic Education of Man*, pp. 46-47.

[183] Schiller, *On the Aesthetic Education of Man*, p. 49.

[184] Burrow, 'Introduction' in *The Limits of State Action,* p. lii.

[185] Schiller, *On the Aesthetic Education of Man*, p. 54.

[186] Immanuel Kant, *On Education,* trans. by Annette Churton (Boston: D.C Heath and Co.,1900), p. 30.

[187] Humboldt, *The Limits of State Action*, p. 12.

[188] Schiller, 'Kallias', p. 164.

[189] Schiller, *Essays Aesthetic and Philosophical*, p. 181.

[190] Schiller, 'Kallias', pp. 173-174.

[191] Ibid., pp. 173-174.

[192] Ibid., pp. 173-174.

[193] Burwick, 'From Aesthetic Teas to the World of Noble Reformers', p. 131.

[194] Spiel, 'Fanny von Arnstein', p. 47.

[195] Arendt, *Rahel Varnhagen*, p. 34.

[196] Weissberg, 'Stepping Out', p. 150.

[197] Ibid., p. 151.

[198] Arendt, *Rahel Varnhagen*, p. 98.

[199] Rahel Levin and David Veit, 'Rahel Levin and David Veit, Correspondence (1793-5)', in *The German-Jewish Dialogue: An Anthology of Literary Texts, 1749-1993,* ed. by Ritchie Robertson (Oxford: Oxford University Press, 1999), pp. 54-63 (p. 62).

[200] Arendt, *Rahel Varnhagen*, p. 67.

[201] Thomann Tewarson, *Rahel Levin Varnhagen,* pp. 188-189.

[202] Arendt, *Rahel Varnhagen,* p. 60.

[203] Giesen,'Cosmopolitans, Patriots, Jacobins, and Romantics', p. 228.

[204] Seyla Benhabib, 'The Pariah and her Shadow: Hannah Arendt's Biography of Rahel Varnhagen', *Political Theory*, vol. 23, no.1 (1995), 5-24, p. 17.

[205] Hertz, *Jewish High Society in Old Regime Berlin,* p. 222.

[206] Tryon Edwards, *The New Dictionary of Thoughts: A Cyclopedia of Quotations* (Montana: Kessinger Publishing, 2008), p. 324.

[207] Norton, *The Beautiful Soul,* p. 210.

[208] Schiller, *Essays Aesthetic and Philosophical*, p. 120.

[209] Joachim Lütkemann, Der Vorschmack göttlicher Güte durch Gottes Gnade, ed. by Philipp Julius Rehtmeyer (Braunschweig: Rudolph Schröder, 1720), p. 543.

[210] Eckermann, *Conversations of Goethe*, p. 108.

[211] Schlegel, 'Ideas', p. 135.

[212] Bruford, *The German Tradition of Self-Cultivation,* pp. 142-143.

[213] Schiller, *Essays Aesthetic and Philosophical*, p. 285.

[214] Schlegel, 'The Concept of Republicanism', p. 103.

[215] Geuss, 'Kultur, Bildung, Geist', p.155.

[216] See Klaus Vondung, Das wilhelminische Bildungsbürgertum: Zur Sozialgeschichte seiner Ideen (Göttingen: Vandenhoeck & Rupreche, 1976)

[217] Norton, *The Beautiful Soul*, p. 123.

[218] Beiser, 'Introduction', in *The Early Political Writings of the German Romantics*, p. xxiv.

[219] Beiser, *Enlightenment, Revolution, and Romanticism*, p. 103.

[220] Ibid., p. 103.

[221] Schleiermacher, 'Monologues II and III', p. 173.

[222] Thomas Fuhr, 'Bildung: An Introduction' in *Transformative Learning Meets Bildung: An International Exchange,* ed. by Anna Laros, Thomas Fuhr, Edward W. Taylor (Rotterdam: Sense Publishers, 2017), pp. 3-17 (p.8).

[223] Goethe, *Werther,* p. 28.

[224] See Sonjeong Cho, *An Ethics of Becoming: Configurations of Feminine Subjectivity in Jane Austen, Charlotte Brontë, and George Eliot* (New York: Routledge, 2005), p. 27.

[225] Humboldt, *The Limits of State Action*, p. 25.

[226] Giovanna Summerfield and Lisa Downward, *New Perspectives on the European Bildungsroman* (London: Continuum International Publishing, 2010), p. 15.

[227] Ibid., p.16.

[228] Arendt, *Rahel Varhagen*, p. 98.

[229] Thomann Tewarson, *Rahel Levin Varnhagen*, p. 80.

[230] Lawler and Richardson 'Introduction' in *Florentin,* p. x.

[231] Key, *Rahel Varnhagen*, p. 196.

[232] Ibid., p. 198.

[233] Ibid., p. 203.

[234] Thomann Tewarson, *Rahel Levin Varnhagen*, p. 209.

[235] Key, *Rahel Varnhagen,* p. 194.

[236] Arendt, *Rahel Varnhagen*, p. 170.

[237] Bilski and Braun, *Jewish Women and their Salons*, p. 44.

[238] Ibid., p. 32.

[239] Key, *Rahel Varnhagen*, p. 185.

[240] Kale, 'Women, Salons and Sociability', p. 320.

[241] Spiel, 'Rahel Varnhagen', p. 53.

[242] Hillman, 'The Conversions of Dorothea Mendelssohn', p. 135.

[243] Lawler and Richardson 'Introduction' in *Florentin,* p. xiv.

[244] Ibid., xiv.

[245] Ibid., pp. lxii-lxiii.

[246] Karin Stuebben Thornton, 'Enlightenment and Romanticism in the Work of Dorothea Schlegel', *The German Quarterly*, vol.39, no.2 (1966), pp.162-172 (p.164).

[247] Arendt, *Rahel Varnhagen*, p. 114.

[248] Ibid., p. 112.

[249] Arendt, *Rahel Varnhagen*, p. 115.

[250] Ibid., p. 112.

[251] Tornius, *Salons*, p. 300.

[252] Schlegel, *Florentin,* p. 97.

[253] Ibid., pp. 99-100.

[254] Hertz, *Jewish High Society in Old Regime Berlin*, p. 7.

[255] Burwick, 'From Aesthetic Teas to the World of Noble Reformers', p. 129.

[256] Spiel, 'Fannny von Arnstein', p. 51.

[257] Hertz, *Jewish High Society in Old Regime Berlin*, p. 13.

[258] Anthony J. La Vopa, 'The Politics of Enlightenment: Friedrich Gedike and German Professional Ideology', *The Journal of Modern History*, vol. 62, no. 1 (1990) 34-56 (p.44).

[259] Key, *Rahel Varnhagen*, p. 220.

[260] Thomann Tewarson, *Rahel Levin Varnhagen*, p.184.

[261] Ibid., p. 37.

[262] Key, *Rahel Varnhagen*, p. 234.

[263] Ibid., p. 204.

[264] Herz, *Ihr Leben und ihre Erinnerungen*, p.81.

[265] Van Horn Melton, *The Rise of the Public in Enlightenment Europe*, p. 197.

[266] Wilhelmy Dollinger, *Berlin Salons*, p. 157.

[267] Hertz, *Jewish High Society in Old Regime Berlin*, p. 106.

[268] Herz, *Ihr Leben und ihre Erinnerungen*, p. 80.

[269] Ibid., p. 81.

[270] Arendt, *Rahel Varnhagen*, p. 38.

[271] Ibid., p. 38.

[272] See Peter Foley, *Friedrich Schleiermacher's Essay on a Theory of Social Behavior (1799): A Contextual Interpretation* (New York: E. Mellen Press, 2006).

[273] Hertz, *Jewish High Society in Old Regime Berlin,* p. 145.

[274] Ibid., p. 13.

[275] Ibid., p. 10.

[276] Ibid., p. 10.

[277] Hertz, 'Salonières and Literary Women', p. 99.

[278] Bilski and Braun, *Jewish Women and their Salons*, p. 16.

[279] Thomann Tewarson, *Rahel Levin Varnhagen*, pp. 72-73.

[280] Ibid., pp. 72-73.

[281] Ibid., p. 88.

[282] Ibid., p. 124.

[283] Ibid., p. 73.

[284] Ibid., p. 4

[285] Ibid., p. 73.

[286] Ibid., p. 44.s

[287] Novalis, 'Fragments from the Notebooks', p. 88.

[288] Bruford, *The German Tradition of Self-Cultivation*, p. 98.

[289] Goethe, *Wilhelm Meister*, p. 325.

[290] Key, *Rahel Varnhagen*, p. 211.

[291] Ibid. p. 221.

[292] Hertz, *Jewish High Society in Old Regime Berlin*, p. 56.

[293] Deborah Hertz, 'Salonières and Literary Women' p. 99.

[294] Van Horn Melton, *The Rise of the Public in Enlightenment Europe*, p. 198.s

[295] Burwick, 'From Aesthetic Teas to the World of Noble Reformers', p. 131.

[296] Bilski and Braun, *Jewish Women and their Salons*, p. 44.

[297] Anderson, 'Franco-German Conversations', p. 567.s

[298] Burrow, 'Introduction' in *The Limits of State Action,* p. lviii.

[299] Geuss, 'Kultur, Bildung, Geist', p.161.

[300] Ibid., p.155.

[301] Elizabeth E. Bohning, 'Goethe's and Schiller's Interpretation of Beauty', *The German Quarterly*, vol. 22, no.4 (1949), 185-194 (p.185).

[302] Hans Reiner, *Duty and Inclination: The Fundamentals of Morality Discussed and Redefined with Special Regard to Kant and Schiller* (The Hague: Martinus Nijhoff Publishers, 1983), p. 519.

[303] Novalis, 'Pollen', p. 30.

[304] Schiller, *On the Aesthetic Education of Man*, pp. 105-106.

[305] Schleiermacher, 'Monologues II and III', p. 187.

[306] Schmidt, 'Introduction', in *On the Aesthetic Education of Man*, p. xxxi.

[307] Geuss, 'Kultur, Bildung, Geist', p.155.

[308] Beiser, *The Romantic Imperative*, p. 105.

[309] Schiller and Goethe, *Correspondence*, p. 285.

[310] Schlegel, 'Lectures on Transcendental Philosophy', p. 153.

[311] Ibid., p. 152.

[312] Schiller, *Essays Aesthetic and Philosophical*, p. 244.

[313] Key, *Rahel Varnhagen*, pp. 260-261.

[314] Ibid., p. 261.

[315] Ibid., p. 261.

316 Key, *Rahel Varnhagen*, p. 47.

317 Wilhelmy Dollinger, *Die Berliner Salons*, p. 64.

318 Hertz, *Jewish High Society in Old Regime Berlin*, p. 100.

319 Ibid., p. 154.

320 Goodman, *The Republic of Letters*, p. 99.

321 Spiel, 'Rahel Varnhagen', p. 15.

322 Thomann Tewarson, *Rahel Levin Varnhagen*, p. 111.

323 Ibid., pp. 74-75.

324 Ibid., p. 74-75.

325 Ibid., p. 75.

326 Ibid., p. 101.

327 Ibid., p. 103.

328 Key, *Rahel Varnhagen*, p. 161.

329 Ibid., p. 169.

330 Ibid., p.163.

331 Deiulio 'The Voice of the schöne Seele', in *Challenging Separate Spheres, p.102*

332 Alexander Schmidt, 'Introduction', in *On the Aesthetic Education of Man*, by Friedrich Schiller, trans. by Keith Tribe (London, Penguin Classics, 2016), pp. vii-xxxv (p. xvii).

333 Humboldt, *The Limits of State Action*, p. 60.

334 Goethe, *The Maxims and Reflections*, p. 147.

335 Humboldt, *The Limits of State Action*, p. 60.

336 Ibid., p. 71.

337 Goethe, *The Maxims and Reflections*, p. 147.

338 Schmidt, 'Introduction', in *On the Aesthetic Education of Man*, p. x.

339 Leonard P. Wessell, 'Schiller and the Genesis of German Romanticism', *Studies in Romanticism,* vol. 10, no.3 (1971), 176-198 (p.179).

340 Johann Wolfgang von Goethe, *The Sorrows of Young Werther,* trans. by Michael Hulse (London: Penguin Classics, 1989), p. 44.

341 Schiller and Goethe, *Correspondence*, pp. 304-305.

342 Paul Barolsky, 'Winckelmann, Ovid, and the Transformation of the "Apollo Belvedere"', *Notes in the History of Art,* vol.33, no.2 (2014), 2-4, p. 2.

343 Jeffrey A. Gauthier, 'Schiller's Critique of Kant's Moral Psychology: Reconciling Practical Reason and an Ethics of Virtue', *Canadian Journal of Philosophy*, vol. 27, no. 4 (1997), 513-543 (pp.535-536).

344 Herder, *Outlines of a Philosophy of the History of Man*, p. 112.ss

345 Norton, *The Beautiful Soul*, p. 40.

346 Schiller, *On the Aesthetic Education of Man*, p. 34
347 Norton, *The Beautiful Soul,* p. 163.
348   See Henry Mackenzie, The Man of Feeling, ed. by Brian Vickers (Oxford: Oxford University Press, 2001)s
349 Schlegel 'Philosophical Fragments from the Philosophical Apprentice- ship (excerpts)', p. 162.
350 Goethe, *Wilhelm Meister*, p. 228.
351 Schiller, 'Kallias', p. 160.
352 Goethe, *Werther,* p. 48.
353 Michael Beddow, *The Fiction of Humanity: Studies in the Bildungsro- man from Wieland to Thomas Mann* (Cambridge: Cambridge University Press, 1982), p. 34.
354 Ibid.,p. 48.
355 Goethe, *Werther,* p. 45.
356 Ibid., p. 55.
357 Schiller, *On the Aesthetic Education of Man*, p. 139.
358 Kant, *On Education*, p. 71.
359 Reed, *Light in Germany*, p.110.
360 Schiller, *Essays Aesthetic and Philosophical*, p. 353.
361 Norton, *The Beautiful Soul*, p. 37.
362 Bruford, *The German Tradition of Self-Cultivation*, p. 16.
363 Beddow, *The Fiction of Humanity,* p. 47.
364 Schiller, *Essays Aesthetic and Philosophical*, p. 155.
365 Robert Edward Norton, 'The Aesthetic Education of Humanity: George Eliot's "Romola" and Schiller's Theory of Tragedy', *The Journal of Aesthetic Education*, vol. 25, no. 4 (1991), 3-20 (p.7).
366 Schiller, *Essays Aesthetic and Philosophical*, p. 204.
367 Ibid., p. 211.
368 Ibid., p. 216.
369 Ibid., p. 152.
370 Ibid., p. 156.
371 Goethe, *Poetry and Truth*, p. 290.
372 Goethe, *Wilhelm Meister*, p. 320.
373 Goethe, *Werther,* p.61.
374 Michael Bell (ed.), *The Cambridge Companion to European Novelists* (Cambridge: Cambridge University Press, 2012), p. 128.
375 Goethe, *Poetry and Truth,* p. 132.
376 Schiller, *Essays Aesthetic and Philosophical*, p. 344.
377 Jürgen Barkhoff, 'Romantic Sociability, Aesthetics and Politics' in *The Cambridge Companion to the Literature of Berlin*, ed. by Andrew J. Webber (Cambridge: Cambridge University Press, 2017), pp. 33-52 (pp. 36-37).

[378] Benhabib, 'The Pariah and her Shadow', p. 11.

[379] Hertz, *Jewish High Society in Old Regime Berlin*, p. 99.

[380] Spiel, 'Rahel Varnhagen', p. 19.

[381] Key, *Rahel Varhagen,* p. 46.

[382] Ibid., p. 48.

[383] Ibid., p. 190.

[384] Ibid., p. 188.

[385] Ibid., p. 214.

[386] Thomann Tewarson, *Rahel Levin Varnhagen*, p. 194.

[387] Ibid., p. 194.

[388] Roy Porter, *Flesh in the Age of Reason* (New York: W.W. Norton & Company, 2004) p. 281.

[389] Thomann Tewarson, *Rahel Levin Varnhagen*, p. 46.

[390] Ibid., p. 51.

[391] Weissberg and Varnhagen, 'Writing on the Wall', p. 165.

[392] Thomann Tewarson, *Rahel Levin Varnhagen*, p. 46.

[393] Goodman, *The Republic of Letters*, p. 303.

[394] Goodman, 'Poesis and Praxis in Rahel Varnhagen's Letters', p. 132.

[395] Van Horn Melton, *The Rise of the Public in Enlightenment Europe*, p. 202.

[396] James Como, 'The Salon: Restoring Conversation', *Arion: A Journal of the Humanities and the Classics,* vol. 22, no. 1 (2014), 33-49 (p. 37).

[397] Giesen,'Cosmopolitans, Patriots, Jacobins, and Romantics', p. 225.

[398] Jane V. Curran, 'Oral Reading, Print Culture, and the German Enlightenment', *The Modern Language Review*, vol. 100, no.3 (2005), 695-708 (p. 699).

[399] Arendt, *Rahel Varnhagen*, p. 171.

[400] Goodman, 'Poesis and Praxis in Rahel Varnhagen's Letters', p. 137.

[401] Weissberg and Varnhagen, 'Writing on the Wall', p. 166.

[402] Hertz, *Jewish High Society in Old Regime Berlin*, p. 185.

[403] Key, *Rahel Varnhagen*, p. 224.

[404] Thomann Tewarson, *Rahel Levin Varnhagen,* p. 131.

[405] Ibid., p. 131.

[406] Spiel, 'Rahel Varnhagen', p. 14.

[407] Weissberg, 'Stepping Out', p. 154.

[408] Thomann Tewarson, *Rahel Levin Varnhagen,* p. 61.

[409] Hertz, *Jewish High Society in Old Regime Berlin*, p. 270.

[410] Key, *Rahel Varnhagen*, p. 176.

[411] Tornius, *Salons*, p. 296.

[412] Levin and Veit, 'Correspondence', p. 56.

[413] Key, *Rahel Varnhagen*, p. 99.

[414] Ibid., p. 38.

[415] Thomann Tewarson, *Rahel Levin Varnhagen*, p. 92.

[416] Novalis, 'Pollen', p. 12.

[417] Burrow, 'Introduction' in *The Limits of State Action*, p. liv.

[418] Schiller, *On the Aesthetic Education of Man*, p. 69.

[419] Burrow, 'Introduction' in *The Limits of State Action*, p. liv.

[420] Eckermann, *Conversations of Goethe*, p. 204.

[421] Schleiermacher, 'Monologues II and III', p. 178.

[422] Eckermann, *Conversations of Goethe*, p. 267.

[423] Paul Guyer, *Kant and the Experience of Freedom: Essays on Aesthetics and Morality* (Cambridge: Cambridge University Press, 1993), p. 126.

[424] Eckermann, *Conversations of Goethe*, p. 412.

[425] Johann Wolfgang von Goethe, *Italian Journey (1786-1788)*, trans. by W. H. Auden and Elizabeth Mayer, (London, Penguin Classics, 1962)

[426] Eckermann, *Conversations of Goethe*, pp. 254-255.

[427] Goethe, *The Maxims and Reflections*, p. 86.

[428] Schiller, *Essays Aesthetic and Philosophical*, p. 334.

[429] Beddow, *The Fiction of Humanity*, p. 88.

[430] See Georg Wilhelm Friedrich Hegel, *The Phenomenology of Spirit*, trans. by Terry Pinkard (Cambridge: Cambridge University Press, 2018), pp. 281-306.

[431] Richard Schacht, *Alienation* (New York: Allen & Unwin, 1971), p. 14.

[432] Ibid., p. 15.

[433] Schiller, *On the Aesthetic Education of Man*, p. 132.

[434] Goethe, Maxims and Reflections, p. 147.

[435] Friedrich Schiller, *The Poems of Schiller*, ed. and trans. by Henry Wireman (Philadelphia: I. Kohler, 1871), p. 109.

[436] Goethe, *Wilhelm Meister*, p. 371.

[437] Goethe, *Poetry and Truth*, p. 400.

[438] Schiller, *The Poems of Schiller*, p. 209.

[439] Eckermann, *Conversations of Goethe*, pp. 102-103.

[440] Humboldt, *The Limits of State Action*, p. 57.

[441] Jeffrey L. High 'Friedrich Schiller, Secular Virtue, and "The Gods of Ancient Greece" (1788)' in *Enlightenment and Secularism*, ed. by Christopher Nadon (Maryland: Lexington Books, 2013), pp. 315-325 (p. 316).

[442] Schlegel, 'Athenaeum Fragments', p. 119.

[443] Humboldt, *The Limits of State Action*, p. 58.

[444] Eckermann, *Conversations of Goethe*, p. 307.

[445] Schiller and Goethe, *Correspondence*, p. 329.

[446] Goethe, *Poetry and Truth*, p. 400.

[447] Beddow, *The Fiction of Humanity*, p. 24.

[448] Marc Redfield, 'Gender, Aesthetics, and the Bildungsroman', *The Wordsworth Circle*, vol. 25, no. 1 (1994), 17-21 (p.19).

[449] Geuss, 'Kultur, Bildung, Geist', p.159.

[450] Schiller and Goethe, *Correspondence*, p. 164.

[451] Drew Milne, 'The Beautiful Soul: From Hegel to Beckett', *Diacritics,* vol. 32, no.1 (2002), 63-82 (p.63).

[452] Norton, *The Beautiful Soul*, p. 209.

[453] Schiller, *Essays Aesthetic and Philosophical*, p. 247.

[454] Ibid., p. 248.

[455] Rüdiger Safranski, *Goethe: Life as a Work of Art*, trans. by David Dollenmayer (New York: Liveright Publishing Corporation, 2017), p. xxiii.

[456] Ibid., p. 42.

[457] Lawler and Richardson 'Introduction' in *Florentin,* p. lv.

[458] Ibid., p. xxxiii.

[459] Hertz, *Jewish High Society in Old Regime Berlin*, p. 138.

[460] Ibid., p. 137.

[461] Spiel, 'Rahel Varnhagen', p. 20.

[462] Key, *Rahel Varnhagen*, p. 195.

[463] Arendt, *Rahel Varnhagen*, p. 171.

[464] Goozé, 'Introduction' in *Challenging Separate Spheres*, p. 24.

[465] Thomann Tewarson, *Rahel Levin Varnhagen*, p. 162.

[466] Ibid., p. 162.

[467] Ibid., p. 162.

[468] Ibid., p. 224.

[469] Key, *Rahel Varnhagen*, p. 208.

[470] Thomann Tewarson, *Rahel Levin Varnhagen*, p. 224.

[471] Key, *Rahel Varnhagen*, p. 206.

[472] Michael Goldfarb, *Emancipation: How Liberating Europe's Jews from the Ghetto Led to Revolution and Renaissance* (New York: Simon & Schuster, 2009), pp. 111

[473] Walter Horace Bruford, *Culture and Society in Classical Weimar, 1775-1806* (Cambridge: Cambridge University Press, 1962), p.286.

[474] Norton, *The Beautiful Soul,* p. 38.

[475] Alexander J.B. Hampton, *Romanticism and the Re-Invention of Modern Religion: The Reconciliation of German Idealism and Platonic Realism* (Cambridge: Cambridge University Press, 2019), p.142.

[476] Norton, *The Beautiful Soul*, p. 38.

[477] Goethe, *The Maxims and Reflections*, p. 186.

[478] Schiller, *On the Aesthetic Education of Man*, pp. 85-87.

[479] Ibid., pp. 74-75.

[480] Wessell, 'Schiller and the Genesis of German Romanticism', p. 179.

[481] Marguerite Heller, 'Goethe and Music', *The German Quarterly*, vol. 22, no. 4 (1949), 205-208 (p.208).

[482] Schiller, *On the Aesthetic Education of Man*, p. 121.

[483] Ibid., p. 122.

[484] Ibid., p. 104-105.

[485] Safranski, *Goethe*, p. 45.

[486] Schiller, *The Poems of Schiller*, p. 83.

[487] Schiller, 'Kallias', p. 148.

[488] Johann Wolfgang von Goethe, *The Metamorphosis of Plants* (Cambridge, MA: MIT Press, 2009), p. 36.

[489] Alexander Nehamas, *Only a Promise of Happiness: The Place of Beauty in a World of Art* (Princeton: Princeton University Press, 2010), p. 3.

[490] Schiller, *On the Aesthetic Education of Man*, pp.136-138.

[491] Immanuel Kant, *Critique of Judgment*, trans. by J.H. Bernard (London: Dover Philosophical Classics, 2005)

[492] See Anthony Ashley Cooper Earl of Shaftesbury, *The Moralists, a Philosophical Rhapsody: Being a Recital of Certain Conversations Upon Natural and Moral Subjects* (London: John Wyat, 1709)

[493] Schiller, *Essays Aesthetic and Philosophical*, pp. 136-137.

[494] Norton, *The Beautiful Soul*, pp. 78-79.

[495] Heinrich von Kleist, *Die heilige Cäcilie oder die Gewalt der Musik* (Berlin: Berliner Abendblätter, 1810)

[496] Schiller, *Essays Aesthetic and Philosophical*, pp. 127-128.

[497] Schlegel, *On the Study of Greek Poetry*, pp. 44-45.

[498] Schiller, *Essays Aesthetic and Philosophical*, p. 125.

[499] Ibid., p. 119.

[500] Ibid., p. 123.

[501] Eckermann, *Conversations of Goethe*, p. 88.

[502] Schlegel, *On the Study of Greek Poetry*, p. 41.

[503] Schiller and Goethe, *Correspondence*, p. 149.

[504] Goethe, *Poetry and Truth*, p. 470.

[505] Marchand, *Down from Olympus,* p. 1.

[506] Guyer, *Kant and the Experience of Freedom,* p. 124.

[507] See Goethe, *Wilhelm Meister*, p. 256.

[508] Helmut Danner, 'Bildung: A Basic Term of German Education', *Educational Sciences*, vol. 9 (1994), p. 16.

[509] Schiller, *Essays Aesthetic and Philosophical*, p. 203.

[510] Beiser, *The Romantic Imperative*, p. 97.

[511] Norton, *The Beautiful Soul*, p. 194.

[512] Susan L. Cocalis, 'The Transformation of "Bildung" from an Image to an Ideal', *Monatshefte,* vol. 70, no. 4 (1978), 399-414, p. 3.

[513] Plotinus, *Complete Works*, trans. by Kenneth Sylvan Guthrie, (California: CreateSpace Independent Publishing Platform, 2017), p. 32.

[514] Safranski, *Goethe*, p. 566.

[515] Schlegel, 'Ideas', p. 126.

[516] Brent W. Sockness, 'Was Schleiermacher a Virtue Ethicist? Tugend and Bildung in the Early Ethical Writings', *Journal for the History of Modern Theology*, vol. 8, no. 1 (2010), 1-33 (p.32).

[517] Schlegel, *On the Study of Greek Poetry*, p. 94.

[518] Goethe, *The Maxims and Reflections*, p. 189.

[519] Schiller, *On the Aesthetic Education of Man*, pp. 52-53.

[520] Schiller, *Essays Aesthetic and Philosophical*, p. 334.

[521] Goethe, *Poetry and Truth,* p. 87.

[522] Schiller, *Essays Aesthetic and Philosophical*, p. 336.

[523] Ibid., pp.338-339.

[524] Kant, *Critique of Judgment*, p. 44.

[525] Schmidt, 'Introduction', in *On the Aesthetic Education of Man*, p. xxxii.

[526] Schiller, *On the Aesthetic Education of Man*, p. 138.

[527] Novalis, 'Pollen', p. 12.

[528] Schiller, 'Kallias', p. 172.

[529] White, 'Beauty of Soul and Speech', p. 80.

[530] Schiller, *Essays Aesthetic and Philosophical*, p. 117.

[531] Schleiermacher, 'Monologues II and III', p. 195.

[532] Ibid.,197.

[533] Schlegel, *On the Study of Greek Poetry,* p. 92.

[534] Chytry, *The Aesthetic State*, p. 58.

[535] Schiller, *Essays Aesthetic and Philosophical*, p. 332.

[536] Chytry, *The Aesthetic State,* p. xliv.

[537] Ibid. p.1.

[538] Ibid. p.7.

[539] Ibid., pp. 39-40.

[540] Ibid., p. 38.

[541] Ibid., pp. 42-43.

[542] Christoph Martin Wieland, *The History of Agathon,* trans. by John Richardson (Oxford: Oxford University Press, 1773), p. 512.

[543] Schiller, *Essays Aesthetic and Philosophical*, pp. 48-49.

[544] Guyer, *Kant and the Experience of Freedom*, p. 117.

[545] Schiller, *On the Aesthetic Education of Man*, p. 33.

[546] Beiser, 'Introduction', in *The Early Political Writings of the German Romantics,* p. xiv.

[547] Schlegel, *On the Study of Greek Poetry*, pp. 44-45.

[548] Beiser, *The Romantic Imperative*, pp. 97-98.

[549] Arendt, *Rahel Varnhagen,* p. 77.

[550] Key, *Rahel Varnhagen,* p. 203.

[551] Bilski and Braun, *Jewish Women and their Salons*, p. 28.

[552] Renata Fuchs, '"Dann ist und Bleibt eine Korrespondenz Lebendig": Romantic Dialogue in the Letters and Works of Rahel Levin Varnhagen, Bettina Brentano von Arnim, and Karoline von Günderrode' (Doctoral Thesis, University of Illinois at Urbana-Champaign, 2015), p. 56.

[553] Wilhelmy Dollinger, *Die Berliner Salons*, p. 154.

[554] Despina Stratigakos, 'Women and the Modern Metropolis', in *Think Space: Approaches to Metropolitanism*, ed. by Dorothee Brantz, Sasha Disko, Georg Wagner-Kyora (New Brunswick: Rutgers University Press, 2012), pp. 279-307 (pp. 297-298).

[555] Hertz, *Jewish High Society in Old Regime Berlin*, p. 18.

[556] Tornius, *Salons,* p. 251.

[557] Thomann Tewarson, *Rahel Levin Varnhagen*, p. 34.

[558] Ibid., p. 181.

[559] Curran, 'Oral Reading, Print Culture, and the German Enlightenment', p. 698.

[560] Ibid., p. 699.

[561] Ibid.,p. 707.

[562] Peter Seibert, *Der literarische Salon. Literatur und Geselligkeit zwischen Aufklärung und Vormärz* (Stuttgart: J.B.Metzler, 1993), p. 170.

[563] Key, *Rahel Varnhagen*, p. 273.

[564] Hertz, *Jewish High Society in Old Regime Berlin*, p. 63.

[565] Benhabib, *The Reluctant Modernism of Hannah Arendt*, p. 17.

[566] Key, *Rahel Varnhagen*, p. 279.

[567] Ibid., p. 171.

[568] Ibid., p. 296.

[569] Thomann Tewarson, *Rahel Levin Varnhagen*, p. 43.

[570] Benhabib, 'The Pariah and her Shadow', p. 11.

[571] Key, *Rahel Varnhagen*, p. 283.

[572] Thomann Tewarson, *Rahel Levin Varnhagen*, p. 44.

[573] Ibid., p. 134.

[574] Ibid., p. 135.

[575] Key, *Rahel Varnhagen*, p. 174.

[576] Ibid., p. 219.

[577] Ibid., p. 238.

[578] Lawler and Richardson 'Introduction' in *Florentin,* p. xiii.

[579] Ibid., p. xiii.

[580] Ibid., p. xiv.

[581] Thomann Tewarson, *Rahel Levin Varnhagen*, p. 49.

[582] Arendt, *Rahel Varnhagen*, p. 57.

583 Key, *Rahel Varnhagen*, p. 238.

584 Thomann Tewarson, *Rahel Levin Varnhagen*, pp. 85-86.

585 Ibid., p. 85.

586 Key, *Rahel Varnhagen*, p. 289.

587 Ibid., p. 283.

588 Ibid., p. 272.

589 Arendt, *Rahel Varnhagen*, p. 38.

590 Ibid., p. 38

591 Thomann Tewarson, *Rahel Levin Varnhagen*, p. 173. .

592 Ibid., p. 173.

593 Key, *Rahel Varnhagen*, p. 214.

594 Bruford, *The German Tradition of Self-Cultivation,* p. 151.

595 Norton, *The Beautiful Soul*, pp. 283-298.

596 For an overview of the *Bildungsbürgertum in the nineteenth century see* Werner Conze, Jürgen Kocka (eds.), *Bildungsbürgertum im 19. Jahrhundert: Bildungssystem und Professionalisierung in internationalen Vergleichen* (Stuttgart: Klett-Cotta, 1985).

597 Norton, *The Beautiful Soul*, p. 284.

598 Hertz, *Jewish High Society in Old Regime Berlin*, p. 279.

599 Ibid., p. 284.

600 Emily Bilski, *Berlin Metropolis: Jews and the New Culture 1890-1918* (Berkeley: University of California Press, 1999), p. 202.

601 Safranski, *Goethe,* p. 565.

602 See Ursula Vogel, 'Liberty is Beautiful: Von Humboldt's Gift to Liberalism', *History of Political Thought*, vol. 3, no. 1 (1982), pp. 77-101.

603 See Terje Rasmussen, 'Internet and the Political Public Sphere', *Sociology Compass*, vol.8, no.12 (2014), 1315-1329

604 Norton, The Beautiful Soul, p. 289.

INDEX

humanist philosophy, 214, 259
Humboldt, Wilhelm von, 16, 21, 27, 101, 104–6, 122, 124, 126, 151–53, 213–15, 261–62, 332–33

I

Italian Journey, 256

J

Jewish, 26, 28, 32–33, 37, 50, 136, 164, 169, 331
Jewish communities, 27, 31
Jewish culture, 31
Jewish gentry (elite), 31—33
Jewish intellectuals, 32
Jewish mercantile class, 26
Jewish scholarship, 27
Jewish societies, 33
Jewish values, 32
justice, 61–62, 80, 86, 136, 142, 154, 156–57, 160, 172, 174–77, 293

K

Kallias Letters, 127
Kant, Immanuel, 21, 63, 123, 282, 284, 296

L

Laocoön, 226–27
Lessing, Gotthold Ephraim, 32, 35, 229, 305
Louis, Prince, 306

M

Madame de Staël, 300

Mendelssohn, Moses, 27, 31–33, 160, 187
modern age, 4, 14, 38, 100, 172, 179, 332–34
Moritz, Karl Philipp, 36
music, 31, 33, 36, 109–10, 159–60, 184–85, 187, 280, 283, 285, 289, 306–9, 311, 314, 316–17
myth of Narcissus, 56

N

noble actions, 161
noble aspirations, 7
noble ideals, 256, 302
noble passions, 294
noble souls, 10–11, 63
noble values, 38
Novalis, 13, 16, 99–100, 122, 196

O

On the Limits of State Action, 213, 261, 300
orchestra, 185, 188, 195

P

Paris, 4, 87
Paul, Jean, 305, 315–16
personal cultivation, 15
philosophy of self-cultivation, 9, 133
Plato, 2, 8, 9, 19, 61, 177, 214
Platonic ideals, 9
Platonic love, 198
Platonic values, 141
Plato's aesthetics, 8

**ANOTHER BOOK FROM DOUBLE A GROUP
PUBLISHING YOU MIGHT ENJOY**

The Gift of Life

by Mel Stein

In 1960s Apartheid South Africa, Black Lives did not matter. Black people were denied all basic freedoms including the right to advanced education.Most people know of South African surgeon, Christiaan Barnard, who carried out the very first successful heart transplant in the world. But very few people know the name of Hamilton Naki. Naki, an uneducated gardener at Barnard's university, doubled up as his laboratory assistant and turned out to have a remarkable natural aptitude for surgery.Even fewer people know that Naki, not Barnard, carried out most of the numerous animal transplant experiments that came before the first human transplant and helped to develop its successful methodology. And sadly, a mere handful of people have heard of Denise Darville, whose tragic car crash made her the first heart donor.

This fluent, moving novel documents the unlikely pairing of Barnard and Naki and their convergence with the short life of Denise – to change the future of heart surgery forever.

Double A Group Publishing,
Barnet,
London